ABOUT THIS PUBLICATION

I0404597

FOR SERVICE ASSISTANCE

Customer Service Department
704.898.0770

North Carolina General Statues is published by The Muliti-Media Group of Greater Charlotte in Charlotte, North Carolina. Copyright 2015 by the Multi-Media Group of Greater Charlotte. This book or parts thereof may not be reproduced in any form, stored in a retrieval system, or transmitted in any form by any means—electronic, mechanical, photocopy, recording or otherwise—without prior written permission of the publisher, except as provided by United States of America copyright law.

The records required by U.S. Code 2257(a) through (c) and the pertinent regulations 28 C.F.R. Cli. 1, Part 75 with respect to this publication and all materials associated with such records are maintained by The Multi-Media Group of Greater Charlotte, Publisher and available for review by Attorney General.

www.visionbooks.org

Copyright © 2015 by MMGGC
All rights reserved!

TID: 4993186
ISBN (10) digit: 1502331284
ISBN (13) digit: 978-1502331281

123-4-56789-01234-Paperback
123-4-56789-01234-Hardback

First Edition

090520140547

Printed in the United States of America

2015 EDITION

North Carolina Criminal Law And Procedure-Pamphlet # 10

Printed In conjunction with the Administration of the Courts

North Carolina Criminal Law and Procedure
Pamphlet Reference Guide

Chapters	Pamphlet
Chapter 1 Civil Procedure	1
Chapter 1 Civil Procedure (Continue)	2
Chapter 1A Rules of Civil Procedure	2
Chapter 1B Contribution.	2
Chapter 1C Enforcement of Judgments.	2
Chapter 1D Punitive Damages.	2
Chapter 1E Eastern Band of Cherokee Indians.	2
Chapter 1F North Carolina Uniform Interstate Depositions and Discovery Act.	2
Chapter 2 - Clerk of Superior Court [Repealed and Transferred.]	3
Chapter 3 - Commissioners of Affidavits and Deeds [Repealed.]	3
Chapter 4 - Common Law	3
Chapter 5 - Contempt [Repealed.]	3
Chapter 5A - Contempt	3
Chapter 6 - Liability for Court Costs	3
Chapter 7 - Courts [Repealed and Transferred.]	3
Chapter 7A – Judicial Department	3
Chapter 7A – Continuation (Judicial Department)	4
Chapter 7A – Continuation (Judicial Department)	5
Chapter 7B - Juvenile Code	5
Chapter 8 - Evidence	6
Chapter 8A - Interpreters for Deaf Persons [Recodified.]	6
Chapter 8B - Interpreters for Deaf Persons	6
Chapter 8C - Evidence Code	6
Chapter 9 - Jurors	6
Chapter 10 - Notaries [Repealed.]	6
Chapter 10A - Notaries [Recodified.]	6
Chapter 10B - Notaries	6
Chapter 11 - Oaths	6
Chapter 12 - Statutory Construction	6
Chapter 13 - Citizenship Restored	6
Chapter 14 - Criminal Law	7
Chapter 14 –Criminal Law (Continuation)	8
Chapter 15 - Criminal Procedure	9
Chapter 15A - Criminal Procedure Act (Continuation)	10
Chapter 15A - Criminal Procedure Act (Continuation)	11
Chapter 15B - Victims Compensation	11
Chapter 15C - Address Confidentiality Program	11
Chapter 16 - Gaming Contracts and Futures	11
Chapter 17 - Habeas Corpus	11

Chapter 17A - Law-Enforcement Officers [Recodified.]	11
Chapter 17B - North Carolina Criminal Justice Education and Training System [Recodified.] Chapter 17C - North Carolina Criminal Justice Education and Training Standards Commission	11
	11
Chapter 17D - North Carolina Justice Academy	11
Chapter 17E - North Carolina Sheriffs' Education and Training Standards Commission	11
Chapter 18 - Regulation of Intoxicating Liquors [Repealed.]	12
Chapter 18A - Regulation of Intoxicating Liquors [Repealed.]	12
Chapter 18B - Regulation of Alcoholic Beverages	12
Chapter 18C - North Carolina State Lottery	12
Chapter 19 - Offenses against Public Morals	12
Chapter 19A - Protection of Animals	12
Chapter 20 - Motor Vehicles	13
Chapter 20 - Motor Vehicles (Continuation)	14
Chapter 20 - Motor Vehicles (Continuation)	15
Chapter 20 - Motor Vehicles (Continuation)	16
Chapter 21 - Bills of Lading	17
Chapter 22 - Contracts Requiring Writing	17
Chapter 22A - Signatures	17
Chapter 22B - Contracts Against Public Policy	17
Chapter 22C - Payments to Subcontractors	17
Chapter 23 - Debtor and Creditor	17
Chapter 24 – Interest	17
Chapter 25 – Uniform Commercial Code	18
Chapter 25 – Uniform Commercial Code (Continuation)	19
Chapter 25A – Retail Installment Sales Act	20
Chapter 25B - Credit	20
Chapter 25C - Sales of Artwork	20
Chapter 26 - Suretyship	20
Chapter 27 - Warehouse Receipts [Repealed.]	20
Chapter 28 - Administration [Repealed.]	20
Chapter 28A - Administration of Decedents' Estates	20
Chapter 28B - Estates of Absentees in Military Service	20
Chapter 28C - Estates of Missing Persons	20
Chapter 29 - Intestate Succession	21
Chapter 30 - Surviving Spouses	21
Chapter 31 - Wills	21
Chapter 31A - Acts Barring Property Rights	21
Chapter 31B - Renunciation of Property and Renunciation of Fiduciary Powers Act	21
Chapter 31C - Uniform Disposition of Community Property Rights at Death Act	21
Chapter 32 - Fiduciaries	21
Chapter 32A - Powers of Attorney	21
Chapter 33 - Guardian and Ward [Repealed and Recodified.]	21

Chapter 33A - North Carolina Uniform Transfers to Minors Act	21
Chapter 33B - North Carolina Uniform Custodial Trust Act	21
Chapter 34 - Veterans' Guardianship Act	22
Chapter 35 - Sterilization Procedures	22
Chapter 35A - Incompetency and Guardianship	22
Chapter 36 - Trusts and Trustees [Repealed.]	22
Chapter 36A - Trusts and Trustees	22
Chapter 36B - Uniform Management of Institutional Funds Act [Repealed.]	22
Chapter 36C - North Carolina Uniform Trust Code	22
Chapter 36D - North Carolina Community Third Party Trusts, Pooled Trusts	23
Chapter 36E - Uniform Prudent Management of Institutional Funds Act	23
Chapter 37 - Allocation of Principal and Income [Repealed.]	23
Chapter 37A - Uniform Principal and Income Act	23
Chapter 38 - Boundaries	23
Chapter 38A - Landowner Liability	23
Chapter 39 - Conveyances	23
Chapter 39A - Transfer Fee Covenants Prohibited	23
Chapter 40 - Eminent Domain [Repealed.]	23
Chapter 40A - Eminent Domain	23
Chapter 41 - Estates	23
Chapter 41A - State Fair Housing Act	23
Chapter 42 - Landlord and Tenant	23
Chapter 42A - Vacation Rental Act	23
Chapter 43 - Land Registration	23
Chapter 44 - Liens	24
Chapter 44A - Statutory Liens and Charges	24
Chapter 45 - Mortgages and Deeds of Trust	24
Chapter 45A - Good Funds Settlement Act	24
Chapter 46 - Partition	24
Chapter 47 - Probate and Registration	25
Chapter 47A - Unit Ownership	25
Chapter 47B - Real Property Marketable Title Act	25
Chapter 47C - North Carolina Condominium Act	25
Chapter 47D - Notice of Settlement Act [Expired.]	25
Chapter 47E - Residential Property Disclosure Act	25
Chapter 47F - North Carolina Planned Community Act	25
Chapter 47G - Option to Purchase Contracts	25
Chapter 47H - Contracts for Deed	25
Chapter 48 - Adoptions	26
Chapter 48A - Minors	26
Chapter 49 - Bastardy	26
Chapter 49A - Rights of Children	26
Chapter 50 - Divorce and Alimony	26
Chapter 50A - Uniform Child-Custody Jurisdiction and	

Enforcement Act	26
Chapter 50B - Domestic Violence	26
Chapter 50C - Civil No-Contact Orders	26
Chapter 51 - Marriage	26
Chapter 52 - Powers and Liabilities of Married Persons	27
Chapter 52A - Uniform Reciprocal Enforcement of Support Act [Repealed.]	27
Chapter 52B - Uniform Premarital Agreement Act	27
Chapter 52C - Uniform Interstate Family Support Act	27
Chapter 53 - Banks	27
Chapter 53A - Business Development Corporations and North Carolina Capital Resource Corporations	28
Chapter 53B - Financial Privacy Act	28
Chapter 54 - Cooperative Organizations	28
Chapter 54A - Capital Stock Savings and Loan Associations [Repealed.]	28
Chapter 54B - Savings and Loan Associations	29
Chapter 54C - Savings Banks	29
Chapter 55 - North Carolina Business Corporation Act	30
Chapter 55A - North Carolina Nonprofit Corporation Act	31
Chapter 55B - Professional Corporation Act	31
Chapter 55C - Foreign Trade Zones	31
Chapter 55D - Filings, Names, and Registered Agents for Corporations, Nonprofit Corporations, and Partnerships	31
Chapter 56 - Electric, Telegraph and Power Companies [Repealed.]	31
Chapter 57 - Hospital, Medical and Dental Service Corporations [Recodified.]	31
Chapter 57A - Health Maintenance Organization Act [Recodified.]	31
Chapter 57B - Health Maintenance Organization Act [Recodified.]	31
Chapter 57C - North Carolina Limited Liability Company Act.	31
Chapter 58 - Insurance.	32
Chapter 58 - Insurance (Continuation)	33
Chapter 58 - Insurance (Continuation)	34
Chapter 58 - Insurance (Continuation)	35
Chapter 58 - Insurance (Continuation)	36
Chapter 58 - Insurance (Continuation)	37
Chapter 58 - Insurance (Continuation)	38
Chapter 58A - North Carolina Health Insurance Trust Commission [Recodified.]	38
Chapter 59 - Partnership.	39
Chapter 59B - Uniform Unincorporated Nonprofit Association Act.	39
Chapter 60 - Railroads and Other Carriers [Repealed and Transferred.]	39
Chapter 61 - Religious Societies	39
Chapter 62 - Public Utilities	39

Chapter 62 - Public Utilities (Continuation)	40
Chapter 62A - Public Safety Telephone Service And Wireless Telephone Service	40
Chapter 63 - Aeronautics	40
Chapter 63A - North Carolina Global TransPark Authority	40
Chapter 64 - Aliens	40
Chapter 65 – Cemeteries	40
Chapter 66 - Commerce and Business	41
Chapter 67 - Dogs	41
Chapter 68 - Fences and Stock Law	41
Chapter 69 - Fire Protection	41
Chapter 70 - Indian Antiquities, Archaeological Resources and Unmarked Human Skeletal Remains Protection	42
Chapter 71 - Indians [Repealed.]	42
Chapter 71A - Indians	42
Chapter 72 - Inns, Hotels and Restaurants	42
Chapter 73 - Mills	42
Chapter 74 - Mines and Quarries	42
Chapter 74A - Company Police [Repealed.]	42
Chapter 74B - Private Protective Services Act [Repealed.]	42
Chapter 74C - Private Protective Services	42
Chapter 74D - Alarm Systems	42
Chapter 74E - Company Police Act	42
Chapter 74F - Locksmith Licensing Act	42
Chapter 74G - Campus Police Act	42
Chapter 75 - Monopolies, Trusts and Consumer Protection	42
Chapter 75A - Boating and Water Safety	43
Chapter 75B - Discrimination in Business	43
Chapter 75C - Motion Picture Fair Competition Act	43
Chapter 75D - Racketeer Influenced and Corrupt Organizations	43
Chapter 75E - Unlawful Activities in Connection With Certain Corporate Transactions	43
Chapter 76 - Navigation	43
Chapter 76A - Navigation and Pilotage Commissions	43
Chapter 77 - Rivers, Creeks, and Coastal Waters	43
Chapter 78 - Securities Law [Repealed.]	43
Chapter 78A - North Carolina Securities Act	43
Chapter 78B - Tender Offer Disclosure Act [Repealed.]	43
Chapter 78C - Investment Advisers	43
Chapter 78D - Commodities Act	43
Chapter 79 - Strays [Repealed.]	43
Chapter 80 - Trademarks, Brands, etc.	44
Chapter 81 - Weights and Measures [Recodified.]	44
Chapter 81A - Weights and Measures Act of 1975.	44
Chapter 82 - Wrecks [Repealed.]	44
Chapter 83 - Architects [Recodified.]	44

Chapter 83A - Architects	44
Chapter 84 - Attorneys-at-Law	44
Chapter 84A - Foreign Legal Consultants	44
Chapter 85 - Auctions and Auctioneers [Repealed.]	44
Chapter 85A - Bail Bondsmen and Runners [Recodified.]	44
Chapter 85B - Auctions and Auctioneers	44
Chapter 85C - Bail Bondsmen and Runners [Recodified.]	44
Chapter 86 - Barbers [Recodified.]	44
Chapter 86A - Barbers	44
Chapter 87 - Contractors	44
Chapter 88 - Cosmetic Art [Repealed.]	44
Chapter 88A - Electrolysis Practice Act	44
Chapter 88B - Cosmetic Art	45
Chapter 89 - Engineering and Land Surveying [Recodified.]	45
Chapter 89A - Landscape Architects	45
Chapter 89B - Foresters	45
Chapter 89C - Engineering and Land Surveying	45
Chapter 89D - Landscape Contractors	45
Chapter 89E - Geologists Licensing Act	45
Chapter 89F - North Carolina Soil Scientist Licensing Act	45
Chapter 89G - Irrigation Contractors	45
Chapter 90 - Medicine and Allied Occupations	45
Chapter 90 - Medicine and Allied Occupations (Continuation)	46
Chapter 90 - Medicine and Allied Occupations (Continuation)	47
Chapter 90 - Medicine and Allied Occupations (Continuation)	48
Chapter 90A - Sanitarians and Water and Wastewater Treatment Facility Operators	48
Chapter 90B - Social Worker Certification and Licensure Act	48
Chapter 90C - North Carolina Recreational Therapy Licensure Act	48
Chapter 90D - Interpreters and Transliterators	48
Chapter 91 - Pawnbrokers [Repealed.]	48
Chapter 91A - Pawnbrokers Modernization Act of 1989	48
Chapter 92 - Photographers [Deleted.]	48
Chapter 93 - Certified Public Accountants	48
Chapter 93A - Real Estate License Law	49
Chapter 93B - Occupational Licensing Boards	49
Chapter 93C - Watchmakers [Repealed.]	49
Chapter 93D - North Carolina State Hearing Aid Dealers and Fitters Board.	49
Chapter 93E - North Carolina Appraisers Act	49
Chapter 94 - Apprenticeship	49
Chapter 95 - Department of Labor and Labor Regulations	49
Chapter 95 - Department of Labor and Labor Regulations (Continuation)	50
Chapter 96 - Employment Security	50
Chapter 97 - Workers' Compensation Act	50
Chapter 97 - Workers' Compensation Act (Continuation)	51

Chapter 98 - Burnt and Lost Records	51
Chapter 99 - Libel and Slander	51
Chapter 99A - Civil Remedies for Criminal Actions	51
Chapter 99B - Products Liability	51
Chapter 99C - Actions Relating to Winter Sports Safety and Accidents	51
Chapter 99D - Civil Rights	51
Chapter 99E - Special Liability Provisions	51
Chapter 100 - Monuments, Memorials and Parks	51
Chapter 101 - Names of Persons	51
Chapter 102 - Official Survey Base	51
Chapter 103 - Sundays, Holidays and Special Days	51
Chapter 104 - United States Lands	51
Chapter 104A - Degrees of Kinship	51
Chapter 104B - Hurricanes or Other Acts of Nature	51
Chapter 104C - Atomic Energy, Radioactivity and Ionizing Radiation [Repealed and Recodified.]	51
Chapter 104D - Southern States Energy Compact	51
Chapter 104E - North Carolina Radiation Protection Act	51
Chapter 104F - Southeast Interstate Low-Level Radioactive Waste Management Compact [Repealed]	51
Chapter 104G - North Carolina Low-Level Radioactive Waste Management Authority Act of 1987 [Repealed]	51
Chapter 105 - Taxation	51
Chapter 105 - Taxation (Continuation)	52
Chapter 105 - Taxation (Continuation)	53
Chapter 105 - Taxation (Continuation)	54
Chapter 105A - Setoff Debt Collection Act	55
Chapter 105B - Defaulted Student Loan Recovery Act	55
Chapter 106 - Agriculture	55
Chapter 106 - Agriculture (Continue)	56
Chapter 106 - Agriculture (Continue)	57
Chapter 107 - Agricultural Development Districts [Repealed.]	57
Chapter 108 - Social Services [Repealed and Recodified.]	57
Chapter 108A - Social Services	57
Chapter 108B - Community Action Programs	58
Chapter 108C Medicaid and Health Choice Provider Requirements.	58
Chapter 108D Medicaid Managed Care for Behavioral Health Services.	58
Chapter 109 - Bonds [Recodified.]	58
Chapter 110 - Child Welfare	58
Chapter 111 - Aid to the Blind	58
Chapter 112 - Confederate Homes and Pensions [Repealed.]	58
Chapter 113 - Conservation and Development	58
Chapter 113 - Conservation and Development (Continuation)	59

Chapter 113A - Pollution Control and Environment	59
Chapter 113A - Pollution Control and Environment (Continuation)	60
Chapter 113B - North Carolina Energy Policy Act of 1975	60
Chapter 114 - Department of Justice	60
Chapter 115 - Elementary and Secondary Education [Repealed.]	60
Chapter 115A - Community Colleges, Technical Institutes, and Industrial Education Centers [Repealed.]	60
Chapter 115B - Tuition and Fee Waivers	60
Chapter 115C - Elementary and Secondary Education	60
Chapter 115C - Elementary and Secondary Education (Continuation)	61
Chapter 115C - Elementary and Secondary Education (Continuation)	62
Chapter 115C - Elementary and Secondary Education (Continuation)	63
Chapter 115D - Community Colleges	63
Chapter 115E - Private Educational Facilities Finance Act [Recodified]	63
Chapter 116 - Higher Education	63
Chapter 116 - Higher Education (Continuation)	63
Chapter 116A - Escheats and Abandoned Property [Repealed.]	64
Chapter 116B - Escheats and Abandoned Property	64
Chapter 116C - Continuum of Education Programs	64
Chapter 116D - Higher Education Bonds	64
Chapter 116E -Education Longitudinal Data System	64
Chapter 117 - Electrification	64
Chapter 118 - Firemen's and Rescue Squad Workers' Relief and Pension Funds [Recodified.]	64
Chapter 118A - Firemen's Death Benefit Act [Repealed.]	64
Chapter 118B - Members of a Rescue Squad Death Benefit Act [Repealed.]	64
Chapter 119 - Gasoline and Oil Inspection and Regulation	64
Chapter 120 - General Assembly	65
Chapter 120 - General Assembly (Continuation)	66
Chapter 120 - General Assembly (Continuation)	67
Chapter 120C - Lobbying	67
Chapter 121 - Archives and History	67
Chapter 122 - Hospitals for the Mentally Disordered [Repealed.]	67
Chapter 122A - North Carolina Housing Finance Agency	67
Chapter 122B - North Carolina Agricultural Facilities Finance Act [Repealed.]	67
Chapter 122C - Mental Health, Developmental Disabilities, and Substance Abuse Act of 1985	67
Chapter 122C - Mental Health, Developmental Disabilities, and Substance Abuse Act of 1985 (Continuation)	68

Chapter 122D - North Carolina Agricultural Finance Act	68
Chapter 122E - North Carolina Housing Trust and Oil Overcharge Act	68
Chapter 123 - Impeachment	69
Chapter 123A - Industrial Development [Repealed.]	69
Chapter 124 - Internal Improvements	69
Chapter 125 - Libraries	69
Chapter 126 - State Personnel System	69
Chapter 127 - Militia [Repealed.]	69
Chapter 127A - Militia	69
Chapter 127B - Military Affairs	69
Chapter 127C - Advisory Commission on Military Affairs	69
Chapter 128 - Offices and Public Officers	69
Chapter 128 - Offices and Public Officers (Continuation)	70
Chapter 129 - Public Buildings and Grounds	70
Chapter 130 - Public Health [Repealed.]	70
Chapter 130A - Public Health	70
Chapter 130A - Public Health (Continuation)	71
Chapter 130A - Public Health (Continuation)	72
Chapter 130B - Hazardous Waste Management Commission [Repealed.]	72
Chapter 131 - Public Hospitals [Repealed.]	72
Chapter 131A - Health Care Facilities Finance Act	72
Chapter 131B - Licensing of Ambulatory Surgical Facilities [Repealed.]	72
Chapter 131C - Charitable Solicitation Licensure Act [Repealed.]	72
Chapter 131D - Inspection and Licensing of Facilities	72
Chapter 131E - Health Care Facilities and Services	72
Chapter 131E - Health Care Facilities and Services (Continuation)	73
Chapter 131F - Solicitation of Contributions	73
Chapter 132 - Public Records	73
Chapter 133 - Public Works	74
Chapter 134 - Youth Development [Recodified.]	74
Chapter 134A - Youth Services [Repealed.]	74
Chapter 135 - Retirement System for Teachers and State Employees; Social Security; Health Insurance Program for Children	74
Chapter 135 - Retirement System for Teachers and State Employees; Social Security; Health Insurance Program for Children	75
Chapter 136 - Transportation	75
Chapter 136 - Transportation (Continuation)	76
Chapter 137 - Rural Rehabilitation [Repealed.]	76
Chapter 138 - Salaries, Fees and Allowances	76
Chapter 138A - State Government Ethics Act	76

Chapter 139 - Soil and Water Conservation Districts	76
Chapter 140 - State Art Museum; Symphony and Art Societies	76
Chapter 140A - State Awards System	76
Chapter 141 - State Boundaries	76
Chapter 142 - State Debt	76
Chapter 143 - State Departments, Institutions, and Commissions	77
Chapter 143 - State Departments, Institutions, and Commissions (Continuation)	78
Chapter 143 - State Departments, Institutions, and Commissions (Continuation)	79
Chapter 143 - State Departments, Institutions, and Commissions (Continuation)	80
Chapter 143A - State Government Reorganization	80
Chapter 143B - Executive Organization Act of 1973	80
Chapter 143B - Executive Organization Act of 1973 (Continuation)	81
Chapter 143B - Executive Organization Act of 1973 (Continuation)	82
Chapter 143C - State Budget Act	83
Chapter 143D - The State Governmental Accountability and Internal Control Act	83
Chapter 144 - State Flag, Official Governmental Flags, Motto, and Colors	83
Chapter 145 - State Symbols and Other Official Adoptions.	83
Chapter 146 - State Lands	83
Chapter 147 - State Officers	83
Chapter 148 - State Prison System	84
Chapter 149 - State Song and Toast	84
Chapter 150 - Uniform Revocation of Licenses [Repealed.]	84
Chapter 150A - Administrative Procedure Act [Recodified.]	84
Chapter 150B - Administrative Procedure Act	84
Chapter 151 - Constables [Repealed.]	84
Chapter 152 - Coroners	84
Chapter 152A - County Medical Examiner [Repealed.]	84
Chapter 152A - County Medical Examiner [Repealed.] (Continuation)	85
Chapter 153 - Counties and County Commissioners [Repealed.]	85
Chapter 153A - Counties	85
Chapter 153B - Mountain Resources Planning Act	85
Chapter 153C - Uwharrie Regional Resources Act	85
Chapter 154 - County Surveyor [Repealed.]	85
Chapter 155 - County Treasurer [Repealed.]	85
Chapter 156 - Drainage	85

Chapter 156 – Drainage (Continuation)	86
Chapter 157 - Housing Authorities and Projects	86
Chapter 157A - Historic Properties Commissions [Transferred.]	86
Chapter 158 - Local Development	86
Chapter 159 - Local Government Finance	86
Chapter 159 - Local Government Finance (Continuation)	87
Chapter 159A - Pollution Abatement and Industrial Facilities Financing Act [Unconstitutional.]	87
Chapter 159B - Joint Municipal Electric Power and Energy Act	87
Chapter 159C - Industrial and Pollution Control Facilities Financing Act	87
Chapter 159D - The North Carolina Capital Facilities Financing Act	87
Chapter 159E - Registered Public Obligations Act	87
Chapter 159F - North Carolina Energy Development Authority [Repealed.]	87
Chapter 159G - Water Infrastructure	87
Chapter 159H - [Reserved.]	87
Chapter 159I - Solid Waste Management Loan Program and Local Government Special Obligation Bonds	87
Chapter 160 - Municipal Corporations [Repealed And Transferred.]	87
Chapter 160A - Cities and Towns	88
Chapter 160A - Cities and Towns (Continuation)	89
Chapter 160B - Consolidated City-County Act	89
Chapter 160C - Baseball Park Districts [Repealed.]	90
Chapter 161 - Register of Deeds	90
Chapter 162 - Sheriff	90
Chapter 162A - Water and Sewer Systems	90
Chapter 162B Continuity of Local Government in Emergency.	90
Chapter 163 Elections and Election Laws.	90
Chapter 163 Elections and Election Laws. (Continuation)	91
Chapter 164 Concerning the General Statutes of North Carolina.	92
Chapter 165 Veterans.	92
Chapter 166 Civil Preparedness Agencies [Repealed.]	92
Chapter 166A North Carolina Emergency Management Act.	92
Chapter 167 State Civil Air Patrol [Repealed.]	92
Chapter 168 Persons with Disabilities.	92
Chapter 168A Persons With Disabilities Protection Act.	92

§ 15A-623. Grand jury proceedings and operation in general.

(a)   The finding of an indictment, the return of a presentment, and every other affirmative official action or decision of the grand jury requires the concurrence of at least 12 members of the grand jury.

(b)   The foreman presides over all hearings and has the power to administer oaths or affirmations to all witnesses.

(c)   The foreman must indicate on each bill of indictment or presentment the witness or witnesses sworn and examined before the grand jury. Failure to comply with this provision does not vitiate a bill of indictment or presentment.

(d)   During the deliberations and voting of a grand jury, only the grand jurors may be present in the grand jury room. During its other proceedings, the following persons, in addition to a witness being examined, may, as the occasion requires, also be present:

(1)   An interpreter, if needed.

(2)   A law-enforcement officer holding a witness in custody.

Any person other than a witness who is permitted in the grand jury room must first take an oath before the grand jury that he will keep secret all matters before it within his knowledge.

(e)   Grand jury proceedings are secret and, except as expressly provided in this Article, members of the grand jury and all persons present during its sessions shall keep its secrets and refrain from disclosing anything which transpires during any of its sessions.

(f)   The presiding judge may direct that a bill of indictment be kept secret until the defendant is arrested or appears before the court. The clerk must seal the bill of indictment and no person including a witness may disclose the finding of the bill of indictment, or the proceedings leading to the finding, except when necessary for the issuance and execution of an order of arrest.

(g)   Any grand juror or other person authorized to attend sessions of the grand jury and bound to keep its secrets who discloses, other than to his attorney, matters occurring before the grand jury other than in accordance with the provisions of this section is in contempt of court and subject to proceedings in accordance with law.

(h)   If a grand jury is convened pursuant to G.S. 15A-622(h), notwithstanding subsection (d) of this section, a prosecutor shall be present to examine witnesses, and a court reporter shall be present and record the examination of witnesses. The record shall be transcribed. If the prosecutor determines that it is necessary to compel testimony from the witness, he may grant use immunity to the witness. The grant of use immunity shall be given to the witness in writing by the prosecutor and shall be signed by the prosecutor. The written grant of use immunity shall also be read into the record by the prosecutor and shall include an explanation of use immunity as provided in G.S. 15A-1051. A witness shall have the right to leave the grand jury room to consult with his counsel at reasonable intervals and for a reasonable period of time upon the request of the witness. Notwithstanding subsection (e) of this section, the record of the examination of witnesses shall be made available to the examining prosecutor, and he may disclose contents of the record to other investigative or law-enforcement officers, the witness or his attorney to the extent that the disclosure is appropriate to the proper performance of his official duties. The record of the examination of a witness may be used in a trial to the extent that it is relevant and otherwise admissible. Further disclosure of grand jury proceedings convened pursuant to this act may be made upon written order of a superior court judge if the judge determines disclosure is essential:

(1)   To prosecute a witness who appeared before the grand jury for contempt or perjury; or

(2)   To protect a defendant's constitutional rights or statutory rights to discovery pursuant to G.S. 15A-903.

Upon the convening of the investigative grand jury pursuant to approval by the three-judge panel, the district attorney shall subpoena the witnesses. The subpoena shall be served by the investigative grand jury officer, who shall be appointed by the court. The name of the person subpoenaed and the issuance and service of the subpoena shall not be disclosed, except that a witness so subpoenaed may divulge that information. The presiding superior court judge shall hear any matter concerning the investigative grand jury in camera to the extent necessary to prevent disclosure of its existence. The court reporter for the investigative grand jury shall be present and record and transcribe the in camera proceeding. The transcription of any in camera proceeding and a copy of all subpoenas and other process shall be returned to the Chief Justice or to such member of the three-judge panel as the Chief Justice may designate, to be filed with the Clerk of the North Carolina Supreme Court. The subpoena shall otherwise be subject to the provisions of G.S. 15A-801 and Article 43 of Chapter 15A. When an investigative grand jury has completed its investigation of the crimes alleged in the petition, the investigative functions of the grand jury shall be dissolved and such investigation shall cease. The District Attorney shall file a notice of dissolution of the investigative functions of the grand jury with the Clerk of the North Carolina Supreme Court. (1973, c. 1286, s. 1; 1985 (Reg. Sess., 1986), c. 843, ss. 3, 6; 1987 (Reg. Sess., 1988), c. 1040, ss. 1, 4; 1989 (Reg. Sess., 1990), c. 1039, s. 4; 1991, c. 686, ss. 2, 3.)

§ 15A-624. Grand jury the judge of facts; judge the source of legal advice.

(a)   The grand jury is the exclusive judge of the facts with respect to any matter before it.

(b)   The legal advisor of the grand jury is the presiding or convening judge. (1973, c. 1286, s. 1.)

§ 15A-625. Reserved for future codification purposes.

§ 15A-626. Who may call witnesses before grand jury; no right to appear without consent of prosecutor or judge.

(a)   Except as provided in this section, no person has a right to call a witness or appear as a witness in a grand jury proceeding.

(b)   In proceedings upon bills of indictment submitted by the prosecutor to the grand jury, the clerk must call as witnesses the persons whose names are listed on the bills by the prosecutor. If the grand jury desires to hear any witness not named on the bill under consideration, it must through its foreman request the prosecutor to call the witness. The prosecutor in his discretion may call, or refuse to call, the witness.

(c) In considering any matter before it a grand jury may swear and hear the testimony of a member of the grand jury.

(d) Any person not called as a witness who desires to testify before the grand jury concerning a criminal matter which may properly be considered by the grand jury must apply to the district attorney or to a superior court judge. The judge or the district attorney in his discretion may call the witness to appear before the grand jury.

(e) An official who is required or authorized to call a witness before the grand jury does so by issuing a subpoena for the witness or by causing one to be issued. If the official is assured that the witness will appear when requested without issuance of a subpoena, he may call the witness simply by notifying him of the time and place his presence is requested before the grand jury. (1973, c. 1286, s. 1; 1975, c. 166, s. 27.)

§ 15A-627. Submission of bill of indictment to grand jury by prosecutor.

(a) When a defendant has been bound over for trial in the superior court upon any charge in the original jurisdiction of such court, the prosecutor, unless he dismisses the charge under the terms of Article 50 of this Chapter, Voluntary Dismissal by the State, or proceeds upon a bill of information, must submit a bill of indictment charging the offense to the grand jury for its consideration.

(b) A prosecutor may submit a bill of indictment charging an offense within the original jurisdiction of the superior court. (1973, c. 1286, s. 1; 1975, c. 166, s. 27.)

§ 15A-628. Functions of grand jury; record to be kept by clerk.

(a) A grand jury:

(1) Must return a bill submitted to it by the prosecutor as a true bill of indictment if it finds from the evidence probable cause for the charge made.

(2) Must return a bill submitted to it by the prosecutor as not a true bill of indictment if it fails to find probable cause for the charge made. Upon returning a

bill of indictment as not a true bill, the grand jury may request the prosecutor to submit a bill of indictment as to a lesser included or related offense.

(3)   May return the bill to the court with an indication that the grand jury has not been able to act upon it because of the unavailability of witnesses.

(4)   May investigate any offense as to which no bill of indictment has been submitted to it by the prosecutor and issue a presentment accusing a named person or named persons with one or more criminal offenses if it has found probable cause for the charges made. An investigation may be initiated upon the concurrence of 12 members of the grand jury itself or upon the request of the presiding or convening judge or the prosecutor.

(5)   Must inspect the jail and may inspect other county offices or agencies and must report the results of its inspections to the court.

(b)   In proceeding under subsection (a), the grand jury may consider any offense which may be prosecuted in the courts of the county, or in the courts of the superior court district or set of districts as defined in G.S. 7A-41.1 when there has been a waiver of venue in accordance with Article 3 of this Chapter, Venue.

(c)   Bills of indictment submitted by the prosecutor to the grand jury, whether found to be true bills or not, must be returned by the foreman of the grand jury to the presiding judge in open court. Presentments must also be returned by the foreman of the grand jury to the presiding judge in open court.

(d)   The clerk must keep a permanent record of all matters returned by the grand jury to the judge under the provisions of this section. (1973, c. 1286, s. 1; 1975, c. 166, s. 27; 1987 (Reg. Sess., 1988), c. 1037, s. 59.)

§ 15A-629. Procedure upon finding of not a true bill; release of defendant, etc.; institution of new charge.

(a)   Upon the return of a bill of indictment as not a true bill, the presiding judge must immediately examine the case records to determine if the defendant is in custody or subject to bail or conditions of pretrial release. If so, except as provided in subsection (b), the judge must immediately order release from custody, exoneration of bail, or release from conditions of pretrial release, as the case may be.

(b)   Upon the return of a bill of indictment as not a true bill but with a request that the prosecutor submit a bill of indictment to a lesser included or related offense, the judge may defer the action required in subsection (a) for a reasonable period, not to extend past the end of that session of superior court, to allow the institution of the new charge. (1973, c. 1286, s. 1; 1975, c. 166, s. 27.)

§ 15A-630. Notice to defendant of true bill of indictment.

Upon the return of a bill of indictment as a true bill the presiding judge must immediately cause notice of the indictment to be mailed or otherwise given to the defendant unless he is then represented by counsel of record. The notice must inform the defendant of the time limitations upon his right to discovery under Article 48 of this Chapter, Discovery in the Superior Court, and a copy of the indictment must be attached to the notice. If the judge directs that the indictment be sealed as provided in G.S. 15A-623(f), he may defer the giving of notice under this section for a reasonable length of time. (1973, c. 1286, s. 1; 1975, 2nd Sess., c. 983, s. 143.)

§ 15A-631. Grand jury venue.

In the General Court of Justice, the place for returning a presentment or indictment is a matter of venue and not jurisdiction. A grand jury shall have venue to present or indict in any case where the county in which it is sitting has venue for trial pursuant to the laws relating to trial venue. (1985, c. 553, s. 1.)

§§ 15A-632 through 15A-640. Reserved for future codification purposes.

Article 32.

Indictment and Related Instruments.

§ 15A-641. Indictment and related instruments; definitions of indictment, information, and presentment.

(a) Any indictment is a written accusation by a grand jury, filed with a superior court, charging a person with the commission of one or more criminal offenses.

(b) An information is a written accusation by a prosecutor, filed with a superior court, charging a person represented by counsel with the commission of one or more criminal offenses.

(c) A presentment is a written accusation by a grand jury, made on its own motion and filed with a superior court, charging a person, or two or more persons jointly, with the commission of one or more criminal offenses. A presentment does not institute criminal proceedings against any person, but the district attorney is obligated to investigate the factual background of every presentment returned in his district and to submit bills of indictment to the grand jury dealing with the subject matter of any presentments when it is appropriate to do so. (1797, c. 474, s. 3, P.R.; R.C., c. 35, s. 6; 1879, c. 12; Code, s. 1175; Rev., s. 3240; C.S., s. 4607; 1973, c. 1286, s. 1; 1975, c. 166, s. 27.)

§ 15A-642. Prosecutions originating in superior court to be upon indictment or information; waiver of indictment.

(a) Prosecutions originating in the superior court must be upon pleadings as provided in Article 49 of this Chapter, Pleadings and Joinder.

(b) Indictment may not be waived in a capital case or in a case in which the defendant is not represented by counsel.

(c) Waiver of indictment must be in writing and signed by the defendant and his attorney. The waiver must be attached to or executed upon the bill of information. (1907, c. 71; C.S., s. 4610; 1951, c. 726, ss. 1, 2; 1971, c. 377, s. 30.1; 1973, c. 1286, s. 1.)

§ 15A-643. Joinder of offenses and defendants and consolidation of indictments and informations.

The rules with respect to joinder of offenses and defendants and the consolidation of charges in indictments and informations are provided in Article 49 of this Chapter, Pleadings and Joinder. (1917, c. 168; C.S., s. 4622; 1921, c. 100; 1973, c. 1286, s. 1.)

§ 15A-644. Form and content of indictment, information or presentment.

(a) An indictment must contain:

(1) The name of the superior court in which it is filed;

(2) The title of the action;

(3) Criminal charges pleaded as provided in Article 49 of this Chapter, Pleadings and Joinder;

(4) The signature of the prosecutor, but its omission is not a fatal defect; and

(5) The signature of the foreman or acting foreman of the grand jury attesting the concurrence of 12 or more grand jurors in the finding of a true bill of indictment.

(b) An information must contain everything required of an indictment in subsection (a) except that the accusation is that of the prosecutor and the provisions of subdivision (a)(5) do not apply. The information must also contain or have attached the waiver of indictment pursuant to G.S. 15A-642(c).

(c) A presentment must contain everything required of an indictment in subsection (a) except that the provisions of subdivisions (a)(4) and (5) do not apply and the foreman must by his signature attest the concurrence of 12 or more grand jurors in the presentment. (1973, c. 1286, s. 1; 1975, c. 166, s. 27.)

§ 15A-644.1. Filing of information when plea of guilty or no contest in district court to Class H or I felony.

A defendant who pleads guilty or no contest in district court pursuant to G.S. 7A-272(c)(1) shall enter that plea to an information complying with G.S. 15A-644(b), except it shall contain the name of the district court in which it is filed. (1995 (Reg. Sess., 1996), c. 725, s. 3.)

§ 15A-645. Allegations of previous convictions.

Trial upon indictments and informations involving allegation of previous convictions is subject to the provisions of G.S. 15A-928. (1973, c. 1286, s. 1.)

§ 15A-646. Superseding indictments and informations.

If at any time before entry of a plea of guilty to an indictment or information, or commencement of a trial thereof, another indictment or information is filed in the same court charging the defendant with an offense charged or attempted to be charged in the first instrument, the first one is, with respect to the offense, superseded by the second and, upon the defendant's arraignment upon the second indictment or information, the count of the first instrument charging the offense must be dismissed by the superior court judge. The first instrument is not, however, superseded with respect to any count contained therein which charged an offense not charged in the second indictment or information. (1973, c. 1286, s. 1.)

Article 33.

§§ 15A-647 through 15A-673. Reserved for future codification purposes.

Article 34.

§§ 15A-674 through 15A-700. Reserved for future codification purposes.

SUBCHAPTER VII. SPEEDY TRIAL; ATTENDANCE OF DEFENDANTS.

Article 35.

Speedy Trial.

§§ 15A-701 through 15A-710: Repealed by Session Laws 1989, c. 688, s. 1.

Article 36.

Special Criminal Process for Attendance of Defendants.

§ 15A-711. Securing attendance of criminal defendants confined in institutions within the State; requiring prosecutor to proceed.

(a)   When a criminal defendant is confined in a penal or other institution under the control of the State or any of its subdivisions and his presence is required for trial, the prosecutor may make written request to the custodian of the institution for temporary release of the defendant to the custody of an appropriate law-enforcement officer who must produce him at the trial. The period of the temporary release may not exceed 60 days. The request of the prosecutor is sufficient authorization for the release, and must be honored, except as otherwise provided in this section.

(b)   If the defendant whose presence is sought is confined pursuant to another criminal proceeding in a different prosecutorial district as defined in G.S. 7A-60, the defendant and the prosecutor prosecuting the other criminal action must be given reasonable notice and opportunity to object to the temporary release. Objections must be heard by a superior court judge having authority to act in criminal cases in the superior court district or set of districts as defined in G.S. 7A-41.1 in which the defendant is confined, and he must make appropriate orders as to the precedence of the actions.

(c)   A defendant who is confined in an institution in this State pursuant to a criminal proceeding and who has other criminal charges pending against him may, by written request filed with the clerk of the court where the other charges are pending, require the prosecutor prosecuting such charges to proceed pursuant to this section. A copy of the request must be served upon the prosecutor in the manner provided by the Rules of Civil Procedure, G.S. 1A-1,

Rule 5(b). If the prosecutor does not proceed pursuant to subsection (a) within six months from the date the request is filed with the clerk, the charges must be dismissed.

(d)   Detainer. -

(1)   When a criminal defendant is imprisoned in this State pursuant to prior criminal proceedings, the clerk upon request of the prosecutor, must transmit to the custodian of the institution in which he is imprisoned, a copy of the charges filed against the defendant and a detainer directing that the prisoner be held to answer to the charges made against him. The detainer must contain a notice of the prisoner's right to proceed pursuant to G.S. 15A-711(c).

(2)   Upon receipt of the charges and the detainer, the custodian must immediately inform the prisoner of its receipt and furnish him copies of the charges and the detainer, must explain to him his right to proceed pursuant to G.S. 15A-711(c).

(3)   The custodian must notify the clerk who transmitted the detainer of the defendant's impending release at least 30 days prior to the date of release. The notice must be given immediately if the detainer is received less than 30 days prior to the date of release. The clerk must direct the sheriff to take custody of the defendant and produce him for trial. The custodian must release the defendant to the custody of the sheriff, but may not hold the defendant in confinement beyond the date on which he is eligible for release.

(4)   A detainer may be withdrawn upon request of the prosecutor, and the clerk must notify the custodian, who must notify the defendant. (1949, c. 303; 1953, c. 603; 1957, c. 349, s. 10; c. 1067, ss. 1, 2; 1967, c. 996, ss. 13, 15; 1973, c. 1286, s. 1; 1975, c. 166, s. 27; 1979, c. 107, s. 1; 1987 (Reg. Sess., 1988), c. 1037, s. 61; 1989, c. 688, s. 3.)

§§ 15A-712 through 15A-720. Reserved for future codification purposes.

Article 37.

Uniform Criminal Extradition Act.

§ 15A-721. Definitions.

Where appearing in this Article the term "Governor" includes any person performing the functions of Governor by authority of the law of this State. The term "executive authority" includes the Governor, and any person performing the functions of governor in a state other than this State. The term "state," referring to a state other than this State, includes any other state or territory, organized or unorganized, of the United States of America. (1937, c. 273, s. 1; 1973, c. 1286, s. 16.)

§ 15A-722. Duty of Governor as to fugitives from justice of other states.

Subject to the provisions of this Article, the provisions of the Constitution of the United States controlling, and any and all acts of Congress enacted in pursuance thereof, it is the duty of the Governor of this State to have arrested and delivered up to the executive authority of any other state of the United States any person charged in that state with treason, felony or other crime, who has fled from justice and is found in this State. (1937, c. 273, s. 2; 1973, c. 1286, s. 16.)

§ 15A-723. Form of demand for extradition.

No demand for the extradition of a person charged with crime in another state shall be recognized by the Governor unless in writing alleging, except in cases arising under G.S. 15A-726, that the accused was present in the demanding state at the time of the commission of the alleged crime, and that thereafter he fled from the state, and accompanied by a copy of an indictment found or by information supported by affidavit in the state having jurisdiction of the crime, or by a copy of an affidavit made before a magistrate there, together with a copy of any warrant which was issued thereupon; or by a copy of a judgment of conviction or of a sentence imposed in execution thereof, together with a statement by the executive authority of the demanding state that the person claimed has escaped from confinement or has broken the terms of his bail, probation or parole. The indictment, information, or affidavit made before the magistrate must substantially charge the person demanded with having committed a crime under the law of that state; and the copy of indictment, information, affidavit, judgment of conviction or sentence must be authenticated by the executive authority making the demand. (1937, c. 273, s. 3; 1973, c. 1286, s. 16.)

§ 15A-724. Governor may cause investigation to be made.

When a demand shall be made upon the Governor of this State by the executive authority of another state for the surrender of a person so charged with crime, the Governor may call upon the Attorney General or any prosecuting officer in this State to investigate or assist in investigating the demand, and to report to him the situation and circumstances of the person so demanded, and whether he ought to be surrendered. (1937, c. 273, s. 4; 1973, c. 1286, s. 16.)

§ 15A-725. Extradition of persons imprisoned or awaiting trial in another state or who have left the demanding state under compulsion.

When it is desired to have returned to this State a person charged in this State with a crime, and such person is imprisoned or is held under criminal proceedings then pending against him in another state, the Governor of this State may agree with the executive authority of such other state for the extradition of such person before the conclusion of such proceedings or his term of sentence in such other state, upon condition that such person be returned to such other state at the expense of this State as soon as the prosecution in this State is terminated.

The Governor of this State may also surrender on demand of the executive authority of any other state any person in this State who is charged in the manner provided in G.S. 15A-743 with having violated the laws of the state whose executive authority is making the demand, even though such person left the demanding state involuntarily. (1937, c. 273, s. 5; 1973, c. 1286, s. 16.)

§ 15A-726. Extradition of persons not present in demanding state at time of commission of crime.

The Governor of this State may also surrender, on demand of the executive authority of any other state, any person in this State charged in such other state in the manner provided in G.S. 15A-723 with committing an act in this State, or in a third state, intentionally resulting in a crime in the state whose executive authority is making the demand, and the provisions of this Article, not otherwise inconsistent, shall apply to such cases, even though the accused was not in that state at the time of the commission of the crime, and has not fled therefrom. (1937, c. 273, s. 6; 1973, c. 1286, s. 16.)

§ 15A-727. Issue of Governor's warrant of arrest; its recitals.

If the Governor decides that the demand should be complied with, he shall sign a warrant of arrest, which shall be sealed with the State seal, and be directed to any peace officer or other person whom he may think fit to entrust with the execution thereof. The warrant must substantially recite the facts necessary to the validity of its issuance. (1937, c. 273, s. 7; 1973, c. 1286, s. 16.)

§ 15A-728. Manner and place of execution of warrant.

Such warrant shall authorize the peace officer or other person to whom directed to arrest the accused at any time and any place where he may be found within the State, and to command the aid of all peace officers or other persons in the execution of the warrant, and to deliver the accused, subject to the provisions of this Article, to the duly authorized agent of the demanding state. (1937, c. 273, s. 8; 1973, c. 1286, s. 16.)

§ 15A-729. Authority of arresting officer.

Every such peace officer or other person empowered to make the arrest shall have the same authority, in arresting the accused, to command assistance therein as peace officers have by law in the execution of any criminal process directed to them, with like penalties against those who refuse their assistance. (1937, c. 273, s. 9; 1973, c. 1286, s. 16.)

§ 15A-730. Rights of accused person; application for writ of habeas corpus.

No person arrested upon such warrant shall be delivered over to the agent whom the executive authority demanding him shall have appointed to receive him unless he shall first be taken forthwith before a judge of a court of record in this State, who shall inform him of the demand made for his surrender and of the crime with which he is charged, and that he has the right to demand and procure legal counsel; and if the prisoner or his counsel shall state that he or they desire to test the legality of his arrest, the judge of such court of record shall fix a reasonable time to be allowed him within which to apply for a writ of habeas corpus. When such writ is applied for, notice thereof, and of the time and place of hearing thereon, shall be given to the prosecuting officer of the county in which the arrest is made and in which the accused is in custody, and to the said agent of the demanding state. (1937, c. 273, s. 10; 1973, c. 1286, s. 16.)

§ 15A-731. Penalty for noncompliance with § 15A-730.

Any officer who shall deliver to the agent for extradition of the demanding state a person in his custody under the Governor's warrant, in willful disobedience to G.S. 15A-730, shall be guilty of a Class 2 misdemeanor. (1937, c. 273, s. 11; 1973, c. 1286, s. 16; 1993, c. 539, s. 302; 1994, Ex. Sess., c. 24, s. 14(c).)

§ 15A-732. Confinement in jail when necessary.

The officer or person executing the Governor's warrant of arrest, or the agent of the demanding state to whom the prisoner may have been delivered, may, when necessary, confine the prisoner in the jail of any county or city through which he may pass; and the keeper of such jail must receive and safely keep the prisoner until the officer or person having charge of him is ready to proceed on his route, such officer or person being chargeable with the expense of keeping.

The officer or agent of a demanding state to whom a prisoner may have been delivered following extradition proceedings in another state, or to whom a prisoner may have been delivered after waiving extradition in such other state, and who is passing through this State with such a prisoner for the purpose of immediately returning such prisoner to the demanding state may, when necessary, confine the prisoner in the jail of any county or city through which he may pass; and the keeper of such jail must receive and safely keep the prisoner until the officer or agent having charge of him is ready to proceed on his route, such officer or agent, however, being chargeable with the expense of keeping: Provided, however, that such officer or agent shall produce and show to the keeper of such jail satisfactory written evidence of the fact that he is actually transporting such prisoner to the demanding state after a requisition by the executive authority of such demanding state. Such prisoner shall not be entitled to demand a new requisition while in this State. (1937, c. 273, s. 12; 1973, c. 1286, s. 16.)

§ 15A-733. Arrest prior to requisition.

Whenever any person within this State shall be charged on the oath of any credible person before any judge or magistrate of this State with the commission of any crime in any other state and, except in cases arising under G.S. 15A-726, with having fled from justice, or with having been convicted of a crime in that state and having escaped from confinement, or having broken the terms of his bail, probation or parole, or whenever complaint shall have been made before any judge or magistrate in this State, setting forth on the affidavit of any credible person in another state that a crime has been committed in such other state, and that the accused has been charged in such state with the commission of the crime, and, except in cases arising under G.S. 15A-726, has fled from justice, or with having been convicted of a crime in that state and having escaped from confinement, or having broken the terms of his bail, probation or parole, and is believed to be in this State, the judge or magistrate shall issue a warrant directed to any peace officer commanding him to apprehend the person named therein, wherever he may be found in this State, and to bring him before the same or any other judge, magistrate or court who or which may be available in or convenient of access to the place where the arrest may be made, to answer the charge or complaint and affidavit, and a certified copy of the sworn charge or complaint and affidavit upon which the warrant is issued shall be attached to the warrant. (1937, c. 273, s. 13; 1973, c. 1286, s. 16.)

§ 15A-734. Arrest without a warrant.

The arrest of a person may be lawfully made also by any peace officer or a private person, without a warrant, upon reasonable information that the accused stands charged in the courts of a state with a crime punishable by death or imprisonment for a term exceeding one year, but when so arrested the accused must be taken before a judge or magistrate with all practicable speed, and complaint must be made against him under oath setting forth the ground for the arrest as in G.S. 15A-733; and thereafter his answer shall be heard as if he had been arrested on a warrant. (1937, c. 273, s. 14; 1973, c. 1286, s. 16.)

§ 15A-735. Commitment to await requisition; bail.

If from the examination before the judge or magistrate it appears that the person held is the person charged with having committed the crime alleged and, except in cases arising under G.S. 15A-726, that he has fled from justice, the judge or magistrate must, by a warrant reciting the accusation, commit him to the county jail for such a time, not exceeding 30 days and specified in the warrant, as will enable the arrest of the accused to be made under a warrant of the Governor on a requisition of the executive authority of the state having jurisdiction of the offense, unless the accused give bail as provided in G.S. 15A-736, or until he shall be legally discharged. (1937, c. 273, s. 15; 1973, c. 1286, s. 16.)

§ 15A-736. Bail in certain cases; conditions of bond.

Unless the offense with which the prisoner is charged is shown to be an offense punishable by death or life imprisonment under the laws of the state in which it was committed, a judge or magistrate in this State may admit the person arrested to bail by bond, with sufficient sureties, and in such sum as he deems proper, conditioned for his appearance before him at a time specified in such bond, and for his surrender, to be arrested upon the warrant of the Governor of this State. (1937, c. 273, s. 16; 1973, c. 1286, s. 16.)

§ 15A-736.1: Recodified as G.S. 15A-534.6 by Session Laws 2007-484, s. 4, effective August 30, 2007.

§ 15A-737. Extension of time of commitment; adjournment.

If the accused is not arrested under warrant of the Governor by the expiration of the time specified in the warrant or bond, a judge or magistrate may discharge him or may recommit him for a further period not to exceed 60 days, or a judge or magistrate may again take bail for his appearance and surrender, as provided in G.S. 15A-736, but within a period not to exceed 60 days after the date of such new bond. (1937, c. 273, s. 17; 1973, c. 1286, s. 16.)

§ 15A-738. Forfeiture of bail.

If the prisoner is admitted to bail and fails to appear and surrender himself according to the conditions of his bond, the judge, or magistrate by proper order, shall declare the bond forfeited and order his immediate arrest without warrant if he be within this State. Recovery may be had on such bond in the name of the State as in the case of other bonds given by the accused in criminal proceedings within this State. (1937, c. 273, s. 18; 1973, c. 1286, s. 16.)

§ 15A-739. Persons under criminal prosecution in this State at time of requisition.

If a criminal prosecution has been instituted against such person under the laws of this State and is still pending, the Governor, in his discretion, either may surrender him on demand of the executive authority of another state or hold him until he has been tried and discharged or convicted and punished in this State. (1937, c. 273, s. 19; 1973, c. 1286, s. 16.)

§ 15A-740. Guilt or innocence of accused, when inquired into.

The guilt or innocence of the accused as to the crime of which he is charged may not be inquired into by the Governor or in any proceeding after the demand for extradition accompanied by a charge of crime in legal form as above provided shall have been presented to the Governor, except as it may be involved in identifying the person held as the person charged with the crime. (1937, c. 273, s. 20; 1973, c. 1286, s. 16.)

§ 15A-741. Governor may recall warrant or issue alias.

The Governor may recall his warrant of arrest or may issue another warrant whenever he deems proper. (1937, c. 273, s. 21; 1973, c. 1286, s. 16.)

§ 15A-742. Fugitives from this State; duty of governors.

Whenever the Governor of this State shall demand a person charged with a crime or with escaping from confinement or breaking the terms of his bail, probation or parole in this State from the executive authority of any other state, or from the chief justice or an associate justice of the Supreme Court of the District of Columbia authorized to receive such demand under the laws of the United States, he shall issue a warrant under the seal of this State, to some agent, commanding him to receive the person so charged if delivered to him and convey him to the proper officer of the county in this State in which the offense was committed. (1937, c. 273, s. 22; 1973, c. 1286, s. 16.)

§ 15A-743. Application for issuance of requisition; by whom made; contents.

(a) When the return to this State of a person charged with crime in this State is required, the prosecuting attorney shall present to the Governor his written application for a requisition for the return of the person charged, in which application shall be stated the name of the person so charged, the crime charged against him, the approximate time, place and circumstances of its commission, the state in which he is believed to be, including the location of the accused therein, at the time the application is made and certifying that, in the opinion of the said prosecuting attorney, the ends of justice require the arrest and return of the accused to this State for trial and that the proceeding is not instituted to enforce a private claim.

(b) When the return to this State is required of a person who has been convicted of a crime in this State and has escaped from confinement or broken the terms of his bail, probation or parole, the prosecuting attorney of the county in which the offense was committed, the parole board, or the Director of Prisons or sheriff of the county from which escape was made, shall present to the Governor a written application for a requisition for the return of such person, in which application shall be stated the name of the person, the crime of which he was convicted, the circumstances of his escape from confinement or of the breach of the terms of his bail, probation or parole, the state in which he is believed to be, including the location of the person therein at the time application is made.

(c) The application shall be verified by affidavit, shall be executed in duplicate and shall be accompanied by two certified copies of the indictment returned, or information and affidavit filed, or of the complaint made to the judge or magistrate, stating the offense with which the accused is charged, or of the judgment of conviction or of the sentence. The prosecuting officer, parole board, warden or sheriff may also attach such further affidavits and other documents in duplicate as he shall deem proper to be submitted with such application. A copy of all papers shall be forwarded with the Governor's requisition. (1937, c. 273, s. 23; 1973, c. 1286, s. 16; 1975, c. 132; 1993, c. 83.)

§ 15A-744. Costs and expenses.

Subject to the requirements and restrictions set forth in this section, if the crime is a felony or if a person convicted in this State of a misdemeanor has broken the terms of his probation or parole, reimbursements for expenses shall be paid out of the State treasury on the certificate of the Governor. In all other cases, such expenses or reimbursements shall be paid out of the county treasury of the county wherein the crime is alleged to have been committed according to such regulations as the board of county commissioners may promulgate. In all cases, the expenses, for which repayment or reimbursement may be claimed, shall consist of the reasonable and necessary travel expense and subsistence costs of the extradition agent or fugitive officer, as well as the fugitive, together with such legal fees as were paid to the officials of the state on whose governor the requisition is made. The person or persons designated to return the fugitive shall not be allowed, paid or reimbursed for any expenses in connection with any requisition or extradition proceeding unless the expenses are itemized, the statement of same be sworn to under oath, and shall not then be paid or reimbursed unless a receipt is obtained showing the amount, the purpose for which said item or sum was expended, the place, date and to whom paid, and said receipt or receipts attached to said sworn statement and filed with the Governor. The Governor shall have the authority, upon investigation, to increase or decrease any item or expenses shown in said sworn statement, or to include items of expenses omitted by mistake or inadvertence. The decision or determination of the Governor as to the correct amount to be paid for such expenses or reimbursements shall be final. When it is deemed necessary for more than one agent, extradition agent, fugitive officer or person, to be designated to return a fugitive from another state to this State, the district attorney or prosecuting officer shall file with his written application to the Governor of this State an affidavit setting forth in detail the grounds or reasons why it is necessary to have more than one extradition agent, fugitive officer or person to be so designated. Among other things, and not by way of limitation, the affidavit shall set forth whether or not the alleged fugitive is a dangerous person, his previous criminal record if any, and any record of said fugitive on file with the Federal Bureau of Investigation or with the prison authorities of this State. As a further ground or reason for more than one extradition agent or fugitive officer to be designated, it may be shown in said affidavit the number of fugitives to be returned to this State and any other grounds or reasons for which more than one extradition agent or fugitive officer is desired. If the Governor finds or determines from his own investigation and from the information made available to him that more than one extradition agent or fugitive officer is necessary for the return of a fugitive or fugitives to this State, he may designate more than one extradition agent or fugitive officer for such purpose. All travel for which expenses or reimbursements are paid or allowed under this section shall be by the nearest, direct, convenient route of travel. If the extradition agent or agents or person or persons designated to return a fugitive or fugitives from another state to this State shall elect to travel by automobile, a sum not exceeding seven cents (7¢) per mile may be allowed in lieu of all travel expense, and which shall be paid upon a basis of mileage for the complete trip. The Governor may promulgate executive orders, rules and regulations governing travel, forms of statements, receipts or any other matter or objective provided for in this section. The Governor may delegate any or all of the duties, powers and responsibilities conferred upon him by this section to any executive agent or executive clerk on his staff or in his office, and such executive agent or executive clerk, when properly authorized, may perform any or all of the duties, powers and responsibilities conferred upon the Governor. Provided that if the fugitive from justice is an alleged felon, and he be returned without the service of extradition papers by the sheriff or the agent of the sheriff of the county in which the felony was alleged to have been committed, the expense of said return shall be borne by the State of North Carolina under the rules and regulations made and promulgated by the Governor of North Carolina or the executive agent or the executive clerk to whom the said Governor may have delegated his duties under this section. (1937, c. 273, s. 24; 1953, c. 1203; 1955, c. 289; 1973, c. 1286, s. 16; 1975, c. 166, s. 27; 1981, c. 859, s. 13.9.)

§ 15A-745. Immunity from service of process in certain civil actions.

A person brought into this State by, or after waiver of, extradition based on a criminal charge shall not be subject to service of personal process in civil actions arising out of the same facts as the criminal proceedings to answer which he is being or has been returned until he has been convicted in the criminal proceeding or, if acquitted, until he has had reasonable opportunity to return to the state from which he was extradited. (1937, c. 273, s. 25; 1973, c. 1286, s. 16.)

§ 15A-746. Written waiver of extradition proceedings.

Any person arrested in this State charged with having committed any crime in another state or alleged to have escaped from confinement, or broken the terms of his bail, probation or parole may waive the issuance and service of the warrant provided for in G.S. 15A-727 and 15A-728 and all other procedure incidental to extradition proceedings, by executing or subscribing in the presence of a judge of any court of record within this State or a clerk of the superior court a writing which states that he consents to return to the demanding state: Provided, however, that before such waiver shall be executed or subscribed by such person it shall be the duty of such judge or clerk of superior court to inform such person of his rights to the issuance and service of a warrant of extradition and to obtain a writ of habeas corpus as provided for in G.S. 15A-730.

If and when such consent has been duly executed it shall forthwith be forwarded to the office of the Governor of this State and filed therein. The judge or clerk of superior court shall direct the officer having such person in custody to deliver forthwith such person to the duly accredited agent or agents of the demanding state, and shall deliver or cause to be delivered to such agent or agents a copy of such consent: Provided, however, that nothing in this section shall be deemed to limit the rights of the accused person to return voluntarily and without formality to the demanding state, nor shall this waiver procedure be deemed to be an exclusive procedure or to limit the powers, rights or duties of the officers of the demanding state or of this State. (1937, c. 273, s. 25a; 1959, c. 271; 1973, c. 1286, s. 16.)

§ 15A-747. Nonwaiver by this State.

Nothing in this Article contained shall be deemed to constitute a waiver by this State of its right, power or privilege to try such demanded person for crime committed within this State, or of its right, power or privilege to regain custody of such person by extradition proceedings or otherwise for the purpose of trial, sentence or punishment for any crime committed within this State, nor shall any proceedings had under this Article which result in, or fail to result in, extradition be deemed a waiver by this State of any of its rights, privileges or jurisdiction in any way whatsoever. (1937, c. 273, s. 25b; 1973, c. 1286, s. 16.)

§ 15A-748. No right of asylum; no immunity from other criminal prosecution while in this State.

After a person has been brought back to this State by, or after waiver of, extradition proceedings, he may be tried in this State for other crimes which he may be charged with having committed here as well as that specified in the requisition for his extradition. (1937, c. 273, s. 26; 1973, c. 1286, s. 16.)

§ 15A-749. Interpretation.

The provisions of this Article shall be so interpreted and construed as to effectuate its general purposes to make uniform the law of those states which enact it. (1937, c. 273, s. 27; 1973, c. 1286, s. 16.)

§ 15A-750. Short title.

This Article may be cited as the Uniform Criminal Extradition Act. (1937, c. 273, s. 30; 1973, c. 1286, s. 16.)

§§ 15A-751 through 15A-760. Reserved for future codification purposes.

Article 38.

Interstate Agreement on Detainers.

§ 15A-761. Agreement on Detainers entered into; form and contents.

This Agreement on Detainers is hereby enacted into law and entered into by this State with all other jurisdictions legally joining therein in the form substantially as follows: The contracting states solemnly agree:

Article I

The party states find that charges outstanding against a prisoner, detainers based on untried indictments, informations or complaints, and difficulties in securing speedy trial of persons already incarcerated in other jurisdictions, produce uncertainties which obstruct programs of prisoner treatment and rehabilitation. Accordingly, it is the policy of the party states and the purpose of this agreement to encourage the expeditious and orderly disposition of such charges and determination of the proper status of any and all detainers based on untried indictments, informations or complaints. The party states also find that proceedings with reference to such charges and detainers, when emanating from another jurisdiction, cannot properly be had in the absence of cooperative procedures. It is the further purpose of this agreement to provide such cooperative procedures.

Article II

As used in this agreement:

(a) "State" shall mean a state of the United States; the United States of America; a territory or possession of the United States; the District of Columbia; the Commonwealth of Puerto Rico.

(b "Sending state" shall mean a state in which a prisoner is incarcerated at the time that he initiates a request for final disposition pursuant to Article III hereof or at the time that a request for custody or availability is initiated pursuant to Article IV hereof.

(c) "Receiving state" shall mean the state in which trial is to be had on an indictment, information or complaint pursuant to Article III or Article IV hereof.

Article III

(a) Whenever a person has entered upon a term of imprisonment in a penal or correctional institution of a party state, and whenever during the continuance of the term of imprisonment there is pending in any other party state any untried indictment, information or complaint on the basis of which a detainer has been lodged against the prisoner, he shall be brought to trial within 180 days after he shall have caused to be delivered to the prosecuting officer and the appropriate court of the prosecuting officer's jurisdiction written notice of the place of his imprisonment and his request for a final disposition to be made of the indictment, information or complaint: Provided that for good cause shown in open court, the prisoner or his counsel being present, the court having jurisdiction of the matter may grant any necessary or reasonable continuance. The request of the prisoner shall be accompanied by a certificate of the appropriate official having custody of the prisoner, stating the term of commitment under which the prisoner is being held, the time already served, the time remaining to be served on the sentence, the amount of good time earned, the time of parole eligibility of the prisoner, and any decisions of the state parole agency relating to the prisoner.

(b) The written notice and request for final disposition referred to in paragraph (a) hereof shall be given or sent by the prisoner to the warden, commissioner of corrections or other official having custody of him, who shall promptly forward it together with the certificate to the appropriate prosecuting official and court by registered or certified mail, return receipt requested.

(c) The warden, commissioner of corrections or other official having custody of the prisoner shall promptly inform him of the source and contents of any detainer lodged against him and shall also inform him of his right to make a request for final disposition of the indictment, information or complaint on which the detainer is based.

(d) Any request for final disposition made by a prisoner pursuant to paragraph (a) hereof shall operate as a request for final disposition of all untried indictments, informations or complaints on the basis of which detainers have been lodged against the prisoner from the state to whose prosecuting official the request for final disposition is specifically directed. The warden, commissioner of corrections or other official having custody of the prisoner shall forthwith notify all appropriate prosecuting officers and courts in the several jurisdictions within the state to which the prisoner's request for final disposition is being sent of the proceeding being initiated by the prisoner. Any notification sent pursuant to this paragraph shall be accompanied by copies of the prisoner's written notice, request and the certificate. If trial is not had on any indictment, information or complaint contemplated hereby prior to the return of the prisoner to the original place of imprisonment, such indictment, information or complaint shall not be of any further force or effect, and the court shall enter an order dismissing the same with prejudice.

(e) Any request for final disposition made by a prisoner pursuant to paragraph (a) hereof shall also be deemed to be a waiver of extradition with respect to any charge or proceeding contemplated thereby or included therein by reason of paragraph (d) hereof, and a waiver of extradition to the receiving state to serve any sentence there imposed upon him, after completion of his term of imprisonment in the sending state. The request for final disposition shall also constitute a consent by the prisoner to the production of his body in any court where his presence may be required in order to effectuate the purposes of this agreement and a further consent voluntarily to be returned to the original place of imprisonment in accordance with the provisions of this agreement. Nothing in this paragraph shall prevent the imposition of a concurrent sentence if otherwise permitted by law.

(f) Escape from custody by the prisoner subsequent to his execution of the request for final disposition referred to in paragraph (a) hereof shall void the request.

Article IV

(a) The appropriate officer of the jurisdiction in which an untried indictment, information or complaint is pending shall be entitled to have a prisoner against whom he has lodged a detainer and who is serving a term of imprisonment in any party state made available in accordance with Article V(a) hereof upon presentation of a written request for temporary custody or availability to the appropriate authorities of the state in which the prisoner is incarcerated: Provided that the court having jurisdiction of such indictment, information or complaint shall have duly approved, recorded and transmitted the request: And provided further that there shall be a period of 30 days after receipt by the appropriate authorities before the request be honored, within which period the governor of the sending state may disapprove the request for temporary custody or availability, either upon his own motion or upon motion of the prisoner.

(b)   Upon receipt of the officer's written request as provided in paragraph (a) hereof, the appropriate authorities having the prisoner in custody shall furnish the officer with a certificate stating the term of commitment under which the prisoner is being held, the time already served, the time remaining to be served on the sentence, the amount of good time earned, the time of parole eligibility of the prisoner, and any decisions of the state parole agency relating to the prisoner. Said authorities simultaneously shall furnish all other officers and appropriate courts in the receiving state who have lodged detainers against the prisoner with similar certificates and with notices informing them of the request for custody or availability and of the reasons therefor.

(c)   In respect of any proceeding made possible by this Article, trial shall be commenced within 120 days of the arrival of the prisoner in the receiving state, but for good cause shown in open court, the prisoner or his counsel being present, the court having jurisdiction of the matter may grant any necessary or reasonable continuance.

(d)   Nothing contained in this Article shall be construed to deprive any prisoner of any right which he may have to contest the legality of his delivery as provided in paragraph (a) hereof, but such delivery may not be opposed or denied on the ground that the executive authority of the sending state has not affirmatively consented to or ordered such delivery.

(e)   If trial is not had on any indictment, information or complaint contemplated hereby prior to the prisoner's being returned to the original place of imprisonment pursuant to Article V(e) hereof, such indictment, information or complaint shall not be of any further force or effect, and the court shall enter an order dismissing the same with prejudice.

Article V

(a)   In response to a request made under Article III or Article IV hereof, the appropriate authority in a sending state shall offer to deliver temporary custody of such prisoner to the appropriate authority in the state where such indictment, information or complaint is pending against such person in order that speedy and efficient prosecution may be had. If the request for final disposition is made by the prisoner, the offer of temporary custody shall accompany the written notice provided for in Article III of this agreement. In the case of a federal prisoner, the appropriate authority in the receiving state shall be entitled to temporary custody as provided by this agreement or to the prisoner's presence in federal custody at the place for trial, whichever custodial arrangement may be approved by the custodian.

(b) The officer or other representative of a state accepting an offer of temporary custody shall present the following upon demand:

(1) Proper identification and evidence of his authority to act for the state into whose temporary custody the prisoner is to be given.

(2) A duly certified copy of the indictment, information or complaint on the basis of which the detainer has been lodged and on the basis of which the request for temporary custody of the prisoner has been made.

(c) If the appropriate authority shall refuse or fail to accept temporary custody of said person, or in the event that an action on the indictment, information or complaint on the basis of which the detainer has been lodged is not brought to trial within the period provided in Article III or Article IV hereof, the appropriate court of the jurisdiction where the indictment, information or complaint has been pending shall enter an order dismissing the same with prejudice, and any detainer based thereon shall cease to be of any force or effect.

(d) The temporary custody referred to in this agreement shall be only for the purpose of permitting prosecution on the charge or charges contained in one or more untried indictments, informations or complaints which form the basis of the detainer or detainers or for prosecution on any other charge or charges arising out of the same transaction. Except for his attendance at court and while being transported to or from any place at which his presence may be required, the prisoner shall be held in a suitable jail or other facility regularly used for persons awaiting prosecution.

(e) At the earliest practicable time consonant with the purposes of this agreement, the prisoner shall be returned to the sending state.

(f)   During the continuance of temporary custody or while the prisoner is otherwise being made available for trial as required by this agreement, time being served on the sentence shall continue to run but good time shall be earned by the prisoner only if, and to the extent that, the law and practice of the jurisdiction which imposed the sentence may allow.

(g)   For all purposes other than that for which temporary custody as provided in this agreement is exercised, the prisoner shall be deemed to remain in the custody of and subject to the jurisdiction of the sending state and any escape from temporary custody may be dealt with in the same manner as an escape from the original place of imprisonment or in any other manner permitted by law.

(h)   From the time that a party state receives custody of a prisoner pursuant to this agreement until such prisoner is returned to the territory and custody of the sending state, the state in which the one or more untried indictments, informations or complaints are pending or in which trial is being had shall be responsible for the prisoner and shall also pay all costs of transporting, caring for, keeping and returning the prisoner. The provisions of this paragraph shall govern unless the states concerned shall have entered into a supplementary agreement providing for a different allocation of costs and responsibilities as between or among themselves. Nothing herein contained shall be construed to alter or affect any internal relationship among the departments, agencies and officers of and in the government of a party state, or between a party state and its subdivisions, as to the payment of costs, or responsibilities therefor.

Article VI

(a)   In determining the duration and expiration dates of the time periods provided in Articles III and IV of this agreement, the running of said time periods shall be tolled whenever and for as long as the prisoner is unable to stand trial, as determined by the court having jurisdiction of the matter.

(b)   No provision of this agreement, and no remedy made available by this agreement, shall apply to any person who is adjudged to be mentally ill.

Article VII

Each state party to this agreement shall designate an officer who, acting jointly with like officers of other party states, shall promulgate rules and regulations to carry out more effectively the terms and provisions of this agreement, and who shall provide, within and without the state, information necessary to the effective operation of this agreement.

Article VIII

This agreement shall enter into full force and effect as to a party state when such state has enacted the same into law. A state party to this agreement may withdraw herefrom by enacting a statute repealing the same. However, the withdrawal of any state shall not affect the status of any proceedings already initiated by inmates or by state officers at the time such withdrawal takes effect, nor shall it affect their rights in respect thereof.

Article IX

This agreement shall be liberally construed so as to effectuate its purposes. The provisions of this agreement shall be severable and if any phrase, clause, sentence or provision of this agreement is declared to be contrary to the constitution of any party state or of the United States or the applicability thereof to any government, agency, person or circumstance is held invalid, the validity of the remainder of this agreement and the applicability thereof to any government, agency, person or circumstance shall not be affected thereby. If this agreement shall be held contrary to the constitution of any state party hereto, the agreement shall remain in full force and effect as to the remaining states and in full force and effect as to the state affected as to all severable matters. (1965, c. 295, s. 1; 1973, c. 1286, s. 22.)

§ 15A-762. Meaning of "appropriate court."

The phrase "appropriate court" as used in the Agreement on Detainers shall, with reference to the courts of this State, mean court of record with criminal jurisdiction. (1965, c. 295, s. 2; 1973, c. 1286, s. 22.)

§ 15A-763. Cooperation in enforcement.

All courts, departments, agencies, officers and employees of this State and its political subdivisions are hereby directed to enforce the Agreement on Detainers and to cooperate with one another and with other party states in enforcing the agreement and effectuating its purpose. (1965, c. 295, s. 3; 1973, c. 1286, s. 22.)

§ 15A-764. Escape from temporary custody.

Any prisoner released to temporary custody under the provisions of the Agreement on Detainers from a place of imprisonment in North Carolina who shall escape or attempt to escape from such temporary custody, whether within or without the borders of this State, shall be dealt with in the same manner as if the escape or attempt to escape were from the original place of imprisonment. (1965, c. 295, s. 4; 1973, c. 1286, s. 22.)

§ 15A-765. Authority and duty of official in charge of institution.

It shall be lawful and mandatory upon the warden or other official in charge of a penal or correctional institution in this State to give over the person of any inmate thereof whenever so required by the operation of the Agreement on Detainers. (1965, c. 295, s. 5; 1973, c. 1286, s. 22.)

§ 15A-766. Designation of central administrator of and information agent for agreement.

The Governor is hereby authorized and empowered to designate the officer who shall serve as central administrator of and information agent for the Agreement on Detainers, pursuant to the provisions of Article VII of the agreement. (1965, c. 295, s. 6; 1973, c. 1286, s. 22.)

§ 15A-767. Distribution of copies of Article.

Copies of this Article shall, upon its approval, be transmitted to the governor of each state, the Attorney General and the Administrator of General Services of the United States, and the Council of State Governments. (1965, c. 295, s. 7; 1973, c. 1286, s. 22.)

§§ 15A-768 through 15A-770. Reserved for future codification purposes.

Article 39.

Other Special Process for Attendance of Defendants.

§ 15A-771. Securing attendance of defendants confined in federal prisons.

(a)　　A defendant against whom a criminal action is pending in this State, and who is confined in a federal prison or custody either within or outside the State, may, with the consent of the Attorney General of the United States, be produced in such court for the purpose of criminal prosecution, pursuant to the provisions of:

(1)　　Section 4085 of Title 18 of the United States Code; or

(2)　　Subsection (b) of this section.

(b)　　When such a defendant is in federal custody as specified in subsection (a), a superior court may, upon application of the prosecutor, issue a certificate, addressed to the Attorney General of the United States, certifying the charges and the court in which they are pending, and that attendance of the defendant in such court for the purpose of criminal prosecution thereon is necessary in the interest of justice, and requesting the Attorney General of the United States to cause such defendant to be produced in such court, under custody of a federal public servant, upon a designated date and for a period of time necessary to complete the prosecution. Upon issuing such a certificate, the court may deliver it, or cause or authorize it to be delivered, together with a certified copy of the charges upon which it is based, to the Attorney General of the United States or to his representative authorized to entertain the request. (1973, c. 1286, s. 1; 1975, c. 166, s. 27.)

§ 15A-772. Securing attendance of defendants who are outside the United States.

(a)   When a criminal action for an offense committed in this State is pending in a criminal court of this State against a defendant who is in a foreign country with which the United States has an extradition treaty, and when the offense charged is one which is declared in such treaty to be an extraditable one, the prosecutor may make an application to the Governor, requesting him to make an application to the President of the United States to institute extradition proceedings for the return of the defendant to this country and State for the purpose of prosecution of such action. The prosecutor's application must comply with rules, regulations, and guidelines established by the Governor for such applications and must be accompanied by all the charges, affidavits, and other documents required thereby.

(b)   Upon receipt of the prosecutor's application, the Governor, if satisfied that the defendant is in the foreign country in question, that the offense charged is an extraditable one pursuant to the treaty in question, and that there are no factors or impediments which in law preclude such an extradition, may in his discretion make an application, addressed to the Secretary of State of the United States, requesting that the President of the United States institute extradition proceedings for the return of the defendant from such foreign country. The Governor's application must comply with applicable treaties and acts of Congress and with rules, regulations, and guidelines established by the Secretary of State for such applications and must be accompanied by all the charges, affidavits, and other documents required thereby.

(c)   The provisions of this section apply equally to extradition or attempted extradition of a person who is a fugitive following the entry of a judgment of conviction against him in a criminal court of this State. (1973, c. 1286, s. 1; 1975, c. 166, s. 27.)

§ 15A-773. Securing attendance of organizations; appearance.

(a)   The court attendance of an organization for purposes of commencing or prosecuting a criminal action against it may be accomplished by:

(1)   Issuance and service of a criminal summons; or

(2)   Issuance of an information and waiver of indictment by an authorized officer or agent of the organization and by counsel for the organization, as provided in G.S. 15A-642(c); or

(3)   Service of the notice of the indictment, as provided in G.S. 15A-630.

The criminal summons or notice of indictment must be directed to the organization, and must be served by delivery to an officer, director, managing or general agent, cashier or assistant cashier of the organization, or to any other agent of the organization authorized by appointment or by law to receive service of process.

(b)   At all stages of a criminal action, an organization may appear by counsel or agent having authority to transact the business of the organization.

(c)   For purposes of this section, "organization" means corporation, unincorporated association, partnership, body politic, consortium, or other group, entity, or organization. (1973, c. 1286, s. 1; 1977, c. 557.)

Article 40.

§§ 15A-774 through 15A-786. Reserved for future codification purposes.

Article 41.

§§ 15A-787 through 15A-800. Reserved for future codification purposes.

SUBCHAPTER VIII. ATTENDANCE OF WITNESSES; DEPOSITIONS.

Article 42.

Attendance of Witnesses Generally.

§ 15A-801. Subpoena for witness.

The presence of a person as a witness in a criminal proceeding may be obtained by subpoena, which must be issued and served in the manner provided in Rule 45 of the Rules of Civil Procedure, G.S. 1A-1, except that subdivision (2) of subsection (b) of the rule does not apply to subpoenas issued under this section. (1973, c. 1286, s. 1; 1975, c. 166, s. 15; 2003-276, s. 2.)

§ 15A-802. Subpoena for the production of documentary evidence.

The production of records, books, papers, documents, or tangible things in a criminal proceeding may be obtained by subpoena which must be issued and served in the manner provided in Rule 45 of the Rules of Civil Procedure, G.S. 1A-1, except that subdivision (2) of subsection (b) of the rule does not apply to subpoenas issued under this section. (1973, c. 1286, s. 1; 1975, c. 166, s. 15; 2003-276, s. 3.)

§ 15A-803. Attendance of witnesses.

(a) Material Witness Order Authorized. - A judge may issue an order assuring the attendance of a material witness at a criminal proceeding. This material witness order may be issued when there are reasonable grounds to believe that the person whom the State or a defendant desires to call as a witness in a pending criminal proceeding possesses information material to the determination of the proceeding and may not be amenable or responsive to a subpoena at a time when his attendance will be sought.

(b) When Order Issued. - A material witness order may be issued by a judge of superior court at any time after the initiation of criminal proceedings. A judge of district court may issue a material witness order only at the time that a defendant is bound over to superior court at a probable-cause hearing.

(c) How Long Effective. - A material witness order remains in effect during the period indicated in the order by the issuing judge unless it is sooner modified or vacated by a judge of superior court. In no event may a material witness order which provides for incarceration of the material witness be issued for a period longer than 20 days, but upon review a superior court judge in his discretion may renew an order one or more times for periods not to exceed five days each.

(d) Procedure. - A material witness order may be obtained upon motion supported by affidavit showing cause for its issuance. The witness must be given reasonable notice, opportunity to be heard and present evidence, and the right of representation by counsel at a hearing on the motion. Counsel for a material witness may be appointed and compensated in the same manner as counsel for an indigent defendant. Appointment of counsel shall be in accordance with rules adopted by the Office of Indigent Defense Services. The order must be based on findings of fact supporting its issuance.

(e) Order. - If the court makes a material witness order:

(1) It may direct release of the witness in the same manner that a defendant may be released under G.S. 15A-534.

(2) It may direct the detention of the witness.

(f) Modification or Vacation. - A material witness order may be modified or vacated by a judge of superior court upon a showing of new or changed facts or circumstances by the witness, the State, or any defendant.

(g) Securing Attendance or Custody of Material Witness. - The witness may be required to attend the hearing by subpoena, or if the court considers it necessary, by order for arrest. An order for arrest also may be issued if it becomes necessary to take the witness into custody after issuance of a material witness order. (1973, c. 1286, s. 1; 2000-144, s. 29.)

§ 15A-804. Voluntary protective custody.

(a) Upon request of a witness, a judge of superior court may determine whether he is a material witness, and may order his protective custody. The order may provide for confinement, custody in other than a penal institution, release to the custody of a law-enforcement officer or other person, or other provisions appropriate to the circumstances.

(b) A person having custody of the witness may not release him without his consent unless directed to do so by a superior court judge, or unless the order so provides.

(c) The issuance of either a material witness order or an order for voluntary protective custody does not preclude the issuance of the other order.

(d) An order for voluntary protective custody may be modified or vacated as appropriate by a superior court judge upon the request of the witness or upon the court's own motion. (1973, c. 1286, s. 1.)

§ 15A-805. Securing attendance of witnesses confined in institutions within the State.

(a) Upon motion of the State or any defendant, the judge of a court in which a criminal proceeding is pending must, for good cause shown, enter an order requiring that any person confined in an institution in this State be produced and compelled to attend as a witness in the action or proceeding.

(b) If the witness is confined pursuant to another pending criminal proceeding, and the judge determines that the production of the witness would result in an unreasonable interference with the conduct of the prior proceeding, he may deny the order. If an order for production is issued, a judge or justice of the appellate division of the General Court of Justice may, upon application of a defendant or prosecutor in the other district for good cause shown, vacate the order for production.

(c) The costs of production of the witness are assessed as are other witness fees. (1973, c. 1286, s. 1; 1975, c. 166, s. 27.)

§§ 15A-806 through 15A-810. Reserved for future codification purposes.

Article 43.

Uniform Act to Secure Attendance of Witnesses from without a State in Criminal Proceedings.

§ 15A-811. Definitions.

The word "state" shall include any territory of the United States and District of Columbia.

The word "summons" shall include a subpoena, order or other notice requiring the appearance of a witness.

"Witness" as used in this Article shall include a person whose testimony is desired in any proceeding or investigation by a grand jury or in a criminal action, prosecution or proceeding. (1937, c. 217, s. 1; 1973, c. 1286, s. 9.)

§ 15A-812. Summoning witness in this State to testify in another state.

If a judge of a court of record in any state which by its laws has made provision for commanding persons within that state to attend and testify in this State certifies, under the seal of such court, that there is a criminal prosecution pending in such court, or that a grand jury investigation has commenced or is about to commence, that a person being within this State is a material witness in such prosecution, or grand jury investigation, and that his presence will be required for a specified number of days, upon presentation of such certificate to any judge of a court of record in the county in which such person is, such judge shall fix a time and place for a hearing, and shall make an order directing the witness to appear at a time and place certain for the hearing.

If at a hearing the judge determines that the witness is material and necessary, that it will not cause undue hardship to the witness to be compelled to attend and testify in the prosecution or a grand jury investigation in the other state, and that the laws of the state in which the prosecution is pending, or grand jury investigation has commenced or is about to commence, and of any other state through which the witness may be required to pass by ordinary course of travel, will give to him protection from arrest and the service of civil and criminal process, he shall issue a summons, with a copy of the certificate attached, directing the witness to attend and testify in the court where the prosecution is pending, or where a grand jury investigation has commenced or is about to commence, at a time and place specified in the summons. In any such hearing the certificate shall be prima facie evidence of all the facts stated therein.

If said certificate recommends that the witness be taken into immediate custody and delivered to an officer of the requesting state to assure his attendance in the requesting state, such judge may, in lieu of notification of the hearing, direct that such witness be forthwith brought before him for said hearing; and the judge at the hearing, being satisfied of the desirability of such custody and delivery, for which determination the certificate shall be prima facie proof of such desirability may, in lieu of issuing subpoena or summons, order that said witness be forthwith taken into custody and delivered to an officer of the requesting state.

If the witness, who is summoned as above provided, after being paid or tendered by some properly authorized person the sum of ten cents (10¢) a mile for each mile by the ordinary traveled route to and from the court where the prosecution is pending and five dollars ($5.00) for each day that he is required to travel and attend as a witness, fails without good cause to attend and testify as directed in the summons, he shall be punished in the manner provided for the punishment of any witness who disobeys a summons issued from a court of record in this State. (1937, c. 217, s. 2; 1973, c. 1286, s. 9.)

§ 15A-813. Witness from another state summoned to testify in this State.

If a person in any state which by its laws has made provision for commanding persons within its borders to attend and testify in criminal prosecutions, or grand jury investigations commenced or about to commence in this State, is a material witness in a prosecution pending in a court of record in this State, or in a grand jury investigation which has commenced or is about to commence, a judge of such court may issue a certificate under the seal of the court, stating these facts and specifying the number of days the witness will be required. Said certificate may include a recommendation that the witness be taken into immediate custody and delivered to an officer of this State to assure his attendance in this State. This certificate shall be presented to a judge of a court of record in the county in which the witness is found.

If the witness is summoned to attend and testify in this State he shall be compensated at the rate allowed to State officers and employees by subdivisions (1) and (2) of G.S. 138-6(a) for each mile by the ordinary traveled route to and from the court where the prosecution is pending, and five dollars ($5.00) for each day that he is required to travel and attend as a witness. A witness who has appeared in accordance with the provisions of the summons shall not be required to remain within this State a longer period of time than the period mentioned in the certificate unless otherwise ordered by the court. If such a witness is required to appear more than one day, he is also entitled to reimbursement for actual expenses incurred for lodging and meals, not to exceed the maximum currently authorized for State employees when traveling in the State. If such witness, after coming into this State, fails without good cause to attend and testify as directed in the summons, he shall be punished in the manner provided for the punishment of any witness who disobeys a summons issued from a court of record in this State. (1937, c. 217, s. 3; 1973, c. 1286, s. 9; 1998-212, s. 16.25(b).)

§ 15A-814. Exemption from arrest and service of process.

If a person comes into this State in obedience to a summons directing him to attend and testify in this State he shall not, while in this State pursuant to such summons, be subject to arrest or the service of process, civil or criminal, in connection with matters which arose before his entrance into this State under the summons.

If a person passes through this State while going to another state in obedience to a summons to attend and testify in that state, or while returning therefrom, he shall not while so passing through this State be subject to arrest or the service of process, civil or criminal, in connection with matters which arose before his entrance into this State under the summons. (1937, c. 217, s. 4; 1973, c. 1286, s. 9.)

§ 15A-815. Uniformity of interpretation.

This Article shall be so interpreted and construed as to effectuate its general purpose to make uniform the law of the states which enact it. (1937, c. 217, s. 5; 1973, c. 1286, s. 9.)

§ 15A-816. Title of Article.

This Article may be cited as "Uniform Act to Secure the Attendance of Witnesses from without a State in Criminal Proceedings." (1937, c. 217, s. 6; 1973, c. 1286, s. 9.)

§§ 15A-817 through 15A-820. Reserved for future codification purposes.

Article 44.

Securing Attendance of Prisoners as Witnesses.

§ 15A-821. Securing attendance of prisoner in this State as witness in proceeding outside the State.

(a) If a judge of a court of general jurisdiction in any other state, which by its laws has made provision for commanding a prisoner within that state to attend and testify in this State, certifies under the seal of that court that there is a criminal prosecution pending in the court or that a grand jury investigation has commenced, and that a person confined in an institution under the control of the Division of Adult Correction of the Department of Public Safety of North Carolina, other than a person confined as criminally insane, is a material witness in the prosecution or investigation and that his presence is required for a specified number of days, upon presentment of the certificate to a superior court judge in the superior court district or set of districts as defined in G.S. 7A-41.1 where the person is confined, upon notice to the Attorney General, the judge must fix a time and place for a hearing and order the person having custody of the prisoner to produce him at the hearing.

(b) If at the hearing the judge determines that the prisoner is a material and necessary witness in the requesting state, the judge must order that the prisoner attend in the court where the prosecution or investigation is pending, upon such terms and conditions as the judge prescribes, including among other things, provision for the return of the prisoner at the conclusion of his testimony, proper safeguard for his custody, and proper financial reimbursement or other payment, including payment in advance, by the demanding jurisdiction for all expenses incurred in the production and return of the prisoner.

(c) The Attorney General may, as agent for the State of North Carolina, enter into such agreements with the demanding jurisdiction as necessary to ensure proper compliance with the order of the court. (1973, c. 1286, s. 1; 1987 (Reg. Sess., 1988), c. 1037, s. 62; 2011-145, s. 19.1(h); 2012-83, s. 27.)

§ 15A-822. Securing attendance of prisoner outside the State as witness in proceeding in the State.

(a) When

(1) A criminal action or proceeding is pending in a court of this State, and

(2) There is reasonable cause to believe that a person confined in a correctional institution or prison of another state, other than a person confined as mentally ill, possesses information material to such criminal action or proceeding, and

(3) The attendance of the person as a witness in such proceeding is desired by a party thereto, and

(4) The state in which such person is confined possesses a statute equivalent to G.S. 15A-821, the court in which such proceeding is pending may issue a certificate under the seal of the court, certifying all such facts and certifying that the attendance of the person as a witness in such court is required for a specified number of days.

(b) The certificate may be issued upon application of either the State or a defendant setting forth the facts specified in subsection (a).

(c) Upon issuing such a certificate, the court may cause it to be delivered to a court of such other state which is authorized to initiate or undertake action for the delivery of such prisoners to this State as witnesses. (1973, c. 1286, s. 1.)

§ 15A-823. Securing attendance of prisoner in federal institution as witness in proceeding in the State.

(a) When

(1) A criminal proceeding is pending in a court of this State; and

(2) There is reasonable cause to believe that a person confined in a federal prison or other federal custody, either within or outside this State, possesses information material to such criminal proceeding; and

(3) His attendance as a witness in such action or proceeding is desired by a party thereto, the court may issue a certificate, known as a writ of habeas corpus ad testificandum, addressed to the Attorney General of the United States certifying all such facts and requesting the Attorney General of the United States to cause the attendance of such person as a witness in such court for a specified number of days under custody of a federal public servant.

(b) The certificate may be issued upon application of either the State or a defendant, setting forth the facts specified in subsection (a).

(c) Upon issuing the certificate, the court may cause it to be delivered to the Attorney General of the United States or to his representative authorized to entertain the request. (1973, c. 1286, s. 1.)

SUBCHAPTER VIII-A. RIGHTS OF CRIME VICTIMS AND WITNESSES.

Article 45.

Fair Treatment for Certain Victims and Witnesses.

§ 15A-824. Definitions.

As used in this Article, unless the context clearly requires otherwise:

(1) "Crime" means a felony or serious misdemeanor as determined in the sole discretion of the district attorney, except those included in Article 46 of this Chapter, or any act committed by a juvenile that, if committed by a competent adult, would constitute a felony or serious misdemeanor.

(2) "Family member" means a spouse, child, parent or legal guardian, or the closest living relative.

(3) "Victim" means a person against whom there is probable cause to believe a crime has been committed.

(4) "Witness" means a person who has been or is expected to be summoned to testify for the prosecution in a criminal action concerning a felony,

or who by reason of having relevant information is subject to being called or is likely to be called as a witness for the prosecution in such an action, whether or not an action or proceeding has been commenced. (1985 (Reg. Sess., 1986), c. 998, s. 1; 1989, c. 596, s. 1; 1998-212, s. 19.4(a), (b).)

§ 15A-825. Treatment due victims and witnesses.

To the extent reasonably possible and subject to available resources, the employees of law-enforcement agencies, the prosecutorial system, the judicial system, and the correctional system should make a reasonable effort to assure that each victim and witness within their jurisdiction:

(1)   Is provided information regarding immediate medical assistance when needed and is not detained for an unreasonable length of time before having such assistance administered.

(2)   Is provided information about available protection from harm and threats of harm arising out of cooperation with law-enforcement prosecution efforts, and receives such protection.

(2a)   Is provided information that testimony as to one's home address is not relevant in every case, and that the victim or witness may request the district attorney to raise an objection should he/she deem it appropriate to this line of questioning in the case at hand.

(3)   Has any stolen or other personal property expeditiously returned by law-enforcement agencies when it is no longer needed as evidence, and its return would not impede an investigation or prosecution of the case. When feasible, all such property, except weapons, currency, contraband, property subject to evidentiary analysis, and property whose ownership is disputed, should be photographed and returned to the owner within a reasonable period of time of being recovered by law-enforcement officials.

(4)   Is provided appropriate employer intercession services to seek the employer's cooperation with the criminal justice system and minimize the employee's loss of pay and other benefits resulting from such cooperation whenever possible.

(5) Is provided, whenever practical, a secure waiting area during court proceedings that does not place the victim or witness in close proximity to defendants and families or friends of defendants.

(6) Is informed of the procedures to be followed to apply for and receive any appropriate witness fees or victim compensation.

(6a) Is informed of the right to be present throughout the entire trial of the defendant, subject to the right of the court to sequester witnesses.

(7) Is given the opportunity to be present during the final disposition of the case or is informed of the final disposition of the case, if he has requested to be present or be informed.

(8) Is notified, whenever possible, that a court proceeding to which he has been subpoenaed will not occur as scheduled.

(9) Has a victim impact statement prepared for consideration by the court.

(9a) Prior to trial, is provided information about plea bargaining procedures and is told that the district attorney may recommend a plea bargain to the court.

(10) Is informed that civil remedies may be available and that statutes of limitation apply in civil cases.

(11) Upon the victim's written request, is notified before a proceeding is held at which the release of the offender from custody is considered, if the crime for which the offender was placed in custody is a Class G or more serious felony.

(12) Upon the victim's written request, is notified if the offender escapes from custody or is released from custody, if the crime for which the offender was placed in custody is a Class G or more serious felony.

(13) Has family members of a homicide victim offered all the guarantees in this section, except those in subdivision (1).

Nothing in this section shall be construed to create a cause of action for failure to comply with its requirements. (1985 (Reg. Sess., 1986), c. 998, s. 1; 1989, c. 596, s. 2.)

§ 15A-826. Assistants for administrative and victim and witness services.

In addition to providing administrative and legal support to the district attorney's office, assistants for administrative and victim and witness services are responsible for coordinating efforts within the law-enforcement and judicial systems to assure that each victim and witness is treated in accordance with this Article. (1985 (Reg. Sess., 1986), c. 998, s. 1; 1997-443, s. 18.7(e).)

§ 15A-827. Scope.

This Article does not create any civil or criminal liability on the part of the State of North Carolina or any criminal justice agency, employee, or volunteer. (1985 (Reg. Sess., 1986), c. 998, s. 1.)

§§ 15A-828 through 15A-829. Reserved for future codification purposes.

Article 46.

Crime Victims' Rights Act.

§ 15A-830. Definitions.

(a)   The following definitions apply in this Article:

(1)   Accused. - A person who has been arrested and charged with committing a crime covered by this Article.

(2)   Arresting law enforcement agency. - The law enforcement agency that makes the arrest of an accused.

(3)   Custodial agency. - The agency that has legal custody of an accused or defendant arising from a charge or conviction of a crime covered by this Article including, but not limited to, local jails or detention facilities, regional jails or detention facilities, facilities designated under G.S. 122C-252 for the custody

and treatment of involuntary clients, or the Division of Adult Correction of the Department of Public Safety.

(4)   Investigating law enforcement agency. - The law enforcement agency with primary responsibility for investigating the crime committed against the victim.

(5)   Law enforcement agency. - An arresting law enforcement agency, a custodial agency, or an investigating law enforcement agency.

(6)   Next of kin. - The victim's spouse, children, parents, siblings, or grandparents. The term does not include the accused unless the charges are dismissed or the person is found not guilty.

(7)   Victim. - A person against whom there is probable cause to believe one of the following crimes was committed:

a.   A Class A, B1, B2, C, D, or E felony.

b.   A Class F felony if it is a violation of one of the following: G.S. 14-16.6(b); 14-16.6(c); 14-18; 14-32.1(e); 14-32.2(b)(3); 14-32.3(a); 14-32.4; 14-34.2; 14-34.6(c); 14-41; 14-43.3; 14-43.11; 14-190.17; 14-190.19; 14-202.1; 14-277.3A; 14-288.9; 20-138.5; or former G.S. 14-277.3.

c.   A Class G felony if it is a violation of one of the following: G.S. 14-32.3(b); 14-51; 14-58; 14-87.1; or 20-141.4.

d.   A Class H felony if it is a violation of one of the following: G.S. 14-32.3(a); 14-32.3(c); 14-33.2; 14-277.3A; or former G.S. 14-277.3.

e.   A Class I felony if it is a violation of one of the following: G.S. 14-32.3(b); 14-34.6(b); or 14-190.17A.

f.   An attempt of any of the felonies listed in this subdivision if the attempted felony is punishable as a felony.

g.   Any of the following misdemeanor offenses when the offense is committed between persons who have a personal relationship as defined in G.S. 50B-1(b): G.S. 14-33(c)(1); 14-33(c)(2); 14-33(a); 14-34; 14-134.3; 14-277.3A; or former G.S. 14-277.3.

h. Any violation of a valid protective order under G.S. 50B-4.1.

(b) If the victim is deceased, then the next of kin, in the order set forth in the definition contained in this section, is entitled to the victim's rights under this Article. However, the right contained in G.S. 15A-834 may only be exercised by the personal representative of the victim's estate. An individual entitled to exercise the victim's rights as a member of the class of next of kin may designate anyone in the class to act on behalf of the class. (1998-212, s. 19.4(c); 2001-433, s. 1; 2001-487, s. 120; 2001-518, s. 2A; 2006-247, s. 20(e); 2007-116, s. 2; 2007-547, s. 2; 2009-58, s. 3; 2011-145, s. 19.1(h).)

§ 15A-831. Responsibilities of law enforcement agency.

(a) As soon as practicable but within 72 hours after identifying a victim covered by this Article, the investigating law enforcement agency shall provide the victim with the following information:

(1) The availability of medical services, if needed.

(2) The availability of crime victims' compensation funds under Chapter 15B of the General Statutes and the address and telephone number of the agency responsible for dispensing the funds.

(3) The address and telephone number of the district attorney's office that will be responsible for prosecuting the victim's case.

(4) The name and telephone number of an investigating law enforcement agency employee whom the victim may contact if the victim has not been notified of an arrest in the victim's case within six months after the crime was reported to the law enforcement agency.

(5) Information about an accused's opportunity for pretrial release.

(6) The name and telephone number of an investigating law enforcement agency employee whom the victim may contact to find out whether the accused has been released from custody.

(7) The informational sheet described in G.S. 50B-3(c1), if there was a personal relationship, as defined in G.S. 50B-1(b), with the accused.

(b)   As soon as practicable but within 72 hours after the arrest of a person believed to have committed a crime covered by this Article, the arresting law enforcement agency shall inform the investigating law enforcement agency of the arrest. As soon as practicable but within 72 hours of being notified of the arrest, the investigating law enforcement agency shall notify the victim of the arrest.

(c)   As soon as practicable but within 72 hours after receiving notification from the arresting law enforcement agency that the accused has been arrested, the investigating law enforcement agency shall forward to the district attorney's office that will be responsible for prosecuting the case the defendant's name and the victim's name, address, date of birth, social security number, race, sex, and telephone number, unless the victim refuses to disclose any or all of the information, in which case, the investigating law enforcement agency shall so inform the district attorney's office.

(d)   Upon receiving the information in subsection (a) of this section, the victim shall, on a form provided by the investigating law enforcement agency, indicate whether the victim wishes to receive any further notices from the investigating law enforcement agency on the status of the accused during the pretrial process. If the victim elects to receive further notices during the pretrial process, the victim shall be responsible for notifying the investigating law enforcement agency of any changes in the victim's name, address, and telephone number. (1998-212, s. 19.4(c); 2001-433, s. 2; 2001-487, s. 120; 2008-4, s. 1.)

§ 15A-831.1. Polygraph examinations of victims of sexual assaults.

(a)   A criminal or juvenile justice agency shall not require a person claiming to be a victim of sexual assault or claiming to be a witness regarding the sexual assault of another person to submit to a polygraph or similar examination as a precondition to the agency conducting an investigation into the matter.

(b)   An agency wishing to perform a polygraph examination of a person claiming to be a victim or witness of sexual assault shall inform the person of the following:

(1)   That taking the polygraph examination is voluntary.

(2) That the results of the examination are not admissible in court.

(3) That the person's decision to submit to or refuse a polygraph examination will not be the sole basis for a decision by the agency not to investigate the matter.

(c) An agency which declines to investigate an alleged case of sexual assault following a decision by a person claiming to be a victim not to submit to a polygraph examination shall provide to that person, in writing, the reasons why the agency did not pursue the investigation at the request of the person. (2007-294, s. 1.)

§ 15A-832. Responsibilities of the district attorney's office.

(a) Within 21 days after the arrest of the accused, but not less than 24 hours before the accused's first scheduled probable-cause hearing, the district attorney's office shall provide to the victim a pamphlet or other written material that explains in a clear and concise manner the following:

(1) The victim's rights under this Article, including the right to confer with the attorney prosecuting the case about the disposition of the case and the right to provide a victim impact statement.

(2) The responsibilities of the district attorney's office under this Article.

(3) The victim's eligibility for compensation under the Crime Victims Compensation Act and the deadlines by which the victim must file a claim for compensation.

(4) The steps generally taken by the district attorney's office when prosecuting a felony case.

(5) Suggestions on what the victim should do if threatened or intimidated by the accused or someone acting on the accused's behalf.

(6) The name and telephone number of a victim and witness assistant in the district attorney's office whom the victim may contact for further information.

(b) Upon receiving the information in subsection (a) of this section, the victim shall, on a form provided by the district attorney's office, indicate whether the victim wishes to receive notices of some, all, or none of the trial and posttrial proceedings involving the accused. If the victim elects to receive notices, the victim shall be responsible for notifying the district attorney's office or any other department or agency that has a responsibility under this Article of any changes in the victim's address and telephone number. The victim may alter the request for notification at any time by notifying the district attorney's office and completing the form provided by the district attorney's office.

(c) The district attorney's office shall notify a victim of the date, time, and place of all trial court proceedings of the type that the victim has elected to receive notice. All notices required to be given by the district attorney's office shall be given in a manner that is reasonably calculated to be received by the victim prior to the date of the court proceeding.

(d) Whenever practical, the district attorney's office shall provide a secure waiting area during court proceedings that does not place the victim in close proximity to the defendant or the defendant's family.

(e) When the victim is to be called as a witness in a court proceeding, the court shall make every effort to permit the fullest attendance possible by the victim in the proceedings. This subsection shall not be construed to interfere with the defendant's right to a fair trial.

(f) Prior to the disposition of the case, the district attorney's office shall offer the victim the opportunity to consult with the prosecuting attorney to obtain the views of the victim about the disposition of the case, including the victim's views about dismissal, plea or negotiations, sentencing, and any pretrial diversion programs.

(g) At the sentencing hearing, the prosecuting attorney shall submit to the court a copy of a form containing the identifying information set forth in G.S. 15A-831(c) about any victim's electing to receive further notices under this Article. The clerk of superior court shall include the form with the final judgment and commitment, or judgment suspending sentence, transmitted to the Division of Adult Correction of the Department of Public Safety or other agency receiving custody of the defendant and shall be maintained by the custodial agency as a confidential file.

(h)   When a person is a victim of a human trafficking offense and is entitled to benefits and services pursuant to G.S. 14-43.11(d), the district attorney's office shall so notify the Office of the Attorney General and Legal Aid of North Carolina, Inc., in addition to providing services under this Article. (1998-212, s. 19.4(c); 2001-433, s. 3; 2001-487, s. 120; 2007-547, s. 3; 2011-145, s. 19.1(h).)

§ 15A-832.1. Responsibilities of judicial officials issuing arrest warrants.

(a)   In issuing a warrant for the arrest of an offender for any of the misdemeanor offenses set forth in G.S. 15A-830(a)(7)g., based on testimony or evidence from a complaining witness rather than from a law enforcement officer, a judicial official shall record the defendant's name and the victim's name, address, and telephone number electronically or on a form separate from the warrant and developed by the Administrative Office of the Courts for the purpose of recording that information, unless the victim refuses to disclose any or all of the information, in which case the judicial official shall so indicate.

(b)   A judicial official issuing a warrant for the arrest of an offender for any of the misdemeanor offenses set forth in G.S. 15A-830(a)(7)g. shall deliver the court's copy of the warrant and the victim-identifying information to the office of the clerk of superior court by the close of the next business day. As soon as practicable, but within 72 hours, the office of the clerk of superior court shall forward to the district attorney's office the victim-identifying information set forth in subsection (a) of this section. (2001-433, s. 4; 2001-487, s. 120.)

§ 15A-833. Evidence of victim impact.

(a)   A victim has the right to offer admissible evidence of the impact of the crime, which shall be considered by the court or jury in sentencing the defendant. The evidence may include the following:

(1)   A description of the nature and extent of any physical, psychological, or emotional injury suffered by the victim as a result of the offense committed by the defendant.

(2)   An explanation of any economic or property loss suffered by the victim as a result of the offense committed by the defendant.

(3)   A request for restitution and an indication of whether the victim has applied for or received compensation under the Crime Victims Compensation Act.

(b)   No victim shall be required to offer evidence of the impact of the crime. No inference or conclusion shall be drawn from a victim's decision not to offer evidence of the impact of the crime. At the victim's request and with the consent of the defendant, a representative of the district attorney's office or a law enforcement officer may proffer evidence of the impact of the crime to the court. (1998-212, s. 19.4(c); 2001-433, s. 5; 2001-487, s. 120.)

§ 15A-834. Restitution.

A victim has the right to receive restitution as ordered by the court pursuant to Article 81C of Chapter 15A of the General Statutes. (1998-212, s. 19.4(c).)

§ 15A-835. Posttrial responsibilities.

(a)   Within 30 days after the final trial court proceeding in the case, the district attorney's office shall notify the victim, in writing, of:

(1)   The final disposition of the case.

(2)   The crimes of which the defendant was convicted.

(3)   The defendant's right to appeal, if any.

(4)   The telephone number of offices to contact in the event of nonpayment of restitution by the defendant.

(b)   Upon a defendant's giving notice of appeal to the Court of Appeals or the Supreme Court, the district attorney's office shall forward to the Attorney General's office the defendant's name and the victim's name, address, and telephone number. Upon receipt of this information, and thereafter as the circumstances require, the Attorney General's office shall provide the victim with the following:

(1)   A clear and concise explanation of how the appellate process works, including information about possible actions that may be taken by the appellate court.

(2)   Notice of the date, time, and place of any appellate proceedings involving the defendant. Notice shall be given in a manner that is reasonably calculated to be received by the victim prior to the date of the proceedings.

(3)   The final disposition of an appeal.

(c)   If the defendant has been released on bail pending the outcome of the appeal, the agency that has custody of the defendant shall notify the investigating law enforcement agency as soon as practicable, and within 72 hours of receipt of the notification the investigating law enforcement agency shall notify the victim that the defendant has been released.

(d)   If the defendant's conviction is overturned, and the district attorney's office decides to retry the case or the case is remanded to superior court for a new trial, the victim shall be entitled to the same rights under this Article as if the first trial did not take place.

(e)   Repealed by Session Laws 2001-302, s. 1. (1998-212, s. 19.4(c); 2001-302, s. 1; 2001-433, s. 6; 2001-487, s. 120.)

§ 15A-836. Responsibilities of agency with custody of defendant.

(a)   When a form is included with the final judgment and commitment pursuant to G.S. 15A-832(g), or when the victim has otherwise filed a written request for notification with the custodial agency, the custodial agency shall notify the victim of:

(1)   The projected date by which the defendant can be released from custody. The calculation of the release date shall be as exact as possible, including earned time and disciplinary credits if the sentence of imprisonment exceeds 90 days.

(2)   An inmate's assignment to a minimum custody unit and the address of the unit. This notification shall include notice that the inmate's minimum custody

status may lead to the inmate's participation in one or more community-based programs such as work release or supervised leaves in the community.

(3)   The victim's right to submit any concerns to the agency with custody and the procedure for submitting such concerns.

(4)   The defendant's escape from custody, within 72 hours, except that if a victim has notified the agency in writing that the defendant has issued a specific threat against the victim, the agency shall notify the victim as soon as possible and within 24 hours at the latest.

(5)   The defendant's capture, within 24 hours.

(6)   The date the defendant is scheduled to be released from the facility. Whenever practical, notice shall be given 60 days before release. In no event shall notice be given less than seven days before release.

(7)   The defendant's death.

(b)   Notifications required in this section shall be provided within 60 days of the date the custodial agency takes custody of the defendant or within 60 days of the event requiring notification, or as otherwise specified in subsection (a) of this section. (1998-212, s. 19.4(c); 2001-433, s. 7; 2001-487, s. 120.)

§ 15A-837. Responsibilities of Section of Community Corrections of the Division of Adult Correction.

(a)   The Section of Community Corrections of the Division of Adult Correction shall notify the victim of:

(1)   The defendant's regular conditions of probation or post-release supervision, special or added conditions, supervision requirements, and any subsequent changes.

(2)   The date and location of any hearing to determine whether the defendant's supervision should be revoked, continued, modified, or terminated.

(3)   The final disposition of any hearing referred to in subdivision (2) of this subsection.

(4) Any restitution modification.

(5) The defendant's movement into or out of any intermediate sanction as defined in G.S. 15A-1340.11(6).

(6) The defendant's absconding supervision, within 72 hours.

(7) The capture of a defendant described in subdivision (6) of this subsection, within 72 hours.

(8) The date when the defendant is terminated or discharged.

(9) The defendant's death.

(b) Notifications required in this section shall be provided within 30 days of the event requiring notification, or as otherwise specified in subsection (a) of this section. (1998-212, s. 19.4(c); 2001-433, s. 8; 2001-487, ss. 47(a), 120; 2011-145, s. 19.1(k).)

§ 15A-838. Notice of commuted sentence or pardon.

The Governor's Clemency Office shall notify a victim when it is considering commuting the defendant's sentence or pardoning the defendant. The Governor's Clemency Office shall also give notice that the victim has the right to present a written statement to be considered by the Office before the defendant's sentence is commuted or the defendant is pardoned. The Governor's Clemency Office shall notify the victim of its decision. Notice shall be given in a manner that is reasonably calculated to allow for a timely response to the commutation or pardon decision. (1998-212, s. 19.4(c).)

§ 15A-839. No money damages.

This Article, including the provision of a service pursuant to this Article through the Statewide Automated Victim Assistance and Notification System established by the Governor's Crime Commission, does not create a claim for damages against the State, a county, or a municipality, or any of its agencies, instrumentalities, officers, or employees. (1998-212, s. 19.4(c); 1999-169, s. 1.)

§ 15A-840. No ground for relief.

The failure or inability of any person to provide a right or service under this Article, including a service provided through the Statewide Automated Victim Assistance and Notification System established by the Governor's Crime Commission, may not be used by a defendant in a criminal case, by an inmate, by any other accused, or by any victim, as a ground for relief in any criminal or civil proceeding, except in suits for a writ of mandamus by the victim. (1998-212, s. 19.4(c); 1999-169, s. 2.)

§ 15A-841. Incompetent victim's rights exercised.

When a victim is mentally or physically incompetent or when the victim is a minor, the victim's rights under this Article, other than the rights provided by G.S. 15A-834, may be exercised by the victim's next of kin or legal guardian. (1998-212, s. 19.4(c).)

§§ 15A-842 through 15A-849. Reserved for future codification purposes.

Article 47.

§§ 15A-850 through 15A-900. Reserved for future codification purposes.

SUBCHAPTER IX. PRETRIAL PROCEDURE.

Article 48.

Discovery in the Superior Court.

§ 15A-901. Application of Article.

This Article applies to cases within the original jurisdiction of the superior court. (1973, c. 1286, s. 1.)

§ 15A-902. Discovery procedure.

(a) A party seeking discovery under this Article must, before filing any motion before a judge, request in writing that the other party comply voluntarily with the discovery request. A written request is not required if the parties agree in writing to voluntarily comply with the provisions of Article 48 of Chapter 15A of the General Statutes. Upon receiving a negative or unsatisfactory response, or upon the passage of seven days following the receipt of the request without response, the party requesting discovery may file a motion for discovery under the provisions of this Article concerning any matter as to which voluntary discovery was not made pursuant to request.

(b) To the extent that discovery authorized in this Article is voluntarily made in response to a request or written agreement, the discovery is deemed to have been made under an order of the court for the purposes of this Article.

(c) A motion for discovery under this Article must be heard before a superior court judge.

(d) If a defendant is represented by counsel, the defendant may as a matter of right request voluntary discovery from the State under subsection (a) of this section not later than the tenth working day after either the probable-cause hearing or the date the defendant waives the hearing. If a defendant is not represented by counsel, or is indicted or consents to the filing of a bill of information before the defendant has been afforded or waived a probable-cause hearing, the defendant may as a matter of right request voluntary discovery from the State under subsection (a) of this section not later than the tenth working day after the later of:

(1) The defendant's consent to be tried upon a bill of information, or the service of notice upon the defendant that a true bill of indictment has been found by the grand jury, or

(2) The appointment of counsel.

For the purposes of this subsection a defendant is represented by counsel only if counsel was retained by or appointed for the defendant prior to or during a probable-cause hearing or prior to execution by the defendant of a waiver of a probable-cause hearing.

(e)   The State may as a matter of right request voluntary discovery from the defendant, when authorized under this Article, at any time not later than the tenth working day after disclosure by the State with respect to the category of discovery in question.

(f)   A motion for discovery made at any time prior to trial may be entertained if the parties so stipulate or if the judge for good cause shown determines that the motion should be allowed in whole or in part. (1973, c. 1286, s. 1; 2004-154, s. 3.)

§ 15A-903. Disclosure of evidence by the State - Information subject to disclosure.

(a)   Upon motion of the defendant, the court must order:

(1)   The State to make available to the defendant the complete files of all law enforcement agencies, investigatory agencies, and prosecutors' offices involved in the investigation of the crimes committed or the prosecution of the defendant.

a.   The term "file" includes the defendant's statements, the codefendants' statements, witness statements, investigating officers' notes, results of tests and examinations, or any other matter or evidence obtained during the investigation of the offenses alleged to have been committed by the defendant. When any matter or evidence is submitted for testing or examination, in addition to any test or examination results, all other data, calculations, or writings of any kind shall be made available to the defendant, including, but not limited to, preliminary test or screening results and bench notes.

b.   The term "prosecutor's office" refers to the office of the prosecuting attorney.

b1.   The term "investigatory agency" includes any public or private entity that obtains information on behalf of a law enforcement agency or prosecutor's office in connection with the investigation of the crimes committed or the prosecution of the defendant.

c.   Oral statements shall be in written or recorded form, except that oral statements made by a witness to a prosecuting attorney outside the presence of a law enforcement officer or investigatorial assistant shall not be required to be in written or recorded form unless there is significantly new or different information in the oral statement from a prior statement made by the witness.

d. The defendant shall have the right to inspect and copy or photograph any materials contained therein and, under appropriate safeguards, to inspect, examine, and test any physical evidence or sample contained therein.

(2) The prosecuting attorney to give notice to the defendant of any expert witnesses that the State reasonably expects to call as a witness at trial. Each such witness shall prepare, and the State shall furnish to the defendant, a report of the results of any examinations or tests conducted by the expert. The State shall also furnish to the defendant the expert's curriculum vitae, the expert's opinion, and the underlying basis for that opinion. The State shall give the notice and furnish the materials required by this subsection within a reasonable time prior to trial, as specified by the court. Standardized fee scales shall be developed by the Administrative Office of the Courts and Indigent Defense Services for all expert witnesses and private investigators who are compensated with State funds.

(3) The prosecuting attorney to give the defendant, at the beginning of jury selection, a written list of the names of all other witnesses whom the State reasonably expects to call during the trial. Names of witnesses shall not be subject to disclosure if the prosecuting attorney certifies in writing and under seal to the court that to do so may subject the witnesses or others to physical or substantial economic harm or coercion, or that there is other particularized, compelling need not to disclose. If there are witnesses that the State did not reasonably expect to call at the time of the provision of the witness list, and as a result are not listed, the court upon a good faith showing shall allow the witnesses to be called. Additionally, in the interest of justice, the court may in its discretion permit any undisclosed witness to testify.

(b) If the State voluntarily provides disclosure under G.S. 15A-902(a), the disclosure shall be to the same extent as required by subsection (a) of this section.

(c) On a timely basis, law enforcement and investigatory agencies shall make available to the prosecutor's office a complete copy of the complete files related to the investigation of the crimes committed or the prosecution of the defendant for compliance with this section and any disclosure under G.S. 15A-902(a). Investigatory agencies that obtain information and materials listed in subdivision (1) of subsection (a) of this section shall ensure that such information and materials are fully disclosed to the prosecutor's office on a timely basis for disclosure to the defendant.

(d)   Any person who willfully omits or misrepresents evidence or information required to be disclosed pursuant to subdivision (1) of subsection (a) of this section, or required to be provided to the prosecutor's office pursuant to subsection (c) of this section, shall be guilty of a Class H felony. Any person who willfully omits or misrepresents evidence or information required to be disclosed pursuant to any other provision of this section shall be guilty of a Class 1 misdemeanor. (1973, c. 1286, s. 1; 1975, c. 166, s. 27; 1983, c. 759, ss. 1-3; 1983, Ex. Sess., c. 6, s. 1; 2001-282, s. 5; 2004-154, s. 4; 2007-183, s. 1; 2007-377, s. 1; 2007-393, s. 1; 2011-19, s. 9; 2011-250, s. 1.)

§ 15A-904. Disclosure by the State - Certain information not subject to disclosure.

(a)   The State is not required to disclose written materials drafted by the prosecuting attorney or the prosecuting attorney's legal staff for their own use at trial, including witness examinations, voir dire questions, opening statements, and closing arguments. Disclosure is also not required of legal research or of records, correspondence, reports, memoranda, or trial preparation interview notes prepared by the prosecuting attorney or by members of the prosecuting attorney's legal staff to the extent they contain the opinions, theories, strategies, or conclusions of the prosecuting attorney or the prosecuting attorney's legal staff.

(a1)   The State is not required to disclose the identity of a confidential informant unless the disclosure is otherwise required by law.

(a2)   The State is not required to provide any personal identifying information of a witness beyond that witness's name, address, date of birth, and published phone number, unless the court determines upon motion of the defendant that such additional information is necessary to accurately identify and locate the witness.

(a3)   The State is not required to disclose the identity of any individual providing information about a crime or criminal conduct to a Crime Stoppers organization under promise or assurance of anonymity unless ordered by the court. For purposes of this Article, a Crime Stoppers organization or similarly named entity means a private, nonprofit North Carolina corporation governed by a civilian volunteer board of directors that is operated on a local or statewide level that (i) offers anonymity to persons providing information to the organization, (ii) accepts and expends donations for cash rewards to persons who report to the organization information about alleged criminal activity and that the organization forwards to the appropriate law enforcement agency, and (iii) is established as a cooperative alliance between the news media, the community, and law enforcement officials.

(a4)   The State is not required to disclose the Victim Impact Statement or its contents unless otherwise required by law. For purposes of this Chapter, a Victim Impact Statement is a document submitted by the victim or the victim's family to the State pursuant to the Victims' Rights Amendment.

(b)   Nothing in this section prohibits the State from making voluntary disclosures in the interest of justice nor prohibits a court from finding that the protections of this section have been waived.

(c)   This section shall have no effect on the State's duty to comply with federal or State constitutional disclosure requirements. (1973, c. 1286, s. 1; 1975, c. 166, s. 27; 2004-154, s. 5; 2007-377, s. 2; 2011-250, s. 2.)

§ 15A-905. Disclosure of evidence by the defendant - Information subject to disclosure.

(a)   Documents and Tangible Objects. - If the court grants any relief sought by the defendant under G.S. 15A-903, the court must, upon motion of the State, order the defendant to permit the State to inspect and copy or photograph books, papers, documents, photographs, motion pictures, mechanical or electronic recordings, tangible objects, or copies or portions thereof which are within the possession, custody, or control of the defendant and which the defendant intends to introduce in evidence at the trial.

(b)   Reports of Examinations and Tests. - If the court grants any relief sought by the defendant under G.S. 15A-903, the court must, upon motion of the State, order the defendant to permit the State to inspect and copy or photograph results or reports of physical or mental examinations or of tests, measurements or experiments made in connection with the case, or copies thereof, within the possession and control of the defendant which the defendant intends to introduce in evidence at the trial or which were prepared by a witness whom the defendant intends to call at the trial, when the results or reports relate to his testimony. In addition, upon motion of the State, the court must order the defendant to permit the State to inspect, examine, and test, subject to appropriate safeguards, any physical evidence or a sample of it available to the defendant if the defendant intends to offer such evidence, or tests or experiments made in connection with such evidence, as an exhibit or evidence in the case.

(c) Notice of Defenses, Expert Witnesses, and Witness Lists. - If the court grants any relief sought by the defendant under G.S. 15A-903, or if disclosure is voluntarily made by the State pursuant to G.S. 15A-902(a), the court must, upon motion of the State, order the defendant to:

(1) Give notice to the State of the intent to offer at trial a defense of alibi, duress, entrapment, insanity, mental infirmity, diminished capacity, self-defense, accident, automatism, involuntary intoxication, or voluntary intoxication. Notice of defense as described in this subdivision is inadmissible against the defendant. Notice of defense must be given within 20 working days after the date the case is set for trial pursuant to G.S. 7A-49.4, or such other later time as set by the court.

a. As to the defense of alibi, the court may order, upon motion by the State, the disclosure of the identity of alibi witnesses no later than two weeks before trial. If disclosure is ordered, upon a showing of good cause, the court shall order the State to disclose any rebuttal alibi witnesses no later than one week before trial. If the parties agree, the court may specify different time periods for this exchange so long as the exchange occurs within a reasonable time prior to trial.

b. As to only the defenses of duress, entrapment, insanity, automatism, or involuntary intoxication, notice by the defendant shall contain specific information as to the nature and extent of the defense.

(2) Give notice to the State of any expert witnesses that the defendant reasonably expects to call as a witness at trial. Each such witness shall prepare, and the defendant shall furnish to the State, a report of the results of the examinations or tests conducted by the expert. The defendant shall also furnish to the State the expert's curriculum vitae, the expert's opinion, and the underlying basis for that opinion. The defendant shall give the notice and furnish the materials required by this subdivision within a reasonable time prior to trial, as specified by the court. Standardized fee scales shall be developed by the

Administrative Office of the Courts and Indigent Defense Services for all expert witnesses and private investigators who are compensated with State funds.

(3) Give the State, at the beginning of jury selection, a written list of the names of all other witnesses whom the defendant reasonably expects to call during the trial. Names of witnesses shall not be subject to disclosure if the defendant certifies in writing and under seal to the court that to do so may subject the witnesses or others to physical or substantial economic harm or coercion, or that there is other particularized, compelling need not to disclose. If there are witnesses that the defendant did not reasonably expect to call at the time of the provision of the witness list, and as a result are not listed, the court upon a good faith showing shall allow the witnesses to be called. Additionally, in the interest of justice, the court may in its discretion permit any undisclosed witness to testify.

(d) If the defendant voluntarily provides discovery under G.S. 15A-902(a), the disclosure shall be to the same extent as required by subsection (c) of this section. (1973, c. 1286, s. 1; 1975, c. 166, s. 27; 2004-154, s. 6; 2011-250, s. 3.)

§ 15A-906. Disclosure of evidence by the defendant - Certain evidence not subject to disclosure.

Except as provided in G.S. 15A-905(b) this Article does not authorize the discovery or inspection of reports, memoranda, or other internal defense documents made by the defendant or his attorneys or agents in connection with the investigation or defense of the case, or of statements made by the defendant, or by prosecution or defense witnesses, or by prospective prosecution witnesses or defense witnesses, to the defendant, his agents, or attorneys. (1973, c. 1286, s. 1.)

§ 15A-907. Continuing duty to disclose.

If a party, who is required to give or who voluntarily gives discovery pursuant to this Article, discovers prior to or during trial additional evidence or witnesses, or decides to use additional evidence or witnesses, and the evidence or witness is or may be subject to discovery or inspection under this Article, the party must promptly notify the attorney for the other party of the existence of the additional evidence or witnesses. (1973, c. 1286, s. 1; 1975, c. 166, s. 16; 2004-154, s. 7.)

§ 15A-908. Regulation of discovery - Protective orders.

(a)   Upon written motion of a party and a finding of good cause, which may include, but is not limited to a finding that there is a substantial risk to any person of physical harm, intimidation, bribery, economic reprisals, or unnecessary annoyance or embarrassment, the court may at any time order that discovery or inspection be denied, restricted, or deferred, or may make other appropriate orders. A party may apply ex parte for a protective order and, if an ex parte order is granted, the opposing party shall receive notice that the order was entered, but without disclosure of the subject matter of the order.

(b)   The court may permit a party seeking relief under subsection (a) to submit supporting affidavits or statements to the court for in camera inspection. If thereafter the court enters an order granting relief under subsection (a), the material submitted in camera must be sealed and preserved in the records of the court to be made available to the appellate court in the event of an appeal. (1973, c. 1286, s. 1; 1983, Ex. Sess., c. 6, s. 2; 2004-154, s. 8.)

§ 15A-909. Regulation of discovery - Time, place, and manner of discovery and inspection.

An order of the court granting relief under this Article must specify the time, place, and manner of making the discovery and inspection permitted and may prescribe appropriate terms and conditions. (1973, c. 1286, s. 1.)

§ 15A-910. Regulation of discovery - Failure to comply.

(a)   If at any time during the course of the proceedings the court determines that a party has failed to comply with this Article or with an order issued pursuant to this Article, the court in addition to exercising its contempt powers may

(1) Order the party to permit the discovery or inspection, or

(2) Grant a continuance or recess, or

(3) Prohibit the party from introducing evidence not disclosed, or

(3a) Declare a mistrial, or

(3b) Dismiss the charge, with or without prejudice, or

(4) Enter other appropriate orders.

(b) Prior to finding any sanctions appropriate, the court shall consider both the materiality of the subject matter and the totality of the circumstances surrounding an alleged failure to comply with this Article or an order issued pursuant to this Article.

(c) For purposes of determining whether to impose personal sanctions for untimely disclosure of law enforcement and investigatory agencies' files, courts and State agencies shall presume that prosecuting attorneys and their staffs have acted in good faith if they have made a reasonably diligent inquiry of those agencies under G.S. 15A-903(c) and disclosed the responsive materials.

(d) If the court imposes any sanction, it must make specific findings justifying the imposed sanction. (1973, c. 1286, s. 1; 1975, c. 166, s. 17; 1983, Ex. Sess., c. 6, s. 3; 2004-154, s. 9; 2011-250, s. 4.)

§§ 15A-911 through 15A-920. Reserved for future codification purposes.

Article 49.

Pleadings and Joinder.

§ 15A-921. Pleadings in criminal cases.

Subject to the provisions of this Article, the following may serve as pleadings of the State in criminal cases:

(1) Citation.

(2) Criminal summons.

(3) Warrant for arrest.

(4) Magistrate's order pursuant to G.S. 15A-511 after arrest without warrant.

(5) Statement of charges.

(6) Information.

(7) Indictment. (1973, c. 1286, s. 1; 1975, c. 166, s. 18.)

§ 15A-922. Use of pleadings in misdemeanor cases generally.

(a) Process as Pleadings. - The citation, criminal summons, warrant for arrest, or magistrate's order serves as the pleading of the State for a misdemeanor prosecuted in the district court, unless the prosecutor files a statement of charges, or there is objection to trial on a citation. When a statement of charges is filed it supersedes all previous pleadings of the State and constitutes the pleading of the State.

(b) Statement of Charges.

(1) A statement of charges is a criminal pleading which charges a misdemeanor. It must be signed by the prosecutor who files it.

(2) Upon appropriate motion, a defendant is entitled to a period of at least three working days for the preparation of his defense after a statement of charges is filed, or the time the defendant is first notified of the statement of charges, whichever is later, unless the judge finds that the statement of charges makes no material change in the pleadings and that no additional time is necessary.

(3) If the judge rules that the pleadings charging a misdemeanor are insufficient and a prosecutor is permitted to file a statement of charges pursuant to subsection (e), the order of the judge must allow the prosecutor three working days, unless the judge determines that a longer period is justified, in which to

file the statement of charges, and must provide that the charges will be dismissed if the statement of charges is not filed within the period allowed.

(c) Objection to Trial on Citation. - A defendant charged in a citation with a criminal offense may by appropriate motion require that the offense be charged in a new pleading. The prosecutor must then file a statement of charges unless it appears that a criminal summons or a warrant for arrest should be secured in order to insure the attendance of the defendant, and in addition serve as the new pleading.

(d) Statement of Charges upon Determination of Prosecutor. -The prosecutor may file a statement of charges upon his own determination at any time prior to arraignment in the district court. It may charge the same offenses as the citation, criminal summons, warrant for arrest, or magistrate's order or additional or different offenses.

(e) Objection to Sufficiency of Criminal Summons; Warrant for Arrest or Magistrate's Order as Pleading. - If the defendant by appropriate motion objects to the sufficiency of a criminal summons, warrant for arrest, or magistrate's order as a pleading, at the time of or after arraignment in the district court or upon trial de novo in the superior court, and the judge rules that the pleading is insufficient, the prosecutor may file a statement of charges, but a statement of charges filed pursuant to this authorization may not change the nature of the offense.

(f) Amendment of Pleadings prior to or after Final Judgment. - A statement of charges, criminal summons, warrant for arrest, citation, or magistrate's order may be amended at any time prior to or after final judgment when the amendment does not change the nature of the offense charged.

(g) Pleadings When Misdemeanor Prosecution Initiated in Superior Court. - When the prosecution of a misdemeanor is initiated in the superior court as permitted by G.S. 7A-271, the prosecution must be upon information or indictment.

(h) Allegations in Superior Court of Prior Convictions. - When charges in the district court involve allegations of prior convictions and there is an appeal to the superior court for trial de novo, a statement of charges must be filed in the superior court to charge the offense in the manner provided in G.S. 15A-928. (1973, c. 1286, s. 1; 1975, c. 166, s. 27; 1979, c. 770; 1985, c. 689, s. 6.)

§ 15A-923. Use of pleadings in felony cases and misdemeanor cases initiated in the superior court division.

(a) Prosecution on Information or Indictment. - The pleading in felony cases and misdemeanor cases initiated in the superior court division must be a bill of indictment, unless there is a waiver of the bill of indictment as provided in G.S. 15A-642. If there is a waiver, the pleading must be an information. A presentment by the grand jury may not serve as the pleading in a criminal case.

(b) Form of Information or Indictment. - An information and a bill of indictment charge the crime or crimes in the same manner. An information has entered upon it or attached to it the defendant's written waiver of a bill of indictment. The bill of indictment has entered upon it the finding of the grand jury that it is a true bill.

(c) Waiver of Indictment. - The defendant may waive a bill of indictment as provided in G.S. 15A-642.

(d) Amendment of Information. - An information may be amended only with the consent of the defendant.

(e) No Amendment of Indictment. - A bill of indictment may not be amended. (1973, c. 1286, s. 1.)

§ 15A-924. Contents of pleadings; duplicity; alleging and proving previous convictions; failure to charge crime; surplusage.

(a) A criminal pleading must contain:

(1) The name or other identification of the defendant but the name of the defendant need not be repeated in each count unless required for clarity.

(2) A separate count addressed to each offense charged, but allegations in one count may be incorporated by reference in another count.

(3) A statement or cross reference in each count indicating that the offense charged therein was committed in a designated county.

(4) A statement or cross reference in each count indicating that the offense charged was committed on, or on or about, a designated date, or during a designated period of time. Error as to a date or its omission is not ground for dismissal of the charges or for reversal of a conviction if time was not of the essence with respect to the charge and the error or omission did not mislead the defendant to his prejudice.

(5) A plain and concise factual statement in each count which, without allegations of an evidentiary nature, asserts facts supporting every element of a criminal offense and the defendant's commission thereof with sufficient precision clearly to apprise the defendant or defendants of the conduct which is the subject of the accusation. When the pleading is a criminal summons, warrant for arrest, or magistrate's order, or statement of charges based thereon, both the statement of the crime and any information showing probable cause which was considered by the judicial official and which has been furnished to the defendant must be used in determining whether the pleading is sufficient to meet the foregoing requirement.

(6) For each count a citation of any applicable statute, rule, regulation, ordinance, or other provision of law alleged therein to have been violated. Error in the citation or its omission is not ground for dismissal of the charges or for reversal of a conviction.

(7) A statement that the State intends to use one or more aggravating factors under G.S. 15A-1340.16(d)(20), with a plain and concise factual statement indicating the factor or factors it intends to use under the authority of that subdivision.

(b) If any count of an indictment or information charges more than one offense, the defendant may by timely filing of a motion require the State to elect and state a single offense alleged in the count upon which the State will proceed to trial. A count may be dismissed for duplicity if the State fails to make timely election.

(c) In trials in superior court, allegations of previous convictions are subject to the provisions of G.S. 15A-928.

(d) In alleging and proving a prior conviction, it is sufficient to state that the defendant was at a certain time and place convicted of the previous offense, without otherwise fully alleging all the elements. A duly certified transcript of the record of a prior conviction is, upon proof of the identity of the person of the defendant, sufficient evidence of a prior conviction. If the surname of a defendant charged is identical to the surname of a defendant previously convicted and there is identity with respect to one given name, or two initials, or two initials corresponding with the first letters of given names, between the two defendants, and there is no evidence that would indicate the two defendants are not one and the same, the identity of name is prima facie evidence that the two defendants are the same person.

(e)   Upon motion of a defendant under G.S. 15A-952(b) the court must dismiss the charges contained in a pleading which fails to charge the defendant with a crime in the manner required by subsection (a), unless the failure is with regard to a matter as to which an amendment is allowable.

(f)   Upon motion of a defendant under G.S. 15A-952(b) the court may strike inflammatory or prejudicial surplusage from the pleading. (1973, c. 1286, s. 1; 1975, c. 642, s. 2; 1989, c. 290, s. 3; 2005-145, s. 3.)

§ 15A-925. Bill of particulars.

(a)   Upon motion of a defendant under G.S. 15A-952, the court in which a charge is pending may order the State to file a bill of particulars with the court and to serve a copy upon the defendant.

(b)   A motion for a bill of particulars must request and specify items of factual information desired by the defendant which pertain to the charge and which are not recited in the pleading, and must allege that the defendant cannot adequately prepare or conduct his defense without such information.

(c)   If any or all of the items of information requested are necessary to enable the defendant adequately to prepare or conduct his defense, the court must order the State to file and serve a bill of particulars. Nothing contained in this section authorizes an order for a bill of particulars which requires the State to recite matters of evidence.

(d)   The bill of particulars must be filed with the court and must recite every item of information required in the order. A copy must be served upon the defendant, or his attorney. The proceedings are stayed pending the filing and service.

(e)   A bill of particulars may not supply an omission or cure a defect in a criminal pleading. The evidence of the State, as to those matters within the scope of the motion, is limited to the items set out in the bill of particulars. The court may permit amendment of a bill of particulars at any time prior to trial. (1973, c. 1286, s. 1.)

§ 15A-926. Joinder of offenses and defendants.

(a)   Joinder of Offenses. - Two or more offenses may be joined in one pleading or for trial when the offenses, whether felonies or misdemeanors or both, are based on the same act or transaction or on a series of acts or transactions connected together or constituting parts of a single scheme or plan. Each offense must be stated in a separate count as required by G.S. 15A-924.

(b)   Separate Pleadings for Each Defendant and Joinder of Defendants for Trial.

(1)   Each defendant must be charged in a separate pleading.

(2)   Upon written motion of the prosecutor, charges against two or more defendants may be joined for trial:

a.   When each of the defendants is charged with accountability for each offense; or

b.   When, even if all of the defendants are not charged with accountability for each offense, the several offenses charged:

1.   Were part of a common scheme or plan; or

2.   Were part of the same act or transaction; or

3.   Were so closely connected in time, place, and occasion that it would be difficult to separate proof of one charge from proof of the others.

(c)   Failure to Join Related Offenses.

(1)   When a defendant has been charged with two or more offenses joinable under subsection (a) his timely motion to join them for trial must be granted unless the court determines that because the prosecutor does not have sufficient evidence to warrant trying some of the offenses at that time or if, for

some other reason, the ends of justice would be defeated if the motion were granted. A defendant's failure to make this motion constitutes a waiver of any right of joinder of offenses joinable under subsection (a) with which the defendant knew he was charged.

(2)   A defendant who has been tried for one offense may thereafter move to dismiss a charge of a joinable offense. The motion to dismiss must be made prior to the second trial, and must be granted unless

a.   A motion for joinder of these offenses was previously denied, or

b.   The court finds that the right of joinder has been waived, or

c.   The court finds that because the prosecutor did not have sufficient evidence to warrant trying this offense at the time of the first trial, or because of some other reason, the ends of justice would be defeated if the motion were granted.

(3)   The right to joinder under this subsection is not applicable when the defendant has pleaded guilty or no contest to the previous charge. (1973, c. 1286, s. 1; 1975, c. 166, ss. 19, 27.)

§ 15A-927. Severance of offenses; objection to joinder of defendants for trial.

(a)   Timeliness of Motion; Waiver; Double Jeopardy.

(1)   A defendant's motion for severance of offenses must be made before trial as provided in G.S. 15A-952, except as provided in G.S. 15A-953, and except that a motion for severance may be made before or at the close of the State's evidence if based upon a ground not previously known. Any right to severance is waived if the motion is not made at the appropriate time.

(2)   If a defendant's pretrial motion for severance is overruled, he may renew the motion on the same grounds before or at the close of all the evidence. Any right to severance is waived by failure to renew the motion.

(3)   Unless consented to by the defendant, a motion by the prosecutor for severance of offenses may be granted only prior to trial.

(4) If a motion for severance of offenses is granted during the trial, a motion by the defendant for a mistrial must be granted.

(b) Severance of Offenses. - The court, on motion of the prosecutor or on motion of the defendant, must grant a severance of offenses whenever:

(1) If before trial, it is found necessary to promote a fair determination of the defendant's guilt or innocence of each offense; or

(2) If during trial, upon motion of the defendant or motion of the prosecutor with the consent of the defendant, it is found necessary to achieve a fair determination of the defendant's guilt or innocence of each offense. The court must consider whether, in view of the number of offenses charged and the complexity of the evidence to be offered, the trier of fact will be able to distinguish the evidence and apply the law intelligently as to each offense.

(c) Objection to Joinder of Charges against Multiple Defendants for Trial; Severance.

(1) When a defendant objects to joinder of charges against two or more defendants for trial because an out-of-court statement of a codefendant makes reference to him but is not admissible against him, the court must require the prosecutor to select one of the following courses:

a. A joint trial at which the statement is not admitted into evidence; or

b. A joint trial at which the statement is admitted into evidence only after all references to the moving defendant have been effectively deleted so that the statement will not prejudice him; or

c. A separate trial of the objecting defendant.

(2) The court, on motion of the prosecutor, or on motion of the defendant other than under subdivision (1) above must deny a joinder for trial or grant a severance of defendants whenever:

a. If before trial, it is found necessary to protect a defendant's right to a speedy trial, or it is found necessary to promote a fair determination of the guilt or innocence of one or more defendants; or

b. If during trial, upon motion of the defendant whose trial is to be severed, or motion of the prosecutor with the consent of the defendant whose trial is to be severed, it is found necessary to achieve a fair determination of the guilt or innocence of that defendant.

(3) The court may order the prosecutor to disclose, out of the presence of the jurors, any statements made by the defendants which he intends to introduce in evidence at the trial when that information would assist the court in ruling on an objection to joinder of defendants for trial or a motion for severance of defendants.

(d) Failure to Prove Grounds for Joinder of Defendants for Trial. - If a defendant moves for severance at the conclusion of the State's case or of all the evidence, and there is not sufficient evidence to support the allegation upon which the moving defendant was joined for trial with the other defendant or defendants, the court must grant a severance if, in view of this lack of evidence, severance is found necessary to achieve a fair determination of that defendant's guilt or innocence.

(e) Severance on Motion of Court. - The court may order a severance of offenses before trial or deny the joinder of defendants for trial if a severance or denial of joinder could be obtained on motion of a defendant or the prosecutor. (1973, c. 1286, s. 1; 1975, c. 166, s. 27.)

§ 15A-928. Allegation and proof of previous convictions in superior court.

(a) When the fact that the defendant has been previously convicted of an offense raises an offense of lower grade to one of higher grade and thereby becomes an element of the latter, an indictment or information for the higher offense may not allege the previous conviction. If a reference to a previous conviction is contained in the statutory name or title of the offense, the name or title may not be used in the indictment or information, but an improvised name or title must be used which labels and distinguishes the offense without reference to a previous conviction.

(b) An indictment or information for the offense must be accompanied by a special indictment or information, filed with the principal pleading, charging that the defendant was previously convicted of a specified offense. At the prosecutor's option, the special indictment or information may be incorporated in the principal indictment as a separate count. Except as provided in subsection (c) below, the State may not refer to the special indictment or information during the trial nor adduce any evidence concerning the previous conviction alleged therein.

(c)   After commencement of the trial and before the close of the State's case, the judge in the absence of the jury must arraign the defendant upon the special indictment or information, and must advise him that he may admit the previous conviction alleged, deny it, or remain silent. Depending upon the defendant's response, the trial of the case must then proceed as follows:

(1)   If the defendant admits the previous conviction, that element of the offense charged in the indictment or information is established, no evidence in support thereof may be adduced by the State, and the judge must submit the case to the jury without reference thereto and as if the fact of such previous conviction were not an element of the offense. The court may not submit to the jury any lesser included offense which is distinguished from the offense charged solely by the fact that a previous conviction is not an element thereof.

(2)   If the defendant denies the previous conviction or remains silent, the State may prove that element of the offense charged before the jury as a part of its case. This section applies only to proof of a prior conviction when it is an element of the crime charged, and does not prohibit the State from introducing proof of prior convictions when otherwise permitted under the rules of evidence.

(d)   When a misdemeanor is tried de novo in superior court in which the fact of a previous conviction is an element of the offense affecting punishment, the State must replace the pleading in the case with superseding statements of charges separately alleging the substantive offense and the fact of any prior conviction, in accordance with the provisions of this section relating to indictments and informations. Any jury trial in superior court on the misdemeanor must be held in accordance with the provisions of subsections (b) and (c).

(e)   Nothing contained in this section precludes the State from proving a prior conviction before a grand jury or relieves the State from the obligation or necessity of so doing in order to submit a legally sufficient case. (1973, c. 1286, s. 1; 1975, c. 166, s. 27.)

§ 15A-929. Reserved for future codification purposes.

§ 15A-930. Reserved for future codification purposes.

Article 50.

Voluntary Dismissal.

§ 15A-931. Voluntary dismissal of criminal charges by the State.

(a) Except as provided in G.S. 20-138.4, the prosecutor may dismiss any charges stated in a criminal pleading including those deferred for prosecution by entering an oral dismissal in open court before or during the trial, or by filing a written dismissal with the clerk at any time. The clerk must record the dismissal entered by the prosecutor and note in the case file whether a jury has been impaneled or evidence has been introduced.

(a1) Unless the defendant or the defendant's attorney has been notified otherwise by the prosecutor, a written dismissal of the charges against the defendant filed by the prosecutor shall be served in the same manner prescribed for motions under G.S. 15A-951. In addition, the written dismissal shall also be served on the chief officer of the custodial facility when the record reflects that the defendant is in custody.

(b) No statute of limitations is tolled by charges which have been dismissed pursuant to this section. (1973, c. 1286, s. 1; 1975, c. 166, s. 27; 1983, c. 435, s. 5; 1991, c. 109, s. 1; 1997-228, s. 1.)

§ 15A-932. Dismissal with leave when defendant fails to appear and cannot be readily found or pursuant to a deferred prosecution agreement.

(a) The prosecutor may enter a dismissal with leave for nonappearance when a defendant:

(1) Cannot be readily found to be served with an order for arrest after the grand jury had indicted him; or

(2) Fails to appear at a criminal proceeding at which his attendance is required, and the prosecutor believes the defendant cannot be readily found.

(a1)   The prosecutor may enter a dismissal with leave pursuant to a deferred prosecution agreement entered into in accordance with the provisions of Article 82 of this Chapter.

(b)   Dismissal with leave for nonappearance or pursuant to a deferred prosecution agreement results in removal of the case from the docket of the court, but all process outstanding retains its validity, and all necessary actions to apprehend the defendant, investigate the case, or otherwise further its prosecution may be taken, including the issuance of nontestimonial identification orders, search warrants, new process, initiation of extradition proceedings, and the like.

(c)   The prosecutor may enter the dismissal with leave for nonappearance or pursuant to a deferred prosecution agreement orally in open court or by filing the dismissal in writing with the clerk. If the dismissal for nonappearance or pursuant to a deferred prosecution agreement is entered orally, the clerk must note the nature of the dismissal in the case records.

(d)   Upon apprehension of the defendant, or in the discretion of the prosecutor when he believes apprehension is imminent, the prosecutor may reinstitute the proceedings by filing written notice with the clerk.

(d1)   If the proceeding was dismissed pursuant to subdivision (2) of subsection (a) of this section and charged only offenses for which written appearance, waiver of trial or hearing, and plea of guilty or admission of responsibility are permitted pursuant to G.S. 7A-148(a), and the defendant later tenders to the court that waiver and payment in full of all applicable fines, costs, and fees, the clerk shall accept said waiver and payment without need for a written reinstatement from the prosecutor. Upon disposition of the case pursuant to this subsection, the clerk shall recall any outstanding criminal process in the case pursuant to G.S. 15A-301(g)(2)b.

(e)   If the defendant fails to comply with the terms of a deferred prosecution agreement, the prosecutor may reinstitute the proceedings by filing written notice with the clerk. (1977, c. 777, s. 1; 1985, c. 250; 1994, Ex. Sess., c. 2, s. 1; 2011-145, s. 31.23B; 2011-192, s. 7(o); 2011-391, s. 63(a); 2011-411, s. 1.)

§§ 15A-933 through 15A-940. Reserved for future codification purposes.

Article 51.

Arraignment.

§ 15A-941. Arraignment before judge only upon written request; use of two-way audio and video transmission; entry of not guilty plea if not arraigned.

(a) Arraignment consists of bringing a defendant in open court or as provided in subsection (b) of this section before a judge having jurisdiction to try the offense, advising him of the charges pending against him, and directing him to plead. The prosecutor must read the charges or fairly summarize them to the defendant. If the defendant fails to plead, the court must record that fact, and the defendant must be tried as if he had pleaded not guilty.

(b) An arraignment in a noncapital case may be conducted by an audio and video transmission between the judge and the defendant in which the parties can see and hear each other. If the defendant has counsel, the defendant shall be allowed to communicate fully and confidentially with his attorney during the proceeding.

(c) Prior to the use of audio and video transmission pursuant to subsection (b) of this section, the procedures and type of equipment for audio and video transmission shall be submitted to the Administrative Office of the Courts by the senior regular resident superior court judge for the judicial district or set of districts and approved by the Administrative Office of the Courts.

(d) A defendant will be arraigned in accordance with this section only if the defendant files a written request with the clerk of superior court for an arraignment not later than 21 days after service of the bill of indictment. If a bill of indictment is not required to be served pursuant to G.S. 15A-630, then the written request for arraignment must be filed not later than 21 days from the date of the return of the indictment as a true bill. Upon the return of the indictment as a true bill, the court must immediately cause notice of the 21-day time limit within which the defendant may request an arraignment to be mailed or otherwise given to the defendant and to the defendant's counsel of record, if any. If the defendant does not file a written request for arraignment, then the court shall enter a not guilty plea on behalf of the defendant.

(e) Nothing in this section shall prevent the district attorney from calendaring cases for administrative purposes. (1973, c. 1286, s. 1; 1975, c. 166, s. 27; 1993, c. 30, s. 3; 1995 (Reg. Sess., 1996), c. 725, s. 7.)

§ 15A-942. Right to counsel.

If the defendant appears at the arraignment without counsel, the court must inform the defendant of his right to counsel, must accord the defendant opportunity to exercise that right, and must take any action necessary to effectuate the right. If the defendant does not file a written request for arraignment, the court, in addition to entering a plea of not guilty on behalf of the defendant, shall also verify that the defendant is aware of the right to counsel, that the defendant has been given the opportunity to exercise that right, and must take any action necessary to effectuate that right on behalf of the defendant. (1777, c. 115, s. 85, P.R.; R.C., c. 35, s. 13; Code, s. 1182; Rev., s. 3150; C.S., s. 4515; 1973, c. 1286, s. 1; 1995 (Reg. Sess., 1996), c. 725, s. 8.)

§ 15A-943. Arraignment in superior court -Required calendaring.

(a)   In counties in which there are regularly scheduled 20 or more weeks of trial sessions of superior court at which criminal cases are heard, and in other counties the Chief Justice designates, the prosecutor must calendar arraignments in the superior court on at least the first day of every other week in which criminal cases are heard. No cases in which the presence of a jury is required may be calendared for the day or portion of a day during which arraignments are calendared.

(b)   When a defendant pleads not guilty at an arraignment required by subsection (a), he may not be tried without his consent in the week in which he is arraigned.

(c)   Notwithstanding the provisions of subsection (a) of this section, in any county where as many as three simultaneous sessions of superior court, whether criminal, civil, or mixed, are regularly scheduled, the prosecutor may calendar arraignments in any of the criminal or mixed sessions, at least every other week, upon any day or days of a session, and jury cases may be calendared for trial in any other court at which criminal cases may be heard, upon such days. (1973, c. 1286, s. 1; 1975, c. 166, s. 27; c. 471.)

§ 15A-944. Arraignment in superior court - Optional calendaring.

In counties other than those described in G.S. 15A-943 the prosecutor may, but is not required to, calendar arraignments in the manner described in that section. (1973, c. 1286, s. 1; 1975, c. 166, s. 27.)

§ 15A-945. Waiver of arraignment.

A defendant who is represented by counsel and who wishes to plead not guilty may waive arraignment prior to the day for which arraignment is calendared by filing a written plea, signed by the defendant and his counsel. (1973, c. 1286, s. 1.)

§§ 15A-946 through 15A-950. Reserved for future codification purposes.

Article 52.

Motions Practice.

§ 15A-951. Motions in general; definition, service, and filing.

(a) A motion must:

(1) Unless made during a hearing or trial, be in writing;

(2) State the grounds of the motion; and

(3) Set forth the relief or order sought.

(b) Each written motion must be served upon the attorney of record for the opposing party or upon the defendant if he is not represented by counsel. Service upon the attorney or upon a party may be made by delivering a copy of the motion to him or by mailing it to him at his address of record. Delivery of a copy within the meaning of this Article means handing it to the attorney or to the party or leaving it at the attorney's office with an associate or employee. Service by mail is complete upon deposit of the motion enclosed in a postpaid, properly addressed wrapper in a post office or official depository under the exclusive care and custody of the Postal Service of the United States.

(c)   All written motions must be filed with the court. Proof of service must be made by filing with the court a certificate:

(1)   By the prosecutor, attorney, or defendant making the motion that the paper was served in the manner prescribed; or

(2)   Of acceptance of service by the prosecutor, attorney, or defendant to be served.

The certificate must show the date and method of service or the date of acceptance of service. (1973, c. 1286, s. 1; 1975, c. 166, s. 27.)

§ 15A-952. Pretrial motions; time for filing; sanction for failure to file; motion hearing date.

(a)   Any defense, objection, or request which is capable of being determined without the trial of the general issue may be raised before trial by motion.

(b)   Except as provided in subsection (d), when the following motions are made in superior court they must be made within the time limitations stated in subsection (c) unless the court permits filing at a later time:

(1)   Motions to continue.

(2)   Motions for a change of venue under G.S. 15A-957.

(3)   Motions for a special venire under G.S. 9-12 or G.S. 15A-958.

(4)   Motions to dismiss under G.S. 15A-955.

(5)   Motions to dismiss for improper venue.

(6)   Motions addressed to the pleadings, including:

a.   Motions to dismiss for failure to plead under G.S. 15A-924(e).

b.   Motions to strike under G.S. 15A-924(f).

c.   Motions for bills of particulars under G.S. 15A-924(b) or G.S. 15A-925.

d. Motions for severance of offenses, to the extent required by G.S. 15A-927.

e. Motions for joinder of related offenses under G.S. 15A-926(c).

(c) Unless otherwise provided, the motions listed in subsection (b) must be made at or before the time of arraignment if a written request is filed for arraignment and if arraignment is held prior to the session of court for which the trial is calendared. If arraignment is to be held at the session for which trial is calendared, the motions must be filed on or before five o'clock P.M. on the Wednesday prior to the session when trial of the case begins.

If a written request for arraignment is not filed, then any motion listed in subsection (b) of this section must be filed not later than 21 days from the date of the return of the bill of indictment as a true bill.

(d) Motions concerning jurisdiction of the court or the failure of the pleading to charge an offense may be made at any time.

(e) Failure to file the motions in subsection (b) within the time required constitutes a waiver of the motion. The court may grant relief from any waiver except failure to move to dismiss for improper venue.

(f) When a motion is made before trial, the court in its discretion may hear the motion before trial, on the date set for arraignment, on the date set for trial before a jury is impaneled, or during trial.

(g) In superior or district court, the judge shall consider at least the following factors in determining whether to grant a continuance:

(1) Whether the failure to grant a continuance would be likely to result in a miscarriage of justice;

(2) Whether the case taken as a whole is so unusual and so complex, due to the number of defendants or the nature of the prosecution or otherwise, that more time is needed for adequate preparation; and

(3) Whether the case involves physical or sexual child abuse when a victim or witness is under 16 years of age, and whether further delay would have an adverse impact on the well-being of the child.

(4) Good cause for granting a continuance shall include those instances when the defendant, a witness, or counsel of record has an obligation of service to the State of North Carolina, including service as a member of the General Assembly or the Rules Review Commission. (1973, c. 1286, s. 1; 1989, c. 688, s. 5; 1995 (Reg. Sess., 1996), c. 725, s. 9; 1997-34, s. 12.)

§ 15A-953. Motions practice in district court.

In misdemeanor prosecutions in the district court motions should ordinarily be made upon arraignment or during the course of trial, as appropriate. A written motion may be made prior to trial in district court. With the consent of other parties and the district court judge, a motion may be heard before trial. Upon trial de novo in superior court, motions are subject to the provisions of G.S. 15A-952, and except as provided in G.S. 15A-135, no motion in superior court is prejudiced by any ruling upon, or a failure to make timely motion on, the subject in district court. (1973, c. 1286, s. 1.)

§ 15A-954. Motion to dismiss - Grounds applicable to all criminal pleadings; dismissal of proceedings upon death of defendant.

(a) The court on motion of the defendant must dismiss the charges stated in a criminal pleading if it determines that:

(1) The statute alleged to have been violated is unconstitutional on its face or as applied to the defendant.

(2) The statute of limitations has run.

(3) The defendant has been denied a speedy trial as required by the Constitution of the United States and the Constitution of North Carolina.

(4) The defendant's constitutional rights have been flagrantly violated and there is such irreparable prejudice to the defendant's preparation of his case that there is no remedy but to dismiss the prosecution.

(5) The defendant has previously been placed in jeopardy of the same offense.

(6) The defendant has previously been charged with the same offense in another North Carolina court of competent jurisdiction, and the criminal pleading charging the offense is still pending and valid.

(7) An issue of fact or law essential to a successful prosecution has been previously adjudicated in favor of the defendant in a prior action between the parties.

(8) The court has no jurisdiction of the offense charged.

(9) The defendant has been granted immunity by law from prosecution.

(10) The pleading fails to charge an offense as provided in G.S. 15A-924(e).

(b) Upon suggestion to the court that the defendant has died, the court upon determining that the defendant is dead must dismiss the charges.

(c) A motion to dismiss for the reasons set out in subsection (a) may be made at any time. (1973, c. 1286, s. 1.)

§ 15A-955. Motion to dismiss - Grounds applicable to indictments.

The court on motion of the defendant may dismiss an indictment if it determines that:

(1) There is ground for a challenge to the array,

(2) The requisite number of qualified grand jurors did not concur in finding the indictment, or

(3) All of the witnesses before the grand jury on the bill of indictment were incompetent to testify. (1973, c. 1286, s. 1.)

§ 15A-956. Deferral of ruling on motion to dismiss when charge to be reinstituted.

If a motion to dismiss is made at arraignment or trial, upon motion of the prosecutor the court may recess the proceedings for a period of time requested by the prosecutor, not to exceed 24 hours, prior to ruling upon the motion. (1973, c. 1286, s. 1; 1975, c. 166, s. 27.)

§ 15A-957. Motion for change of venue.

If, upon motion of the defendant, the court determines that there exists in the county in which the prosecution is pending so great a prejudice against the defendant that he cannot obtain a fair and impartial trial, the court must either:

(1) Transfer the proceeding to another county in the prosecutorial district as defined in G.S. 7A-60 or to another county in an adjoining prosecutorial district as defined in G.S. 7A-60, or

(2) Order a special venire under the terms of G.S. 15A-958.

The procedure for change of venue is in accordance with the provisions of Article 3 of this Chapter, Venue. (1973, c. 1286, s. 1; 1987 (Reg. Sess., 1988), c. 1037, s. 63.)

§ 15A-958. Motion for a special venire from another county.

Upon motion of the defendant or the State, or on its own motion, a court may issue an order for a special venire of jurors from another county if in its discretion it determines the action to be necessary to insure a fair trial. The procedure for securing this special venire is governed by G.S. 9-12. (1973, c. 1286, s. 1.)

§ 15A-959. Notice of defense of insanity; pretrial determination of insanity.

(a) If a defendant intends to raise the defense of insanity, the defendant must file a notice of the defendant's intention to rely on the defense of insanity as provided in G.S. 15A-905(c) and, if the case is not subject to that section, within a reasonable time prior to trial. The court may for cause shown allow late filing of the notice or grant additional time to the parties to prepare for trial or make other appropriate orders.

(b)   In cases not subject to the requirements of G.S. 15A-905(c), if a defendant intends to introduce expert testimony relating to a mental disease, defect, or other condition bearing upon the issue of whether the defendant had the mental state required for the offense charged, the defendant must within a reasonable time prior to trial file a notice of that intention. The court may for cause shown allow late filing of the notice or grant additional time to the parties to prepare for trial or make other appropriate orders.

(c)   Upon motion of the defendant and with the consent of the State the court may conduct a hearing prior to the trial with regard to the defense of insanity at the time of the offense. If the court determines that the defendant has a valid defense of insanity with regard to any criminal charge, it may dismiss that charge, with prejudice, upon making a finding to that effect. The court's denial of relief under this subsection is without prejudice to the defendant's right to rely on the defense at trial. If the motion is denied, no reference to the hearing may be made at the trial, and recorded testimony or evidence taken at the hearing is not admissible as evidence at the trial. (1973, c. 1286, s. 1; 1977, c. 711, s. 25; 2004-154, s. 10.)

§§ 15A-960 through 15A-970. Reserved for future codification purposes.

Article 53.

Motion to Suppress Evidence.

§ 15A-971. Definitions.

As used in this Article the following definitions apply unless the context clearly requires otherwise:

(1)   Evidence. - When referring to matter in the possession of or available to a prosecutor, any tangible property or potential testimony which may be offered in evidence in a criminal action.

(2) Potential Testimony. - Information or factual knowledge of a person who is or may be available as a witness. (1973, c. 1286, s. 1; 1975, c. 166, s. 27.)

§ 15A-972. Motion to suppress evidence before trial in superior court in general.

When an indictment has been returned or an information has been filed in the superior court, or a defendant has been bound over for trial in superior court, a defendant who is aggrieved may move to suppress evidence in accordance with the terms of this Article. (1973, c. 1286, s. 1.)

§ 15A-973. Motion to suppress evidence in district court.

In misdemeanor prosecutions in the district court, motions to suppress evidence should ordinarily be made during the course of the trial. A motion to suppress may be made prior to trial. With the consent of the prosecutor and the district court judge, the motion may be heard prior to trial. (1973, c. 1286, s. 1; 1975, c. 166, s. 27.)

§ 15A-974. Exclusion or suppression of unlawfully obtained evidence.

(a) Upon timely motion, evidence must be suppressed if:

(1) Its exclusion is required by the Constitution of the United States or the Constitution of the State of North Carolina; or

(2) It is obtained as a result of a substantial violation of the provisions of this Chapter. In determining whether a violation is substantial, the court must consider all the circumstances, including:

    a. The importance of the particular interest violated;

    b. The extent of the deviation from lawful conduct;

    c. The extent to which the violation was willful;

d. The extent to which exclusion will tend to deter future violations of this Chapter.

Evidence shall not be suppressed under this subdivision if the person committing the violation of the provision or provisions under this Chapter acted under the objectively reasonable, good faith belief that the actions were lawful.

(b) The court, in making a determination whether or not evidence shall be suppressed under this section, shall make findings of fact and conclusions of law which shall be included in the record, pursuant to G.S. 15A-977(f). (1973, c. 1286, s. 1; 2011-6, s. 1.)

§ 15A-975. Motion to suppress evidence in superior court prior to trial and during trial.

(a) In superior court, the defendant may move to suppress evidence only prior to trial unless the defendant did not have reasonable opportunity to make the motion before trial or unless a motion to suppress is allowed during trial under subsection (b) or (c).

(b) A motion to suppress may be made for the first time during trial when the State has failed to notify the defendant's counsel or, if he has none, the defendant, sooner than 20 working days before trial, of its intention to use the evidence, and the evidence is:

(1) Evidence of a statement made by a defendant;

(2) Evidence obtained by virtue of a search without a search warrant; or

(3) Evidence obtained as a result of search with a search warrant when the defendant was not present at the time of the execution of the search warrant.

(c) If, after a pretrial determination and denial of the motion, the judge is satisfied, upon a showing by the defendant, that additional pertinent facts have been discovered by the defendant which he could not have discovered with reasonable diligence before the determination of the motion, he may permit the defendant to renew the motion before the trial or, if not possible because of the time of discovery of alleged new facts, during trial.

When a misdemeanor is appealed by the defendant for trial de novo in superior court, the State need not give the notice required by this section. (1973, c. 1286, s. 1.)

§ 15A-976. Timing of pretrial suppression motion and hearing.

(a) A motion to suppress evidence in superior court may be made at any time prior to trial except as provided in subsection (b).

(b) If the State gives notice not later than 20 working days before trial of its intention to use evidence and if the evidence is of a type listed in G.S. 15A-975(b), the defendant may move to suppress the evidence only if its motion is made not later than 10 working days following receipt of the notice from the State.

(c) When the motion is made before trial, the judge in his discretion may hear the motion before trial, on the date set for arraignment, on the date set for trial before a jury is impaneled, or during trial. He may rule on the motion before trial or reserve judgment until trial. (1973, c. 1286, s. 1.)

§ 15A-977. Motion to suppress evidence in superior court; procedure.

(a) A motion to suppress evidence in superior court made before trial must be in writing and a copy of the motion must be served upon the State. The motion must state the grounds upon which it is made. The motion must be accompanied by an affidavit containing facts supporting the motion. The affidavit may be based upon personal knowledge, or upon information and belief, if the source of the information and the basis for the belief are stated. The State may file an answer denying or admitting any of the allegations. A copy of the answer must be served on the defendant's counsel, or on the defendant if he has no counsel.

(b) The judge must summarily grant the motion to suppress evidence if:

(1) The motion complies with the requirements of subsection (a), it states grounds which require exclusion of the evidence, and the State concedes the truth of allegations of fact which support the motion; or

(2) The State stipulates that the evidence sought to be suppressed will not be offered in evidence in any criminal action or proceeding against the defendant.

(c) The judge may summarily deny the motion to suppress evidence if:

(1) The motion does not allege a legal basis for the motion; or

(2) The affidavit does not as a matter of law support the ground alleged.

(d) If the motion is not determined summarily the judge must make the determination after a hearing and finding of facts. Testimony at the hearing must be under oath.

(e) A motion to suppress made during trial may be made in writing or orally and may be determined in the same manner as when made before trial. The hearing, if held, must be out of the presence of the jury.

(f) The judge must set forth in the record his findings of facts and conclusions of law. (1973, c. 1286, s. 1.)

§ 15A-978. Motion to suppress evidence in superior court or district court; challenge of probable cause supporting search on grounds of truthfulness; when identity of informant must be disclosed.

(a) A defendant may contest the validity of a search warrant and the admissibility of evidence obtained thereunder by contesting the truthfulness of the testimony showing probable cause for its issuance. The defendant may contest the truthfulness of the testimony by cross-examination or by offering evidence. For the purposes of this section, truthful testimony is testimony which reports in good faith the circumstances relied on to establish probable cause.

(b) In any proceeding on a motion to suppress evidence pursuant to this section in which the truthfulness of the testimony presented to establish probable cause is contested and the testimony includes a report of information furnished by an informant whose identity is not disclosed in the testimony, the defendant is entitled to be informed of the informant's identity unless:

(1) The evidence sought to be suppressed was seized by authority of a search warrant or incident to an arrest with warrant; or

(2) There is corroboration of the informant's existence independent of the testimony in question.

The provisions of subdivisions (b)(1) and (b)(2) do not apply to situations in which disclosure of an informant's identity is required by controlling constitutional decisions.

(c) This section does not limit the right of a defendant to contest the truthfulness of testimony offered in support of a search made without a warrant. (1973, c. 1286, s. 1.)

§ 15A-979. Motion to suppress evidence in superior and district court; orders of suppression; effects of orders and of failure to make motion.

(a) Upon granting a motion to suppress evidence the judge must order that the evidence in question be excluded in the criminal action pending against the defendant. When the order is based upon the ground of an unlawful search and seizure and excludes tangible property unlawfully taken from the defendant's possession, and when the property is not contraband or otherwise subject to lawful retention by the State or another, the judge must order that the property be restored to the defendant at the conclusion of the trial including all appeals.

(b) An order finally denying a motion to suppress evidence may be reviewed upon an appeal from a judgment of conviction, including a judgment entered upon a plea of guilty.

(c) An order by the superior court granting a motion to suppress prior to trial is appealable to the appellate division of the General Court of Justice prior to trial upon certificate by the prosecutor to the judge who granted the motion that the appeal is not taken for the purpose of delay and that the evidence is essential to the case. The appeal is to the appellate court that would have jurisdiction if the defendant were found guilty of the charge and received the maximum punishment. If there are multiple charges affected by a motion to suppress, the ruling is appealable to the court with jurisdiction over the offense carrying the highest punishment.

(d) A motion to suppress evidence made pursuant to this Article is the exclusive method of challenging the admissibility of evidence upon the grounds specified in G.S. 15A-974. (1973, c. 1286, s. 1; 1975, c. 166, s. 27; 1979, c. 723.)

§ 15A-980. Right to suppress use of certain prior convictions obtained in violation of right to counsel.

(a) A defendant has the right to suppress the use of a prior conviction that was obtained in violation of his right to counsel if its use by the State is to impeach the defendant or if its use will:

(1) Increase the degree of crime of which the defendant would be guilty; or

(2) Result in a sentence of imprisonment that otherwise would not be imposed; or

(3) Result in a lengthened sentence of imprisonment.

(b) A defendant who has grounds to suppress the use of a conviction in evidence at a trial or other proceeding as set forth in (a) must do so by motion made in accordance with the procedure in this Article. A defendant waives his right to suppress use of a prior conviction if he does not move to suppress it.

(c) When a defendant has moved to suppress use of a prior conviction under the terms of subsection (a), he has the burden of proving by the preponderance of the evidence that the conviction was obtained in violation of his right to counsel. To prevail, he must prove that at the time of the conviction he was indigent, had no counsel, and had not waived his right to counsel. If the defendant proves that a prior conviction was obtained in violation of his right to counsel, the judge must suppress use of the conviction at trial or in any other proceeding if its use will contravene the provisions of subsection (a). (1983, c. 513, s. 1.)

Article 54.

§§ 15A-981 through 15A-990. Reserved for future codification purposes.

Article 55.

§§ 15A-991 through 15A-1000. Reserved for future codification purposes.

SUBCHAPTER X. GENERAL TRIAL PROCEDURE.

Article 56.

Incapacity to Proceed.

§ 15A-1001. No proceedings when defendant mentally incapacitated; exception.

(a) No person may be tried, convicted, sentenced, or punished for a crime when by reason of mental illness or defect he is unable to understand the nature and object of the proceedings against him, to comprehend his own situation in reference to the proceedings, or to assist in his defense in a rational or reasonable manner. This condition is hereinafter referred to as "incapacity to proceed."

(b) This section does not prevent the court from going forward with any motions which can be handled by counsel without the assistance of the defendant. (1973, c. 1286, s. 1.)

§ 15A-1002. Determination of incapacity to proceed; evidence; temporary commitment; temporary orders.

(a) The question of the capacity of the defendant to proceed may be raised at any time on motion by the prosecutor, the defendant, the defense counsel, or the court. The motion shall detail the specific conduct that leads the moving party to question the defendant's capacity to proceed.

(b) (1) When the capacity of the defendant to proceed is questioned, the court shall hold a hearing to determine the defendant's capacity to proceed. If an examination is ordered pursuant to subdivision (1a) or (2) of this subsection, the hearing shall be held after the examination. Reasonable notice shall be given to the defendant and prosecutor, and the State and the defendant may introduce evidence.

(1a)   In the case of a defendant charged with a misdemeanor or felony, the court may appoint one or more impartial medical experts, including forensic evaluators approved under rules of the Commission for Mental Health, Developmental Disabilities, and Substance Abuse Services, to examine the defendant and return a written report describing the present state of the defendant's mental health. Reports so prepared are admissible at the hearing. The court may call any expert so appointed to testify at the hearing with or without the request of either party.

(2)   At any time in the case of a defendant charged with a felony, the court may order the defendant to a State facility for the mentally ill for observation and treatment for the period, not to exceed 60 days, necessary to determine the defendant's capacity to proceed. If a defendant is ordered to a State facility without first having an examination pursuant to subsection (b)(1a) of this section, the judge shall make a finding that an examination pursuant to this subsection would be more appropriate to determine the defendant's capacity. The sheriff shall return the defendant to the county when notified that the evaluation has been completed. The director of the facility shall direct his report on defendant's condition to the defense attorney and to the clerk of superior court, who shall bring it to the attention of the court. The report is admissible at the hearing.

(3)   Repealed by Session Laws 1989, c. 486, s. 1.

(4)   A presiding district or superior court judge of this State who orders an examination pursuant to subdivision (1a) or (2) of this subsection shall order the release of relevant confidential information to the examiner, including, but not limited to, the warrant or indictment, arrest records, the law enforcement incident report, the defendant's criminal record, jail records, any prior medical and mental health records of the defendant, and any school records of the defendant after providing the defendant with reasonable notice and an opportunity to be heard and then determining that the information is relevant and necessary to the hearing of the matter before the court and unavailable from any other source. This subdivision shall not be construed to relieve any court of its duty to conduct hearings and make findings required under relevant federal law before ordering the release of any private medical or mental health information or records related to substance abuse or HIV status or treatment. The records may be surrendered to the court for in camera review if surrender is

necessary to make the required determinations. The records shall be withheld from public inspection and, except as provided in this subdivision, may be examined only by order of the court.

(b1) The order of the court shall contain findings of fact to support its determination of the defendant's capacity to proceed. The parties may stipulate that the defendant is capable of proceeding but shall not be allowed to stipulate that the defendant lacks capacity to proceed. If the court concludes that the defendant lacks capacity to proceed, proceedings for involuntary civil commitment under Chapter 122C of the General Statutes may be instituted on the basis of the report in either the county where the criminal proceedings are pending or, if the defendant is hospitalized, in the county in which the defendant is hospitalized.

(b2) Reports made to the court pursuant to this section shall be completed and provided to the court as follows:

(1) The report in a case of a defendant charged with a misdemeanor shall be completed and provided to the court no later than 10 days following the completion of the examination for a defendant who was in custody at the time the examination order was entered and no later than 20 days following the completion of the examination for a defendant who was not in custody at the time the examination order was entered.

(2) The report in the case of a defendant charged with a felony shall be completed and provided to the court no later than 30 days following the completion of the examination.

(3) In cases where the defendant challenges the determination made by the court-ordered examiner or the State facility and the court orders an independent psychiatric examination, that examination and report to the court must be completed within 60 days of the entry of the order by the court.

The court may, for good cause shown, extend the time for the provision of the report to the court for up to 30 additional days. The court may renew an extension of time for an additional 30 days upon request of the State or the defendant prior to the expiration of the previous extension. In no case shall the court grant extensions totaling more than 120 days beyond the time periods otherwise provided in this subsection.

(c)   The court may make appropriate temporary orders for the confinement or security of the defendant pending the hearing or ruling of the court on the question of the capacity of the defendant to proceed.

(d)   Any report made to the court pursuant to this section shall be forwarded to the clerk of superior court in a sealed envelope addressed to the attention of a presiding judge, with a covering statement to the clerk of the fact of the examination of the defendant and any conclusion as to whether the defendant has or lacks capacity to proceed. If the defendant is being held in the custody of the sheriff, the clerk shall send a copy of the covering statement to the sheriff. The sheriff and any persons employed by the sheriff shall maintain the copy of the covering statement as a confidential record. A copy of the full report shall be forwarded to defense counsel, or to the defendant if he is not represented by counsel. If the question of the defendant's capacity to proceed is raised at any time, a copy of the full report must be forwarded to the district attorney, as provided in G.S. 122C-54(b). Until such report becomes a public record, the full report to the court shall be kept under such conditions as are directed by the court, and its contents shall not be revealed except as directed by the court. Any report made to the court pursuant to this section shall not be a public record unless introduced into evidence. (1973, c. 1286, s. 1; 1975, c. 166, ss. 20, 27; 1977, cc. 25, 860; 1979, 2nd Sess., c. 1313; 1985, c. 588; c. 589, s. 9; 1989, c. 486, s. 1; 1991, c. 636, s. 19(b); 1995, c. 299, s. 1; 1995 (Reg. Sess., 1996), c. 742, ss. 13, 14; 2013-18, s. 1.)

§ 15A-1003. Referral of incapable defendant for civil commitment proceedings.

(a)   When a defendant is found to be incapable of proceeding, the presiding judge, upon such additional hearing, if any, as he determines to be necessary, shall determine whether there are reasonable grounds to believe the defendant meets the criteria for involuntary commitment under Part 7 of Article 5 of Chapter 122C of the General Statutes. If the presiding judge finds reasonable grounds to believe that the defendant meets the criteria, he shall make findings of fact and issue a custody order in the same manner, upon the same grounds and with the same effect as an order issued by a clerk or magistrate pursuant to G.S. 122C-261. Proceedings thereafter are in accordance with Part 7 of Article 5 of Chapter 122C of the General Statutes. If the defendant was charged with a violent crime, including a crime involving assault with a deadly weapon, the judge's custody order shall require a law-enforcement officer to take the defendant directly to a 24-hour facility as described in G.S. 122C-252; and the order must indicate that the defendant was charged with a violent crime and that he was found incapable of proceeding.

(b)   The court may make appropriate orders for the temporary detention of the defendant pending that proceeding.

(c)   Evidence used at the hearing with regard to capacity to proceed is admissible in the involuntary civil commitment proceedings. (1973, c. 1286, s. 1; 1975, c. 166, s. 20; 1983, c. 380, s. 1; 1985, c. 589, s. 10; 1987, c. 596, s. 5.)

§ 15A-1004. Orders for safeguarding of defendant and return for trial.

(a)   When a defendant is found to be incapable of proceeding, the trial court must make appropriate orders to safeguard the defendant and to ensure his return for trial in the event that he subsequently becomes capable of proceeding.

(b)   If the defendant is not placed in the custody of a hospital or other institution in a proceeding for involuntary civil commitment, appropriate orders may include any of the procedures, orders, and conditions provided in Article 26 of this Chapter, Bail, specifically including the power to place the defendant in the custody of a designated person or organization agreeing to supervise him.

(c)   If the defendant is placed in the custody of a hospital or other institution in a proceeding for involuntary civil commitment, the orders must provide for reporting to the clerk if the defendant is to be released from the custody of the hospital or institution. The original or supplemental orders may make provisions as in subsection (b) in the event that the defendant is released. The court shall also order that the defendant shall be examined to determine whether the defendant has the capacity to proceed prior to release from custody. A report of the examination shall be provided pursuant to G.S. 15A-1002. If the defendant was charged with a violent crime, including a crime involving assault with a deadly weapon, and that charge has not been dismissed, the order must require that if the defendant is to be released from the custody of the hospital or other institution, he is to be released only to the custody of a specified law enforcement agency. If the original or supplemental orders do not specify to whom the respondent shall be released, the hospital or other institution may release the defendant to whomever it thinks appropriate.

(d) If the defendant is placed in the custody of a hospital or institution pursuant to proceedings for involuntary civil commitment, or if the defendant is placed in the custody of another person pursuant to subsection (b), the orders of the trial court must require that the hospital, institution, or individual report the condition of the defendant to the clerk at the same times that reports on the condition of the defendant-respondent are required under Part 7 of Article 5 of Chapter 122C of the General Statutes, or more frequently if the court requires, and immediately if the defendant gains capacity to proceed. The order must also require the report to state the likelihood of the defendant's gaining capacity to proceed, to the extent that the hospital, institution, or individual is capable of making such a judgment.

(e) The orders must require and provide for the return of the defendant to stand trial in the event that he gains capacity to proceed, unless the charges have been dismissed pursuant to G.S. 15A-1008, and may also provide for the confinement or pretrial release of the defendant in that event.

(f) The orders of the court may be amended or supplemented from time to time as changed conditions require. (1973, c. 1286, s. 1; 1975, c. 166, s. 20; 1983, c. 380, s. 2; c. 460, s. 2; 1985, c. 589, s. 11; 2013-18, s. 2.)

§ 15A-1005. Reporting to court with regard to defendants incapable of proceeding.

The clerk of the court in which the criminal proceeding is pending must keep a docket of defendants who have been determined to be incapable of proceeding. The clerk must submit the docket to the senior resident superior court judge in his district at least semiannually. (1973, c. 1286, s. 1.)

§ 15A-1006. Return of defendant for trial upon gaining capacity.

If a defendant who has been determined to be incapable of proceeding, and who is in the custody of an institution or an individual, has been determined by the institution or individual having custody to have gained capacity to proceed, the individual or institution shall provide written notification to the clerk in the county in which the criminal proceeding is pending. The clerk shall provide written notification to the district attorney, the defendant's attorney, and the sheriff. The sheriff shall return the defendant to the county for a supplemental hearing pursuant to G.S. 15A-1007, if conducted, and trial and hold the defendant for a supplemental hearing and trial, subject to the orders of the court entered pursuant to G.S. 15A-1004. (1973, c. 1286, s. 1; 2013-18, s. 3.)

§ 15A-1007. Supplemental hearings.

(a) When it has been reported to the court that a defendant has gained capacity to proceed, or when the defendant has been determined by the individual or institution having custody of him to have gained capacity and has been returned for trial, in accordance with G.S. 15A-1004(e) and G.S. 15A-1006, the clerk shall notify the district attorney. Upon receiving the notification, the district attorney shall calendar the matter for hearing at the next available term of court but no later than 30 days after receiving the notification. The court may hold a supplemental hearing to determine whether the defendant has capacity to proceed. The court may take any action at the supplemental hearing that it could have taken at an original hearing to determine the capacity of the defendant to proceed.

(b) The court may hold a supplemental hearing any time upon its own determination that a hearing is appropriate or necessary to inquire into the condition of the defendant.

(c) The court must hold a supplemental hearing if it appears that any of the conditions for dismissal of the charges have been met.

(d) If the court determines in a supplemental hearing that a defendant has gained the capacity to proceed, the case shall be calendared for trial at the earliest practicable time. Continuances that extend beyond 60 days after initial calendaring of the trial shall be granted only in extraordinary circumstances when necessary for the proper administration of justice, and the court shall issue a written order stating the grounds for granting the continuance. (1973, c. 1286, s. 1; 2013-18, s. 4.)

§ 15A-1008. Dismissal of charges.

(a) When a defendant lacks capacity to proceed, the court shall dismiss the charges upon the earliest of the following occurrences:

(1) When it appears to the satisfaction of the court that the defendant will not gain capacity to proceed.

(2) When as a result of incarceration, involuntary commitment to an inpatient facility, or other court-ordered confinement, the defendant has been substantially deprived of his liberty for a period of time equal to or in excess of the maximum term of imprisonment permissible for prior record Level VI for felonies or prior conviction Level III for misdemeanors for the most serious offense charged.

(3) Upon the expiration of a period of five years from the date of determination of incapacity to proceed in the case of misdemeanor charges and a period of 10 years in the case of felony charges.

(b) A dismissal entered pursuant to subdivision (2) of subsection (a) of this section shall be without leave.

(c) A dismissal entered pursuant to subdivision (1) or (3) of subsection (a) of this section shall be issued without prejudice to the refiling of the charges. Upon the defendant becoming capable of proceeding, the prosecutor may reinstitute proceedings dismissed pursuant to subdivision (1) or (3) of subsection (a) of this section by filing written notice with the clerk, with the defendant, and with the defendant's attorney of record.

(d) Dismissal of criminal charges pursuant to this section shall be upon motion of the prosecutor or the defendant or upon the court's own motion. (1973, c. 1286, s. 1; 2013-18, s. 5.)

§ 15A-1009: Repealed by Session Laws 2013-18, s. 6, effective December 1, 2013.

§ 15A-1010. Reserved for future codification purposes.

Article 57.

Pleas.

§ 15A-1011. Pleas in district and superior courts; waiver of appearance.

(a) A defendant may plead not guilty, guilty, or no contest "(nolo contendere)." A plea may be received only from the defendant himself in open court except when:

(1) The defendant is a corporation, in which case the plea may be entered by counsel or a corporate officer; or

(2) There is a waiver of arraignment and a filing of a written plea of not guilty under G.S. 15A-945; or

(3) In misdemeanor cases there is a written waiver of appearance submitted with the approval of the presiding judge; or

(4) Written pleas in traffic cases, hunting and fishing offenses under Chapter 113, and boating offenses under Chapter 75A are authorized under G.S. 7A-146(8); or

(5) The defendant executes a waiver and plea of not guilty as provided in G.S. 15A-1011(d).

(6) The defendant, before a magistrate or clerk of court, enters a written appearance, waiver of trial and plea of guilty and at the same time makes restitution in a case wherein the sole allegation is a violation of G.S. 14-107, the check is in an amount provided in G.S. 7A-273(8), and the warrant does not charge a fourth or subsequent violation of this statute.

(b) A defendant may plead no contest only with the consent of the prosecutor and the presiding judge.

(c) Upon entry of a plea of guilty or no contest or after conviction on a plea of not guilty, the defendant may request permission to enter a plea of guilty or no contest as to other crimes with which he is charged in the same or another prosecutorial district as defined in G.S. 7A-60. A defendant may not enter any plea to crimes charged in another prosecutorial district as defined in G.S. 7A-60 unless the district attorney of that district consents in writing to the entry of such plea. The prosecutor or his representative may appear in person or by filing an affidavit as to the nature of the evidence gathered as to these other crimes. Entry of a plea under this subsection constitutes a waiver of venue. A superior court is granted jurisdiction to accept the plea, upon an appropriate indictment or information, even though the case may otherwise be within the exclusive original jurisdiction of the district court. A district court may accept pleas under this section only in cases within the original jurisdiction of the district court and in cases within the concurrent jurisdiction of the district and superior courts pursuant to G.S. 7A-272(c).

(d)   A defendant may execute a written waiver of appearance and plead not guilty and designate legal counsel to appear in his behalf in the following circumstances:

(1)   The defendant agrees in writing to waive the right to testify in person and waives the right to face his accusers in person and agrees to be bound by the decision of the court as in any other case of adjudication of guilty and entry of judgment, subject to the right of appeal as in any other case; and

(2)   The defendant submits in writing circumstances to justify the request and submits in writing a request to proceed under this section; and

(3)   The judge allows the absence of the defendant because of distance, infirmity or other good cause.

(e)   In the event the judge shall permit the procedure set forth in the foregoing subsection (d), the State may offer evidence and the defendant may offer evidence, with right of cross-examination of witnesses, and the other procedures, including the right of the prosecutor to dismiss the charges, shall be the same as in any other criminal case, except for the absence of defendant. (1973, c. 1286, s. 1; 1975, c. 166, s. 27; c. 626, s. 1; 1983, c. 586, s. 3; 1987, c. 355, s. 4; 1987 (Reg. Sess., 1988), c. 1037, s. 64; 1995 (Reg. Sess., 1996), c. 725, s. 5.)

§ 15A-1012. Aid of counsel; time for deliberation.

(a)   A defendant may not be called upon to plead until he has had an opportunity to retain counsel or, if he is eligible for assignment of counsel, until counsel has been assigned or waived in accordance with Article 36 of Chapter 7A of the General Statutes.

(b) In cases in the original jurisdiction of the superior court a defendant who has waived counsel may not plead within less than seven days following the date he was arrested or was otherwise informed of the charge. (1973, c. 1286, s. 1.)

§§ 15A-1013 through 15A-1020. Reserved for future codification purposes.

Article 58.

Procedures Relating to Guilty Pleas in Superior Court.

§ 15A-1021. Plea conference; improper pressure prohibited; submission of arrangement to judge; restitution and reparation as part of plea arrangement agreement, etc.

(a) In superior court, the prosecution and the defense may discuss the possibility that, upon the defendant's entry of a plea of guilty or no contest to one or more offenses, the prosecutor will not charge, will dismiss, or will move for the dismissal of other charges, or will recommend or not oppose a particular sentence. If the defendant is represented by counsel in the discussions the defendant need not be present. The trial judge may participate in the discussions.

(b) No person representing the State or any of its political subdivisions may bring improper pressure upon a defendant to induce a plea of guilty or no contest.

(c) If the parties have reached a proposed plea arrangement in which the prosecutor has agreed to recommend a particular sentence, they may, with the permission of the trial judge, advise the judge of the terms of the arrangement and the reasons therefor in advance of the time for tender of the plea. The proposed plea arrangement may include a provision for the defendant to make restitution or reparation to an aggrieved party or parties for the damage or loss caused by the offense or offenses committed by the defendant. The judge may indicate to the parties whether he will concur in the proposed disposition. The judge may withdraw his concurrence if he learns of information not consistent with the representations made to him.

(d)   When restitution or reparation by the defendant is a part of the plea arrangement agreement, if the judge concurs in the proposed disposition he may order that restitution or reparation be made as a condition of special probation pursuant to the provisions of G.S. 15A-1351, or probation pursuant to the provisions of G.S. 15A-1343(d). If an active sentence is imposed the court may recommend that the defendant make restitution or reparation out of any earnings gained by the defendant if he is granted work release privileges under the provisions of G.S. 148-33.1, or that restitution or reparation be imposed as a condition of parole in accordance with the provisions of G.S. 148-57.1. The order or recommendation providing for restitution or reparation shall be in accordance with the applicable provisions of G.S. 15A-1343(d) and Article 81C of this Chapter.

If the offense is one in which there is evidence of physical, mental or sexual abuse of a minor, the court should encourage the minor and the minor's parents or custodians to participate in rehabilitative treatment and the plea agreement may include a provision that the defendant will be ordered to pay for such treatment.

When restitution or reparation is recommended as part of a plea arrangement that results in an active sentence, the sentencing court shall enter as a part of the commitment that restitution or reparation is recommended as part of the plea arrangement. The Administrative Office of the Courts shall prepare and distribute forms which provide for ample space to make restitution or reparation recommendations incident to commitments. (1973, c. 1286, s. 1; 1975, c. 117; c. 166, s. 27; 1977, c. 614, ss. 3, 4; 1977, 2nd Sess., c. 1147, s. 1; 1979, c. 760, s. 3; 1985, c. 474, s. 2; 1987, c. 598, s. 3; 1997-80, s. 2; 1998-212, s. 19.4(e).)

§ 15A-1022. Advising defendant of consequences of guilty plea; informed choice; factual basis for plea; admission of guilt not required.

(a)   Except in the case of corporations or in misdemeanor cases in which there is a waiver of appearance under G.S. 15A-1011(a)(3), a superior court judge may not accept a plea of guilty or no contest from the defendant without first addressing him personally and:

(1) Informing him that he has a right to remain silent and that any statement he makes may be used against him;

(2) Determining that he understands the nature of the charge;

(3) Informing him that he has a right to plead not guilty;

(4) Informing him that by his plea he waives his right to trial by jury and his right to be confronted by the witnesses against him;

(5) Determining that the defendant, if represented by counsel, is satisfied with his representation;

(6) Informing him of the maximum possible sentence on the charge for the class of offense for which the defendant is being sentenced, including that possible from consecutive sentences, and of the mandatory minimum sentence, if any, on the charge; and

(7) Informing him that if he is not a citizen of the United States of America, a plea of guilty or no contest may result in deportation, the exclusion from admission to this country, or the denial of naturalization under federal law.

(b) By inquiring of the prosecutor and defense counsel and the defendant personally, the judge must determine whether there were any prior plea discussions, whether the parties have entered into any arrangement with respect to the plea and the terms thereof, and whether any improper pressure was exerted in violation of G.S. 15A-1021(b). The judge may not accept a plea of guilty or no contest from a defendant without first determining that the plea is a product of informed choice.

(c) The judge may not accept a plea of guilty or no contest without first determining that there is a factual basis for the plea. This determination may be based upon information including but not limited to:

(1) A statement of the facts by the prosecutor.

(2) A written statement of the defendant.

(3) An examination of the presentence report.

(4) Sworn testimony, which may include reliable hearsay.

(5) A statement of facts by the defense counsel.

(d) The judge may accept the defendant's plea of no contest even though the defendant does not admit that he is in fact guilty if the judge is nevertheless satisfied that there is a factual basis for the plea. The judge must advise the defendant that if he pleads no contest he will be treated as guilty whether or not he admits guilt. (1973, c. 1286, s. 1; 1975, c. 166, s. 27; 1989, c. 280; 1993, c. 538, s. 10; 1994, Ex. Sess., c. 24, s. 14(b).)

§ 15A-1022.1. Procedure in accepting admissions of the existence of aggravating factors in felonies.

(a) Before accepting a plea of guilty or no contest to a felony, the court shall determine whether the State intends to seek a sentence in the aggravated range. If the State does intend to seek an aggravated sentence, the court shall determine which factors the State seeks to establish. The court shall determine whether the State seeks a finding that a prior record level point should be found under G.S. 15A-1340.14(b)(7). The court shall also determine whether the State has provided the notice to the defendant required by G.S. 15A-1340.16(a6) or whether the defendant has waived his or her right to such notice.

(b) In all cases in which a defendant admits to the existence of an aggravating factor or to a finding that a prior record level point should be found under G.S. 15A-1340.14(b)(7), the court shall comply with the provisions of G.S. 15A-1022(a). In addition, the court shall address the defendant personally and advise the defendant that:

(1) He or she is entitled to have a jury determine the existence of any aggravating factors or points under G.S. 15A-1340.14(b)(7); and

(2) He or she has the right to prove the existence of any mitigating factors at a sentencing hearing before the sentencing judge.

(c) Before accepting an admission to the existence of an aggravating factor or a prior record level point under G.S. 15A-1340.14(b)(7), the court shall determine that there is a factual basis for the admission, and that the admission is the result of an informed choice by the defendant. The court may base its determination on the factors specified in G.S. 15A-1022(c), as well as any other appropriate information.

(d)   A defendant may admit to the existence of an aggravating factor or to the existence of a prior record level point under G.S. 15A-1340.14(b)(7) before or after the trial of the underlying felony.

(e)   The procedures specified in this Article for the handling of pleas of guilty are applicable to the handling of admissions to aggravating factors and prior record points under G.S. 15A-1340.14(b)(7), unless the context clearly indicates that they are inappropriate. (2005-145, s. 4.)

§ 15A-1023. Action by judge in plea arrangements relating to sentence; no approval required when arrangement does not relate to sentence.

(a)   If the parties have agreed upon a plea arrangement pursuant to G.S. 15A-1021 in which the prosecutor has agreed to recommend a particular sentence, they must disclose the substance of their agreement to the judge at the time the defendant is called upon to plead.

(b)   Before accepting a plea pursuant to a plea arrangement in which the prosecutor has agreed to recommend a particular sentence, the judge must advise the parties whether he approves the arrangement and will dispose of the case accordingly. If the judge rejects the arrangement, he must so inform the parties, refuse to accept the defendant's plea of guilty or no contest, and advise the defendant personally that neither the State nor the defendant is bound by the rejected arrangement. The judge must advise the parties of the reasons he rejected the arrangement and afford them an opportunity to modify the arrangement accordingly. Upon rejection of the plea arrangement by the judge the defendant is entitled to a continuance until the next session of court. A decision by the judge disapproving a plea arrangement is not subject to appeal. If a judge rejects a plea arrangement disclosed, in open court, pursuant to subsection (a) of this section, then the judge shall order that the rejection be noted on the plea transcript and shall order that the plea transcript with the notation of the rejection be made a part of the record.

(c)   If the parties have entered a plea arrangement relating to the disposition of charges in which the prosecutor has not agreed to make any recommendations concerning sentence, the substance of the arrangement must be disclosed to the judge at the time the defendant is called upon to plead. The judge must accept the plea if he determines that the plea is the product of the informed choice of the defendant and that there is a factual basis for the plea. (1973, c. 1286, s. 1; 1975, c. 166, s. 27; 1977, c. 186; 2009-179, s. 1.)

§ 15A-1024. Withdrawal of guilty plea when sentence not in accord with plea arrangement.

If at the time of sentencing, the judge for any reason determines to impose a sentence other than provided for in a plea arrangement between the parties, the judge must inform the defendant of that fact and inform the defendant that he may withdraw his plea. Upon withdrawal, the defendant is entitled to a continuance until the next session of court. (1973, c. 1286, s. 1.)

§ 15A-1025. Plea discussion and arrangement inadmissible.

The fact that the defendant or his counsel and the prosecutor engaged in plea discussions or made a plea arrangement may not be received in evidence against or in favor of the defendant in any criminal or civil action or administrative proceedings. (1973, c. 1286, s. 1; 1975, c. 166, s. 27.)

§ 15A-1026. Record of proceedings.

A verbatim record of the proceedings at which the defendant enters a plea of guilty or no contest and of any preliminary consideration of a plea arrangement by the judge pursuant to G.S. 15A-1021(c) must be made and preserved. This record must include the judge's advice to the defendant, and his inquiries of the defendant, defense counsel, and the prosecutor, and any responses. If the plea arrangement has been reduced to writing, it must be made a part of the record; otherwise the judge must require that the terms of the arrangement be stated for the record and that the assent of the defendant, his counsel, and the prosecutor be recorded. If the judge rejects the plea arrangement under G.S. 15A-1023(b), then the rejection of the plea arrangement must also be made part of the record pursuant to G.S. 15A-1023(b). (1973, c. 1286, s. 1; 1975, c. 166, s. 27; 1975, 2nd Sess., c. 983, s. 144; 2009-179, s. 2.)

§ 15A-1027. Limitation on collateral attack on conviction.

Noncompliance with the procedures of this Article may not be a basis for review of a conviction after the appeal period for the conviction has expired. (1973, c. 1286, s. 1; 1975, c. 166, s. 21; 1989, c. 290, s. 4.)

§ 15A-1028. Reserved for future codification purposes.

§ 15A-1029. Reserved for future codification purposes.

Article 58A.

Procedures Relating to Felony Guilty Pleas in District Court.

§ 15A-1029.1. Transfer of case from superior court to district court to accept guilty and no contest pleas for certain felony offenses.

(a)   With the consent of both the prosecutor and the defendant, the presiding superior court judge may order a transfer of the defendant's case to the district court for the purpose of allowing the defendant to enter a plea of guilty or no contest to a Class H or I felony.

(b)   The provisions of Article 58 of this Chapter apply to a case transferred under this section from superior court to district court in the same manner as if the plea were entered in superior court. Appeals that are authorized in these matters are to the appellate division. (1995 (Reg. Sess., 1996), c. 725, s. 6.)

§ 15A-1030. Reserved for future codification purposes.

Article 59.

Maintenance of Order in the Courtroom.

§ 15A-1031. Custody and restraint of defendant and witnesses.

A trial judge may order a defendant or witness subjected to physical restraint in the courtroom when the judge finds the restraint to be reasonably necessary to maintain order, prevent the defendant's escape, or provide for the safety of persons. If the judge orders a defendant or witness restrained, he must:

(1)   Enter in the record out of the presence of the jury and in the presence of the person to be restrained and his counsel, if any, the reasons for his action; and

(2)   Give the restrained person an opportunity to object; and

(3)   Unless the defendant or his attorney objects, instruct the jurors that the restraint is not to be considered in weighing evidence or determining the issue of guilt.

If the restrained person controverts the stated reasons for restraint, the judge must conduct a hearing and make findings of fact. (1977, c. 711, s. 1.)

§ 15A-1032. Removal of disruptive defendant.

(a)   A trial judge, after warning a defendant whose conduct is disrupting his trial, may order the defendant removed from the trial if he continues conduct which is so disruptive that the trial cannot proceed in an orderly manner. When practicable, the judge's warning and order for removal must be issued out of the presence of the jury.

(b)   If the judge orders a defendant removed from the courtroom, he must:

(1)   Enter in the record the reasons for his action; and

(2)   Instruct the jurors that the removal is not to be considered in weighing evidence or determining the issue of guilt.

A defendant removed from the courtroom must be given the opportunity of learning of the trial proceedings through his counsel at reasonable intervals as directed by the court and must be given opportunity to return to the courtroom during the trial upon assurance of his good behavior. (1977, c. 711, s. 1.)

§ 15A-1033. Removal of disruptive witnesses and spectators.

The judge in his discretion may order any person other than a defendant removed from a courtroom when his conduct disrupts the conduct of the trial. (1977, c. 711, s. 1.)

§ 15A-1034. Controlling access to the courtroom.

(a) The presiding judge may impose reasonable limitations on access to the courtroom when necessary to ensure the orderliness of courtroom proceedings or the safety of persons present.

(b) The judge may order that all persons entering or any person present and choosing to remain in the courtroom be searched for weapons or devices that could be used to disrupt or impede the proceedings and may require that belongings carried by persons entering the courtroom be inspected. An order under this subsection must be entered on the record. (1977, c. 711, s. 1.)

§ 15A-1035. Other powers.

In addition to the use of the powers provided in this Article, a presiding judge may maintain courtroom order through the use of his contempt powers as provided in Chapter 5A, Contempt, and through the use of other inherent powers of the court. (1977, c. 711, s. 1.)

§§ 15A-1036 through 15A-1039. Reserved for future codification purposes.

Article 60.

§§ 15A-1040 through 15A-1050. Reserved for future codification purposes.

Article 61.

Granting of Immunity to Witnesses.

§ 15A-1051. Immunity; general provisions.

(a) A witness who asserts his privilege against self-incrimination in a hearing or proceeding in court or before a grand jury of North Carolina may be ordered to testify or produce other information as provided in this Article. He may not thereafter be excused from testifying or producing other information on the ground that his testimony or other information required of him may tend to incriminate him. Except as provided in G.S. 15A-623(h), no testimony or other information so compelled, or any information directly or indirectly derived from the testimony or other information, may be used against the witness in a criminal case, except a prosecution for perjury or contempt arising from a failure to comply with an order of the court. In the event of a prosecution of the witness he shall be entitled to a record of his testimony.

(b) An order to testify or produce other information authorized by this Article may be issued prior to the witness's assertion of his privilege against self-incrimination, but the order is not effective until the witness asserts his privilege against self-incrimination and the person presiding over the inquiry communicates the order to him.

(c) As used in this Article, "other information" includes any book, paper, document, record, recordation, tangible object, or other material. (1973, c. 1286, s. 1; 1985 (Reg. Sess., 1986), c. 843, s. 4; 1991, c. 636, s. 3.)

§ 15A-1052. Grant of immunity in court proceedings.

(a) When the testimony or other information is to be presented to a court of the trial division of the General Court of Justice, the order to the witness to testify or produce other information must be issued by a superior court judge, upon application of the district attorney:

(1) Be in writing and filed with the permanent records of the case; or

(2) If orally made in open court, recorded and transcribed and made a part of the permanent records of the case.

(b) The application may be made whenever, in the judgment of the district attorney, the witness has asserted or is likely to assert his privilege against self-incrimination and his testimony or other information is or will be necessary to the public interest. Before making application to the judge, the district attorney must inform the Attorney General, or a deputy or assistant attorney general designated by him, of the circumstances and his intent to make an application.

(c) In a jury trial the judge must inform the jury of the grant of immunity and the order to testify prior to the testimony of the witness under the grant of immunity. During the charge to the jury, the judge must instruct the jury as in the case of interested witnesses. (1973, c. 1286, s. 1; 1975, c. 166, s. 27.)

§ 15A-1053. Grant of immunity before grand jury.

(a) When the testimony or other information is to be presented to a grand jury, the order to the witness to testify or produce other information must be issued by the presiding or convening superior court judge, upon application of the district attorney. The order of a superior court judge under this section must be in writing and filed as a part of the permanent records of the court.

(b) The application may be made when the district attorney has been informed by the foreman of the grand jury that the witness has asserted his privilege against self-incrimination and the district attorney determines that the testimony or other information is necessary to the public interest. Before making application to the judge, the district attorney must inform the Attorney General, or a deputy or assistant attorney general designated by him, of the circumstances and his intent to make an application. (1973, c. 1286, s. 1; 1975, c. 166, s. 27.)

§ 15A-1054. Charge reductions or sentence concessions in consideration of truthful testimony.

(a) Whether or not a grant of immunity is conferred under this Article, a prosecutor, when the interest of justice requires, may exercise his discretion not to try any suspect for offenses believed to have been committed within the prosecutorial district as defined in G.S. 7A-60, to agree to charge reductions, or to agree to recommend sentence concessions, upon the understanding or agreement that the suspect will provide truthful testimony in one or more criminal proceedings.

(b)   Recommendations as to sentence concessions must be made to the trial judge by the prosecutor in accordance with the provisions of Article 58 of this Chapter, Procedure[s] Relating to Guilty Pleas in Superior Court.

(c)   When a prosecutor enters into any arrangement authorized by this section, written notice fully disclosing the terms of the arrangement must be provided to defense counsel, or to the defendant if not represented by counsel, against whom such testimony is to be offered, a reasonable time prior to any proceeding in which the person with whom the arrangement is made is expected to testify. Upon motion of the defendant or his counsel on grounds of surprise or for other good cause or when the interests of justice require, the court must grant a recess. (1973, c. 1286, s. 1; 1975, c. 166, s. 27; 1987 (Reg. Sess., 1988), c. 1037, s. 65.)

§ 15A-1055. Evidence of grant of immunity or testimonial arrangement may be fully developed; impact may be argued to the jury.

(a)   Notwithstanding any other rule of evidence to the contrary, any party may examine a witness testifying under a grant of immunity or pursuant to an arrangement under G.S. 15A-1054 with respect to that grant of immunity or arrangement. A party may also introduce evidence or examine other witnesses in corroboration or contradiction of testimony or evidence previously elicited by himself or another party concerning the grant of immunity or arrangement.

(b)   A party may argue to the jury with respect to the impact of a grant of immunity or an arrangement under G.S. 15A-1054 upon the credibility of a witness. (1973, c. 1286, s. 1.)

§§ 15A-1056 through 15A-1060. Reserved for future codification purposes.

Article 62.

Mistrial.

§ 15A-1061. Mistrial for prejudice to defendant.

Upon motion of a defendant or with his concurrence the judge may declare a mistrial at any time during the trial. The judge must declare a mistrial upon the defendant's motion if there occurs during the trial an error or legal defect in the proceedings, or conduct inside or outside the courtroom, resulting in substantial and irreparable prejudice to the defendant's case. If there are two or more defendants, the mistrial may not be declared as to a defendant who does not make or join in the motion. (1977, c. 711, s. 1.)

§ 15A-1062. Mistrial for prejudice to the State.

Upon motion of the State, the judge may declare a mistrial if there occurs during the trial, either inside or outside the courtroom, misconduct resulting in substantial and irreparable prejudice to the State's case and the misconduct was by a juror or the defendant, his lawyer, or someone acting at the behest of the defendant or his lawyer. If there are two or more defendants, the mistrial may not be declared as to a defendant who does not join in the motion of the State if:

(1)   Neither he, his lawyer, nor a person acting at his or his lawyer's behest participated in the misconduct; or

(2)   The State's case is not substantially and irreparably prejudiced as to him. (1977, c. 711, s. 1.)

§ 15A-1063. Mistrial for impossibility of proceeding.

Upon motion of a party or upon his own motion, a judge may declare a mistrial if:

(1)   It is impossible for the trial to proceed in conformity with law; or

(2)   It appears there is no reasonable probability of the jury's agreement upon a verdict. (1977, c. 711, s. 1.)

§ 15A-1064. Mistrial; finding of facts required.

Before granting a mistrial, the judge must make finding of facts with respect to the grounds for the mistrial and insert the findings in the record of the case. (1977, c. 711, s. 1.)

§ 15A-1065. Procedure following mistrial.

When a mistrial is ordered, the judge must direct that the case be retained for trial or such other proceedings as may be proper. (1977, c. 711, s. 1.)

§§ 15A-1066 through 15A-1070. Reserved for future codification purposes.

Article 63.

§§ 15A-1071 through 15A-1080. Reserved for future codification purposes.

Article 64.

§§ 15A-1081 through 15A-1100. Reserved for future codification purposes.

SUBCHAPTER XI. TRIAL PROCEDURE IN DISTRICT COURT.

Article 65.

In General.

§ 15A-1101. Applicability of superior court procedure.

Trial procedure in the district court is in accordance with the provisions of Subchapter XII, Trial in Superior Court, except for provisions:

(1)　　Relating to jury trial.

(2)   Requiring recordation of proceedings unless they specify their applicability to the district court.

(3)   That specify their applicability to superior court. (1977, c. 711, s. 1.)

§§ 15A-1102 through 15A-1110. Reserved for future codification purposes.

Article 66.

Procedure for Hearing and Disposition of Infractions.

§ 15A-1111. General procedure for disposition of infractions.

The procedure for the disposition of an infraction, as defined in G.S. 14-3.1, is as provided in this Article. If a question of procedure is not governed by this Article, the procedures applicable to the conduct of pretrial and trial proceedings for misdemeanors in district court are applicable unless the procedure is clearly inapplicable to the hearing of an infraction. (1985, c. 764, s. 3.)

§ 15A-1112. Venue.

Venue for the conduct of infraction hearings lies in any county where any act or omission constituting part of the alleged infraction occurred. (1985, c. 764, s. 3.)

§ 15A-1113. Prehearing procedure.

(a)   Process. - A law enforcement officer may issue a citation for an infraction in accordance with the provisions of G.S. 15A-302. A judicial official may issue a summons for an infraction in accordance with the provisions of G.S. 15A-303.

(b) Detention of Person Charged. - A law enforcement officer who has probable cause to believe a person has committed an infraction may detain the person for a reasonable period in order to issue and serve him a citation.

(c) Appearance Bond May Be Required. - A person charged with an infraction may not be required to post an appearance bond if:

(1) He is licensed to drive by a state that subscribes to the nonresident violator compact as defined in Article 1B of Chapter 20 of the General Statutes, the infraction charged is subject to the provisions of that compact, and he executes a personal recognizance as defined by that compact.

(2) He is a resident of North Carolina.

Any other person charged with an infraction may be required to post a bond to secure his appearance and a charging officer may require such a person charged to accompany him to a judicial official's office to allow the official to determine if a bond is necessary to secure the person's court appearance, and if so, what kind of bond is to be used. If the judicial official finds that the person is unable to post a secured bond, he must allow the person to be released on execution of an unsecured bond. The provisions of Article 26 of this Chapter relating to issuance and forfeiture of bail bonds are applicable to bonds required pursuant to this subsection.

(d) Territorial Jurisdiction. - A law enforcement officer's territorial jurisdiction to charge a person with an infraction is the same as his jurisdiction to arrest specified in G.S. 15A-402.

(e) Use of Same Process for Two Offenses. - A person may be charged with a criminal offense and an infraction in the same pleading. (1985, c. 764, s. 3; 1985 (Reg. Sess., 1986), c. 852, s. 12.)

§ 15A-1114. Hearing procedure for infractions.

(a) Jurisdiction. - Jurisdiction for the adjudication and disposition of infractions is as specified in G.S. 7A-253 and G.S. 7A-271(d).

(b) No Trial by Jury. - In adjudicatory hearings for infractions, no party has a right to a trial by jury in district court.

(c) Infractions Heard in Civil or Criminal Session. - A district court judge may conduct proceedings relating to traffic infractions in a civil or criminal session of court, unless the infraction is joined with a criminal offense arising out of the same transaction or occurrence. In such a case, the criminal offense and the infraction must be heard at a session in which criminal matters may be heard.

(d) Pleas. - A person charged with an infraction may admit or deny responsibility for the infraction. The plea must be made by the person charged in open court, unless he submits a written waiver of appearance which is approved by the presiding judge, or, if authorized by G.S. 7A-146, he waives his right to a hearing and admits responsibility for the infraction in writing and pays the specified penalty and costs.

(e) Duty of District Attorney. - The district attorney is responsible for ensuring that infractions are calendared and prosecuted efficiently.

(f) Burden of Proof. - The State must prove beyond a reasonable doubt that the person charged is responsible for the infraction unless the person admits responsibility.

(g) Recording Not Necessary. - The State does not have to record the proceedings at infraction hearings. With the approval of the court, a party may, at his expense, record any proceeding. (1985, c. 764, s. 3.)

§ 15A-1115. Review of infractions originally disposed of in superior court.

(a) Repealed by Session Laws 2013-385, s. 1, effective December 1, 2013.

(b) Review of Infractions Originally Disposed of in Superior Court. - If the superior court disposes of an infraction pursuant to its jurisdiction in G.S. 7A-271(d), appeal from that judgment is as provided for criminal actions in the superior court. (1985, c. 764, s. 3; 1985 (Reg. Sess., 1986), c. 852, s. 10; 2013-385, s. 1.)

§ 15A-1116. Enforcement of sanctions.

(a) Use of Contempt or Fine Collection Procedures: Notification of DMV. - If the person does not comply with a sanction ordered by the court, the court may proceed in accordance with Chapter 5A of the General Statutes. If the person fails to pay a penalty or costs, the court may proceed in accordance with Article 84 of this Chapter. If the infraction is a motor vehicle infraction, the court must report a failure to pay the applicable penalty and costs to the Division of Motor Vehicles as specified in G.S. 20-24.2.

(b) No Order for Arrest. - If a person served with a citation for an infraction fails to appear to answer the charge, the court may issue a criminal summons to secure the person's appearance, but an order for arrest may not be used in such cases. (1985, c. 764, s. 3; 1985 (Reg. Sess., 1986), c. 852, ss. 1, 2, 15.)

§ 15A-1117: Recodified as § 20-24.2 by Session Laws 1985 (Reg. Sess., 1986), c. 852, s. 3.

§ 15A-1118. Costs.

Costs assessed for an infraction are as specified in G.S. 7A-304. (1985, c. 764, s. 3.)

ARTICLES 67 to 70.

§§ 15A-1119 through 15A-1200. Reserved for future codification purposes.

SUBCHAPTER XII. TRIAL PROCEDURE IN SUPERIOR COURT.

Article 71.

Right to Trial by Jury.

§ 15A-1201. (Effective until December 1, 2014, contingent upon approval of constitutional amendment) Right to trial by jury.

In all criminal cases the defendant has the right to be tried by a jury of 12 whose verdict must be unanimous. In the district court the judge is the finder of fact in criminal cases, but the defendant has the right to appeal for trial de novo in superior court as provided in G.S. 15A-1431. In superior court all criminal trials in which the defendant enters a plea of not guilty must be tried before a jury. (1977, c. 711, s. 1.)

§ 15A-1201. (Effective December 1, 2014, contingent upon approval of constitutional amendment) Right to trial by jury; waiver of jury trial.

(a) In all criminal cases the defendant has the right to be tried by a jury of 12 whose verdict must be unanimous. In the district court the judge is the finder of fact in criminal cases, but the defendant has the right to appeal for trial de novo in superior court as provided in G.S. 15A-1431. In superior court all criminal trials in which the defendant enters a plea of not guilty must be tried before a jury, unless the defendant waives the right to a jury trial, as provided in subsection (b) of this section.

(b) A defendant accused of any criminal offense for which the State is not seeking a sentence of death in superior court may, knowingly and voluntarily, in writing or on the record in the court and with the consent of the trial judge, waive the right to trial by jury. When a defendant waives the right to trial by jury under this section, the jury is dispensed with as provided by law, and the whole matter of law and fact shall be heard and judgment given by the court. (1977, c. 711, s. 1; 2013-300, s. 4.)

§§ 15A-1202 through 15A-1210. Reserved for future codification purposes.

Article 72.

Selecting and Impaneling the Jury.

§ 15A-1211. Selection procedure generally; role of judge; challenge to the panel; authority of judge to excuse jurors.

(a) The provisions of Chapter 9 of the General Statutes, Jurors, pertinent to criminal cases apply except when this Chapter specifically provides a different procedure.

(b) The trial judge must decide all challenges to the panel and all questions concerning the competency of jurors.

(c) The State or the defendant may challenge the jury panel. A challenge to the panel:

(1) May be made only on the ground that the jurors were not selected or drawn according to law.

(2) Must be in writing.

(3) Must specify the facts constituting the ground of challenge.

(4) Must be made and decided before any juror is examined.

If a challenge to the panel is sustained, the judge must discharge the panel.

(d) The judge may excuse a juror without challenge by any party if he determines that grounds for challenge for cause are present. (1977, c. 711, s. 1.)

§ 15A-1212. Grounds for challenge for cause.

A challenge for cause to an individual juror may be made by any party on the ground that the juror:

(1) Does not have the qualifications required by G.S. 9-3.

(2) Is incapable by reason of mental or physical infirmity of rendering jury service.

(3) Has been or is a party, a witness, a grand juror, a trial juror, or otherwise has participated in civil or criminal proceedings involving a transaction which relates to the charge against the defendant.

(4) Has been or is a party adverse to the defendant in a civil action, or has complained against or been accused by him in a criminal prosecution.

(5) Is related by blood or marriage within the sixth degree to the defendant or the victim of the crime.

(6) Has formed or expressed an opinion as to the guilt or innocence of the defendant. It is improper for a party to elicit whether the opinion formed is favorable or adverse to the defendant.

(7) Is presently charged with a felony.

(8) As a matter of conscience, regardless of the facts and circumstances, would be unable to render a verdict with respect to the charge in accordance with the law of North Carolina.

(9) For any other cause is unable to render a fair and impartial verdict. (1977, c. 711, s. 1.)

§ 15A-1213. Informing prospective jurors of case.

Prior to selection of jurors, the judge must identify the parties and their counsel and briefly inform the prospective jurors, as to each defendant, of the charge, the date of the alleged offense, the name of any victim alleged in the pleading, the defendant's plea to the charge, and any affirmative defense of which the defendant has given pretrial notice as required by Article 52, Motions Practice. The judge may not read the pleadings to the jury. (1977, c. 711, s. 1.)

§ 15A-1214. Selection of jurors; procedure.

(a) The clerk, under the supervision of the presiding judge, must call jurors from the panel by a system of random selection which precludes advance knowledge of the identity of the next juror to be called. When a juror is called and he is assigned to the jury box, he retains the seat assigned until excused.

(b) The judge must inform the prospective jurors of the case in accordance with G.S. 15A-1213. He may briefly question prospective jurors individually or as a group concerning general fitness and competency to determine whether there is cause why they should not serve as jurors in the case.

(c)   The prosecutor and the defense counsel, or the defendant if not represented by counsel, may personally question prospective jurors individually concerning their fitness and competency to serve as jurors in the case to determine whether there is a basis for a challenge for cause or whether to exercise a peremptory challenge. The prosecution or defense is not foreclosed from asking a question merely because the court has previously asked the same or similar question.

(d)   The prosecutor must conduct his examination of the first 12 jurors seated and make his challenges for cause and exercise his peremptory challenges. If the judge allows a challenge for cause, or if a peremptory challenge is exercised, the clerk must immediately call a replacement into the box. When the prosecutor is satisfied with the 12 in the box, they must then be tendered to the defendant. Until the prosecutor indicates his satisfaction, he may make a challenge for cause or exercise a peremptory challenge to strike any juror, whether an original or replacement juror.

(e)   Each defendant must then conduct his examination of the jurors tendered him, making his challenges for cause and his peremptory challenges. If a juror is excused, no replacement may be called until all defendants have indicated satisfaction with those remaining, at which time the clerk must call replacements for the jurors excused. The judge in his discretion must determine order of examination among multiple defendants.

(f)   Upon the calling of replacement jurors, the prosecutor must examine the replacement jurors and indicate satisfaction with a completed panel of 12 before the replacement jurors are tendered to a defendant. Only replacement jurors may be examined and challenged. This procedure is repeated until all parties have accepted 12 jurors.

(g)   If at any time after a juror has been accepted by a party, and before the jury is impaneled, it is discovered that the juror has made an incorrect statement during voir dire or that some other good reason exists:

(1)   The judge may examine, or permit counsel to examine, the juror to determine whether there is a basis for challenge for cause.

(2) If the judge determines there is a basis for challenge for cause, he must excuse the juror or sustain any challenge for cause that has been made.

(3) If the judge determines there is no basis for challenge for cause, any party who has not exhausted his peremptory challenges may challenge the juror.

Any replacement juror called is subject to examination, challenge for cause, and peremptory challenge as any other unaccepted juror.

(h) In order for a defendant to seek reversal of the case on appeal on the ground that the judge refused to allow a challenge made for cause, he must have:

(1) Exhausted the peremptory challenges available to him;

(2) Renewed his challenge as provided in subsection (i) of this section; and

(3) Had his renewal motion denied as to the juror in question.

(i) A party who has exhausted his peremptory challenges may move orally or in writing to renew a challenge for cause previously denied if the party either:

(1) Had peremptorily challenged the juror; or

(2) States in the motion that he would have challenged that juror peremptorily had his challenges not been exhausted.

The judge may reconsider his denial of the challenge for cause, reconsidering facts and arguments previously adduced or taking cognizance of additional facts and arguments presented. If upon reconsideration the judge determines that the juror should have been excused for cause, he must allow the party an additional peremptory challenge.

(j) In capital cases the trial judge for good cause shown may direct that jurors be selected one at a time, in which case each juror must first be passed by the State. These jurors may be sequestered before and after selection. (1977, c. 711, s. 1.)

§ 15A-1215. Alternate jurors.

(a) The judge may permit the seating of one or more alternate jurors. Alternate jurors must be sworn and seated near the jury with equal opportunity to see and hear the proceedings. They must attend the trial at all times with the jury, and obey all orders and admonitions of the judge. When the jurors are ordered kept together, the alternate jurors must be kept with them. If before final submission of the case to the jury, any juror dies, becomes incapacitated or disqualified, or is discharged for any other reason, an alternate juror becomes a juror, in the order in which selected, and serves in all respects as those selected on the regular trial panel. Alternate jurors receive the same compensation as other jurors and, unless they become jurors, must be discharged upon the final submission of the case to the jury.

(b) In all criminal actions in which one or more defendants is to be tried for a capital offense, or enter a plea of guilty to a capital offense, the presiding judge shall provide for the selection of at least two alternate jurors, or more as he deems appropriate. The alternate jurors shall be retained during the deliberations of the jury on the issue of guilt or innocence under such restrictions, regulations and instructions as the presiding judge shall direct. In case of sequestration of a jury during deliberations in a capital case, alternates shall be sequestered in the same manner as is the trial jury, but such alternates shall also be sequestered from the trial jury. In no event shall more than 12 jurors participate in the jury's deliberations. (1977, c. 711, s. 1; 1979, c. 711, s. 1.)

§ 15A-1216. Impaneling jury.

After all jurors, including alternate jurors, have been selected, the clerk impanels the jury by instructing them as follows: "Members of the jury, you have been sworn and are now impaneled to try the issue in the case of State of North Carolina versus _____. You will sit together, hear the evidence, and render your verdict accordingly." (1977, c. 711, s. 1.)

§ 15A-1217. Number of peremptory challenges.

(a) Capital cases.

(1) Each defendant is allowed 14 challenges.

(2) The State is allowed 14 challenges for each defendant.

(b) Noncapital cases.

(1) Each defendant is allowed six challenges.

(2) The State is allowed six challenges for each defendant.

(c) Each party is entitled to one peremptory challenge for each alternate juror in addition to any unused challenges. (1977, c. 711, s. 1.)

§§ 15A-1218 through 15A-1220. Reserved for future codification purposes.

Article 73.

Criminal Jury Trial in Superior Court.

§ 15A-1221. Order of proceedings in jury trial; reading of indictment prohibited.

(a) The order of a jury trial, in general, is as follows:

(1) Repealed by Session Laws 1995 (Regular Session 1996), c. 725, s. 10.

(1a) Unless the defendant has filed a written request for an arraignment, the court must enter a not guilty plea on behalf of the defendant in accordance with G.S. 15A-941. If a defendant does file a written request for an arraignment, then the defendant must be arraigned and must have his or her plea recorded out of the presence of the prospective jurors in accordance with G.S. 15A-941.

(2) The judge must inform the prospective jurors of the case in accordance with G.S. 15A-1213.

(3) The jury must be sworn, selected and impaneled in accordance with Article 72, Selecting and Impaneling the Jury.

(4) Each party must be given the opportunity to make a brief opening statement, but the defendant may reserve his opening statement.

(5) The State must offer evidence.

(6) The defendant may offer evidence and, if he has reserved his opening statement, may precede his evidence with that statement.

(7) The State and the defendant may then offer successive rebuttals as provided in G.S. 15A-1226.

(8) At the conclusion of the evidence, the parties may make arguments to the jury in accordance with the provisions of G.S. 15A-1230.

(9) The judge must deliver a charge to the jury in accordance with the provisions of G.S. 15A-1231 and 15A-1232.

(10) The jury must retire to deliberate, and alternate jurors who have not been seated must be excused as provided in G.S. 15A-1215.

(b) At no time during the selection of the jury or during trial may any person read the indictment to the prospective jurors or to the jury. (1977, c. 711, s. 1; 1977, 2nd Sess., c. 1147, s. 2; 1995 (Reg. Sess., 1996), c. 725, s. 10.)

§ 15A-1222. Expression of opinion prohibited.

The judge may not express during any stage of the trial, any opinion in the presence of the jury on any question of fact to be decided by the jury. (1977, c. 711, s. 1.)

§ 15A-1223. Disqualification of judge.

(a) A judge on his own motion may disqualify himself from presiding over a criminal trial or other criminal proceeding.

(b) A judge, on motion of the State or the defendant, must disqualify himself from presiding over a criminal trial or other criminal proceeding if he is:

(1) Prejudiced against the moving party or in favor of the adverse party; or

(2) Repealed by Session Laws 1983 (Regular Session 1984), c. 1037, s. 6.

(3) Closely related to the defendant by blood or marriage; or

(4) For any other reason unable to perform the duties required of him in an impartial manner.

(c) A motion to disqualify must be in writing and must be accompanied by one or more affidavits setting forth facts relied upon to show the grounds for disqualification.

(d) A motion to disqualify a judge must be filed no less than five days before the time the case is called for trial unless good cause is shown for failure to file within that time. Good cause includes the discovery of facts constituting grounds for disqualification less than five days before the case is called for trial.

(e) A judge must disqualify himself from presiding over a criminal trial or proceeding if he is a witness for or against one of the parties in the case. (1977, c. 711, s. 1; 1983 (Reg. Sess., 1984), c. 1037, s. 6.)

§ 15A-1224. Death or disability of trial judge.

(a) If by reason of sickness or other disability a judge before whom the defendant is being tried is unable to continue presiding over the trial without the necessity of a continuance, he may in his discretion order a mistrial.

(b) If by reason of absence, death, sickness, or other disability, the judge before whom the defendant is being or has been tried is unable to perform the duties required of him before entry of judgment, and has not ordered a mistrial, any other judge assigned to the court may perform those duties, but if the other judge is satisfied that he cannot perform those duties because he did not preside at an earlier stage of the proceedings or for any other reason, he must order a mistrial. (1977, c. 711, s. 1.)

§ 15A-1225. Exclusion of witnesses.

Upon motion of a party the judge may order all or some of the witnesses other than the defendant to remain outside of the courtroom until called to testify, except when a minor child is called as a witness the parent or guardian may be present while the child is testifying even though his parent or guardian is to be called subsequently. (1977, c. 711, s. 1.)

§ 15A-1225.1. Child witnesses; remote testimony.

(a) Definitions:

(1) Child. - For the purposes of this section, a minor who is under the age of 16 years old at the time of the testimony.

(2) Criminal proceeding. - Any hearing or trial in a prosecution of a person charged with violating a criminal law of this State, and any hearing or proceeding conducted under Subchapter II of Chapter 7B of the General Statutes where a juvenile is alleged to have committed an offense that would be a criminal offense if committed by an adult.

(3) Remote testimony. - A method by which a child witness testifies in a criminal proceeding outside of the physical presence of the defendant.

(b) Remote Testimony Authorized. - In a criminal proceeding, a child witness who has been found competent to testify may testify, under oath or affirmation, other than in an open forum when the court determines:

(1) That the child witness would suffer serious emotional distress, not by the open forum in general, but by testifying in the defendant's presence, and

(2) That the child's ability to communicate with the trier of fact would be impaired.

(c) Hearing Procedure. - Upon motion of a party or the court's own motion, and for good cause shown, the court shall hold an evidentiary hearing to determine whether to allow remote testimony. Hearings in the superior court division, and hearings conducted under Subchapter II of Chapter 7B of the General Statutes, shall be recorded. The presence of the child witness is not required at the hearing unless ordered by the presiding judge.

(d) Order. - An order allowing or disallowing the use of remote testimony shall state the findings of fact and conclusions of law that support the court's determination. An order allowing the use of remote testimony shall do the following:

(1) State the method by which the child is to testify.

(2) List any individual or category of individuals allowed to be in, or required to be excluded from, the presence of the child during the testimony.

(3) State any special conditions necessary to facilitate the cross-examination of the child.

(4) State any condition or limitation upon the participation of individuals in the child's presence during his or her testimony.

(5) State any other condition necessary for taking or presenting the testimony.

(e) Testimony. - The method used for remote testimony shall allow the judge, jury, and defendant or juvenile respondent to observe the demeanor of the child as the child testifies in a similar manner as if the child were in the open forum. The court shall ensure that the defense counsel, except a pro se defendant, is physically present where the child testifies, has a full and fair opportunity for cross-examination of the child witness, and has the ability to communicate privately with the defendant or juvenile respondent during the remote testimony. Nothing in this section shall be construed to limit the provisions of G.S. 15A-1225.

(f) Nonexclusive Procedure and Standard. - Nothing in this section shall:

(1) Prohibit the use or application of any other method or procedure authorized or required by statute, common law, or rule for the introduction into evidence of the statements or testimony of a child in a criminal or noncriminal proceeding.

(2) Be construed to require a court, in noncriminal proceedings, to apply the standard set forth in subsection (b) of this section, or to deviate from a standard or standards authorized by statute, common law, or rule, for allowing the use of remote testimony in noncriminal proceedings.

(g) This section does not apply if the defendant is an attorney pro se, unless the defendant has a court-appointed attorney assisting the defendant in the defense, in which case only the court-appointed attorney shall be permitted in the room with the child during the child's testimony. (2009-356, s. 1.)

§ 15A-1225.2. Witnesses with developmental disabilities or mental retardation; remote testimony.

(a) Definitions. - The following definitions apply to this section:

(1) The definitions set out in G.S. 122C-3.

(2) "Remote testimony" means a method by which a witness testifies outside of an open forum and outside of the physical presence of a party or parties.

(b) Remote Testimony Authorized. - A person with a developmental disability or a person with mental retardation who is competent to testify may testify by remote testimony in a prosecution of a person charged with violating a criminal law of this State and in any hearing or proceeding conducted under Subchapter II of Chapter 7B of the General Statutes where a juvenile is alleged to have committed an offense that would be a criminal offense if committed by an adult if the court determines by clear and convincing evidence that the witness would suffer serious emotional distress from testifying in the presence of the defendant and that the ability of the witness to communicate with the trier of fact would be impaired by testifying in the presence of the defendant.

(c) Hearing Procedure. - Upon motion of a party or the court's own motion, and for good cause shown, the court shall hold an evidentiary hearing to determine whether to allow remote testimony. The hearing shall be recorded unless recordation is waived by all parties. The presence of the witness is not required at the hearing unless so ordered by the presiding judge.

(d) Order. - An order allowing or disallowing the use of remote testimony shall state the findings and conclusions of law that support the court's determination. An order allowing the use of remote testimony also shall do all of the following:

(1) State the method by which the witness is to testify.

(2) List any individual or category of individuals allowed to be in or required to be excluded from the presence of the witness during testimony.

(3) State any special conditions necessary to facilitate the cross-examination of the witness.

(4) State any condition or limitation upon the participation of individuals in the presence of the witness during the testimony.

(5) State any other conditions necessary for taking or presenting testimony.

(e) Testimony. - The method of remote testimony shall allow the trier of fact and all parties to observe the demeanor of the witness as the witness testifies in a similar manner as if the witness were testifying in the open forum. The court shall ensure that the counsel for all parties, except a pro se defendant, is physically present where the witness testifies and has a full and fair opportunity for examination and cross-examination of the witness. The court shall ensure that the defendant or juvenile respondent has the ability to communicate privately with defense counsel during the remote testimony. A party may waive the right to have counsel physically present where the witness testifies. Nothing in this section shall be construed to limit the provisions of G.S. 15A-1225.

(f) Nonexclusive Procedure and Standard. - Nothing in this section shall prohibit the use or application of any other method or procedure authorized or required by law for the introduction into evidence of statements or testimony of a person with a developmental disability or a person with mental retardation. (2009-514, s. 2.)

§ 15A-1226. Rebuttal evidence; additional evidence.

(a) Each party has the right to introduce rebuttal evidence concerning matters elicited in the evidence in chief of another party. The judge may permit a party to offer new evidence during rebuttal which could have been offered in the party's case in chief or during a previous rebuttal, but if new evidence is allowed, the other party must be permitted further rebuttal.

(b) The judge in his discretion may permit any party to introduce additional evidence at any time prior to verdict. (1977, c. 711, s. 1.)

§ 15A-1227. Motion for dismissal.

(a) A motion for dismissal for insufficiency of the evidence to sustain a conviction may be made at the following times:

(1) Upon close of the State's evidence.

(2) Upon close of all the evidence.

(3) After return of a verdict of guilty and before entry of judgment.

(4) After discharge of the jury without a verdict and before the end of the session.

(b) Failure to make the motion at the close of the State's evidence or after all the evidence is not a bar to making the motion at a later time as provided in subsection (a).

(c) The judge must rule on a motion to dismiss for insufficiency of the evidence before the trial may proceed.

(d) The sufficiency of all evidence introduced in a criminal case is reviewable on appeal without regard to whether a motion has been made during trial, as provided in G.S. 15A-1446(d)(5). (1977, c. 711, s. 1.)

§ 15A-1228. Notes by the jury.

Except where the judge, on the judge's own motion or the motion of any party, directs otherwise, jurors may make notes and take them into the jury room during their deliberations. (1977, c. 711, s. 1; 1993, c. 498.)

§ 15A-1229. View by jury.

(a) The trial judge in his discretion may permit a jury view. If a view is ordered, the judge must order the jury to be conducted to the place in question in the custody of an officer. The officer must be instructed to permit no person to communicate with the jury on any subject connected with the trial, except as provided in subsection (b), nor to do so himself, and to return the jurors to the courtroom without unnecessary delay or at a specified time. The judge, prosecutor, and counsel for the defendant must be present at the view by the jury. The defendant is entitled to be present at the view by the jury.

(b) A judge in his discretion may permit a witness under oath to testify at the site of the jury view and point out objects and physical characteristics material to his testimony. The testimony must be recorded. (1977, c. 711, s. 1.)

§ 15A-1230. Limitations on argument to the jury.

(a) During a closing argument to the jury an attorney may not become abusive, inject his personal experiences, express his personal belief as to the truth or falsity of the evidence or as to the guilt or innocence of the defendant, or make arguments on the basis of matters outside the record except for matters concerning which the court may take judicial notice. An attorney may, however, on the basis of his analysis of the evidence, argue any position or conclusion with respect to a matter in issue.

(b) Length, number, and order of arguments allotted to the parties are governed by G.S. 7A-97. (1977, c. 711, s. 1; 2010-96, s. 4.)

§ 15A-1231. Jury instructions.

(a) At the close of the evidence or at an earlier time directed by the judge, any party may tender written instructions. A party tendering instructions must furnish copies to the other parties at the time he tenders them to the judge.

(b) Before the arguments to the jury, the judge must hold a recorded conference on instructions out of the presence of the jury. At the conference the judge must inform the parties of the offenses, lesser included offenses, and affirmative defenses on which he will charge the jury and must inform them of what, if any, parts of tendered instructions will be given. A party is also entitled to be informed, upon request, whether the judge intends to include other particular instructions in his charge to the jury. The failure of the judge to comply fully with the provisions of this subsection does not constitute grounds for appeal unless his failure, not corrected prior to the end of the trial, materially prejudiced the case of the defendant.

(c)   After the arguments are completed, the judge must instruct the jury in accordance with G.S. 15A-1232.

(d)   All instructions given and tendered instructions which have been refused become a part of the record. Failure to object to an erroneous instruction or to the erroneous failure to give an instruction does not constitute a waiver of the right to appeal on that error in accordance with G.S. 15A-1446(d)(13). (1977, c. 711, s. 1; 1983, c. 635.)

§ 15A-1232. Jury instructions; explanation of law; opinion prohibited.

In instructing the jury, the judge shall not express an opinion as to whether or not a fact has been proved and shall not be required to state, summarize or recapitulate the evidence, or to explain the application of the law to the evidence. (1977, c. 711, s. 1; 1985, c. 537, s. 1.)

§ 15A-1233. Review of testimony; use of evidence by the jury.

(a)   If the jury after retiring for deliberation requests a review of certain testimony or other evidence, the jurors must be conducted to the courtroom. The judge in his discretion, after notice to the prosecutor and defendant, may direct that requested parts of the testimony be read to the jury and may permit the jury to reexamine in open court the requested materials admitted into evidence. In his discretion the judge may also have the jury review other evidence relating to the same factual issue so as not to give undue prominence to the evidence requested.

(b)   Upon request by the jury and with consent of all parties, the judge may in his discretion permit the jury to take to the jury room exhibits and writings which have been received in evidence. If the judge permits the jury to take to the jury room requested exhibits and writings, he may have the jury take additional material or first review other evidence relating to the same issue so as not to give undue prominence to the exhibits or writings taken to the jury room. If the judge permits an exhibit to be taken to the jury room, he must, upon request, instruct the jury not to conduct any experiments with the exhibit. (1977, c. 711, s. 1.)

§ 15A-1234. Additional instructions.

(a) After the jury retires for deliberation, the judge may give appropriate additional instructions to:

(1) Respond to an inquiry of the jury made in open court; or

(2) Correct or withdraw an erroneous instruction; or

(3) Clarify an ambiguous instruction; or

(4) Instruct the jury on a point of law which should have been covered in the original instructions.

(b) At any time the judge gives additional instructions, he may also give or repeat other instructions to avoid giving undue prominence to the additional instructions.

(c) Before the judge gives additional instructions, he must inform the parties generally of the instructions he intends to give and afford them an opportunity to be heard. The parties upon request must be permitted additional argument to the jury if the additional instructions change, by restriction or enlargement, the permissible verdicts of the jury. Otherwise, the allowance of additional argument is within the discretion of the judge.

(d) All additional instructions must be given in open court and must be made a part of the record. (1977, c. 711, s. 1.)

§ 15A-1235. Length of deliberations; deadlocked jury.

(a) Before the jury retires for deliberation, the judge must give an instruction which informs the jury that in order to return a verdict, all 12 jurors must agree to a verdict of guilty or not guilty.

(b) Before the jury retires for deliberation, the judge may give an instruction which informs the jury that:

(1) Jurors have a duty to consult with one another and to deliberate with a view to reaching an agreement, if it can be done without violence to individual judgment;

(2) Each juror must decide the case for himself, but only after an impartial consideration of the evidence with his fellow jurors;

(3) In the course of deliberations, a juror should not hesitate to reexamine his own views and change his opinion if convinced it is erroneous; and

(4) No juror should surrender his honest conviction as to the weight or effect of the evidence solely because of the opinion of his fellow jurors, or for the mere purpose of returning a verdict.

(c) If it appears to the judge that the jury has been unable to agree, the judge may require the jury to continue its deliberations and may give or repeat the instructions provided in subsections (a) and (b). The judge may not require or threaten to require the jury to deliberate for an unreasonable length of time or for unreasonable intervals.

(d) If it appears that there is no reasonable possibility of agreement, the judge may declare a mistrial and discharge the jury. (1977, c. 711, s. 1.)

§ 15A-1236. Admonitions to jurors; regulation and separation of jurors.

(a) The judge at appropriate times must admonish the jurors that it is their duty:

(1) Not to talk among themselves about the case except in the jury room after their deliberations have begun;

(2) Not to talk to anyone else, or to allow anyone else to talk with them or in their presence about the case and that they must report to the judge immediately the attempt of anyone to communicate with them about the case;

(3) Not to form an opinion about the guilt or innocence of the defendant, or express any opinion about the case until they begin their deliberations;

(4) To avoid reading, watching, or listening to accounts of the trial; and

(5) Not to talk during trial to parties, witnesses, or counsel.

The judge may also admonish them with respect to other matters which he considers appropriate.

(b) The judge in his discretion may direct that the jurors be sequestered.

(c) If the jurors are committed to the charge of an officer, he must be sworn by the clerk to keep the jurors together and not to permit any person to speak or otherwise communicate with them on any subject connected with the trial nor to do so himself, and to return the jurors to the courtroom as directed by the judge. (1977, c. 711, s. 1; 1977, 2nd Sess., c. 1147, s. 3.)

§ 15A-1237. Verdict.

(a) The verdict must be in writing, signed by the foreman, and made a part of the record of the case.

(b) The verdict must be unanimous, and must be returned by the jury in open court.

(c) If the jurors find the defendant not guilty on the ground that he was insane at the time of the commission of the offense charged, their verdict must so state.

(d) If there are two or more defendants, the jury must return a separate verdict with respect to each defendant. If the jury agrees upon a verdict for one defendant but not another, it must return that verdict upon which it agrees.

(e) If there are two or more offenses for which the jury could return a verdict, it may return a verdict with respect to any offense, including a lesser included offense on which the judge charged, as to which it agrees. (1977, c. 711, s. 1.)

§ 15A-1238. Polling the jury.

Upon the motion of any party made after a verdict has been returned and before the jury has dispersed, the jury must be polled. The judge may also upon his own motion require the polling of the jury. The poll may be conducted by the judge or by the clerk by asking each juror individually whether the verdict announced is his verdict. If upon the poll there is not unanimous concurrence, the jury must be directed to retire for further deliberations. (1977, c. 711, s. 1.)

§ 15A-1239. Judicial comment on verdict.

The trial judge may not comment upon the verdict of a jury in open court in the presence or hearing of any member of the jury panel. If he does so, any defendant whose case is calendared for that session of court is entitled, upon motion, to a continuance of his case to a time when all members of the entire jury panel are no longer serving. (1977, c. 711, s. 1.)

§ 15A-1240. Impeachment of the verdict.

(a) Upon an inquiry into the validity of a verdict, no evidence may be received to show the effect of any statement, conduct, event, or condition upon the mind of a juror or concerning the mental processes by which the verdict was determined.

(b) The limitations in subsection (a) do not bar evidence concerning whether the verdict was reached by lot.

(c) After the jury has dispersed, the testimony of a juror may be received to impeach the verdict of the jury on which he served, subject to the limitations in subsection (a), only when it concerns:

(1) Matters not in evidence which came to the attention of one or more jurors under circumstances which would violate the defendant's constitutional right to confront the witnesses against him; or

(2) Bribery, intimidation, or attempted bribery or intimidation of a juror. (1977, c. 711, s. 1.)

§ 15A-1241. Record of proceedings.

(a)   The trial judge must require that the reporter make a true, complete, and accurate record of all statements from the bench and all other proceedings except:

(1)   Selection of the jury in noncapital cases;

(2)   Opening statements and final arguments of counsel to the jury; and

(3)   Arguments of counsel on questions of law.

(b)   Upon motion of any party or on the judge's own motion, proceedings excepted under subdivisions (1) and (2) of subsection (a) must be recorded. The motion for recordation of jury arguments must be made before the commencement of any argument and if one argument is recorded all must be. Upon suggestion of improper argument, when no recordation has been requested or ordered, the judge in his discretion may require the remainder to be recorded.

(c)   When a party makes an objection to unrecorded statements or other conduct in the presence of the jury, upon motion of either party the judge must reconstruct for the record, as accurately as possible, the matter to which objection was made.

(d)   The trial judge may review the accuracy of the reporter's record of the proceedings, but may not make substantive changes in the transcript concerning his charge, rulings, and comments without notice to the State, the defense, and the reporter. When any correction of a transcript is ordered made by a judge, each party is entitled to receive, upon request, a copy of the transcript indicating the text as submitted by the reporter and as changed by the judge. Upon motion of any party, the judge must afford the parties a hearing upon any change ordered by the judge. (1977, c. 711, s. 1.)

§ 15A-1242. Defendant's election to represent himself at trial.

A defendant may be permitted at his election to proceed in the trial of his case without the assistance of counsel only after the trial judge makes thorough inquiry and is satisfied that the defendant:

(1) Has been clearly advised of his right to the assistance of counsel, including his right to the assignment of counsel when he is so entitled;

(2) Understands and appreciates the consequences of this decision; and

(3) Comprehends the nature of the charges and proceedings and the range of permissible punishments. (1977, c. 711, s. 1.)

§ 15A-1243. Standby counsel for defendant representing himself.

When a defendant has elected to proceed without the assistance of counsel, the trial judge in his discretion may determine that standby counsel should be appointed to assist the defendant when called upon and to bring to the judge's attention matters favorable to the defendant upon which the judge should rule upon his own motion. Appointment and compensation of standby counsel shall be in accordance with rules adopted by the Office of Indigent Defense Services. (1977, c. 711, s. 1; 2000-144, s. 30.)

§§ 15A-1244 through 15A-1250. Reserved for future codification purposes.

Article 74.

§§ 15A-1251 through 15A-1260. Reserved for future codification purposes.

Article 75.

§§ 15A-1261 through 15A-1280. Reserved for future codification purposes.

Article 76.

§§ 15A-1281 through 15A-1290. Reserved for future codification purposes.

Article 77.

§§ 15A-1291 through 15A-1300. Reserved for future codification purposes.

SUBCHAPTER XIII. DISPOSITION OF DEFENDANTS.

Article 78.

Order of Commitment to Imprisonment.

§ 15A-1301. Order of commitment to imprisonment when not otherwise specified.

When a judicial official orders that a defendant be imprisoned he must issue an appropriate written commitment order. When the commitment is to a sentence of imprisonment, the commitment must include the identification and class of the offense or offenses for which the defendant was convicted and, if the sentences are consecutive, the maximum sentence allowed by law upon conviction of each offense for the punishment range used to impose the sentence for the class of offense and prior record or conviction level, and, if the sentences are concurrent or consolidated, the longest of the maximum sentences allowed by law for the classes of offense and prior record or conviction levels upon conviction of any of the offenses. (1977, c. 711, s. 1; 1977, 2nd Sess., c. 1147, s. 4; 1993, c. 538, s. 11; 1994, Ex. Sess., c. 24, s. 14(b).)

§§ 15A-1302 through 15A-1310. Reserved for future codification purposes.

Article 79.

§§ 15A-1311 through 15A-1320: Reserved for future codification purposes.

Article 80.

Defendants Found Not Guilty by Reason of Insanity.

§ 15A-1321. Automatic civil commitment of defendants found not guilty by reason of insanity.

(a) When a defendant charged with a crime, wherein it is not alleged that the defendant inflicted or attempted to inflict serious physical injury or death, is found not guilty by reason of insanity by verdict or upon motion pursuant to G.S. 15A-959(c), the presiding judge shall enter an order finding that the defendant has been found not guilty by reason of insanity of a crime and committing the defendant to a State 24-hour facility designated pursuant to G.S. 122C-252. The court order shall also grant custody of the defendant to a law enforcement officer who shall take the defendant directly to that facility. Proceedings thereafter are in accordance with Part 7 of Article 5 of Chapter 122C of the General Statutes.

(b) When a defendant charged with a crime, wherein it is alleged that the defendant inflicted or attempted to inflict serious physical injury or death, is found not guilty by reason of insanity, by verdict, or upon motion pursuant to G.S. 15A-959(c), notwithstanding any other provision of law, the presiding judge shall enter an order finding that the defendant has been found not guilty by reason of insanity of a crime and committing the defendant to a Forensic Unit operated by the Department of Health and Human Services, where the defendant shall reside until the defendant's release in accordance with Chapter 122C of the General Statutes. The court order shall also grant custody of the defendant to a law enforcement officer who shall take the defendant directly to the facility. Proceedings not inconsistent with this section shall thereafter be in accordance with Part 7 of Article 5 of Chapter 122C of the General Statutes. (1977, c. 711, s. 1; 1983, c. 380, s. 3; 1985, c. 589, s. 10; 1987, c. 596, s. 6; 1991, c. 37, s. 1; 1998-212, s. 12.35B(a).)

§ 15A-1322. Temporary restraint.

If the judge finds that there are reasonable grounds to believe that the defendant-respondent is mentally ill, as defined in G.S. 122C-3, and is dangerous to himself or others, and the judge determines upon appropriate findings of fact that it is appropriate to proceed under the provisions of this Article, he may order that the respondent be held under appropriate restraint pending proceedings under G.S. 15A-1321. (1977, c. 711, s. 1; 1985, c. 589, s. 12.)

§§ 15A-1323 through 15A-1330. Reserved for future codification purposes.

Article 81.

General Sentencing Provisions.

§ 15A-1331. Authorized sentences; conviction.

(a) The criminal judgment entered against a person in either district or superior court shall be consistent with the provisions of Article 81B of this Chapter and contain a sentence disposition consistent with that Article, unless the offense for which his guilt has been established is not covered by that Article.

(b) For the purpose of imposing sentence, a person has been convicted when he has been adjudged guilty or has entered a plea of guilty or no contest. (1977, c. 711, s. 1; 1993, c. 538, s. 12; 1994, Ex. Sess., c. 24, s. 14(b).)

§ 15A-1331.1. Forfeiture of licensing privileges after conviction of a felony.

(a) The following definitions apply in this section:

(1) Licensing agency. - Any department, division, agency, officer, board, or other unit of State or local government that issues licenses for licensing privileges.

(2) Licensing privilege. - The privilege of an individual to be authorized to engage in an activity as evidenced by the following licenses: regular and commercial drivers licenses, occupational licenses, hunting licenses and permits, and fishing licenses and permits.

(3) Occupational license. - A licensure, permission, certification, or similar authorization required by statute or rule to practice an occupation or business. The term does not include a tax license issued under Chapter 105 of the

General Statutes, Article 7 of Chapter 153A of the General Statutes, or Article 9 of Chapter 160A of the General Statutes.

(b)   Upon conviction of a felony, an individual automatically forfeits the individual's licensing privileges for the full term of the period the individual is placed on probation by the sentencing court at the time of conviction for the offense, if:

(1)   The individual is offered a suspended sentence on condition the individual accepts probation and the individual refuses probation, or

(2)   The individual's probation is revoked or suspended, and the judge makes findings in the judgment that the individual failed to make reasonable efforts to comply with the conditions of probation.

(c)   Whenever an individual's licensing privileges are forfeited under this section, the judge shall make findings in the judgment of the licensing privileges held by the individual known to the court at that time, the drivers license number and social security number of the individual, and the beginning and ending date of the period of time of the forfeiture. The terms and conditions of the forfeiture shall be transmitted by the clerk of court to the Division of Motor Vehicles, in accordance with G.S. 20-24 and to the licensing agencies specified by the judge in the judgment. A licensing agency, upon receiving notice from the clerk of court, shall require the individual whose licensing privileges were forfeited to surrender the forfeited license issued by the agency and shall not reissue a license to that individual during the period of forfeiture as stated in the notice. Licensing agencies are authorized to establish procedures to implement this section.

(d)   Notwithstanding any other provision of this section, the court may order that an individual whose licensing privileges are forfeited under this section be granted a limited driving privilege in accordance with the provisions of G.S. 20-179.3. (1994, Ex. Sess., c. 20, ss. 1, 5; 2012-194, s. 45(a).)

§ 15A-1331.2. Prayer for judgment continued for a period of time that exceeds 12 months is an improper disposition of a Class B1, B2, C, D, or E felony.

The court shall not dispose of any criminal action that is a Class B1, B2, C, D, or E felony by ordering a prayer for judgment continued that exceeds 12 months. If the court orders a prayer for judgment continued in any criminal action that is a Class B1, B2, C, D, or E felony, the court shall include as a condition that the State shall pray judgment within a specific period of time not to exceed 12 months. At the time the State prays judgment, or 12 months from the date of the prayer for judgment continued order, whichever is earlier, the court shall enter a final judgment unless the court finds that it is in the interest of justice to continue the order for prayer for judgment continued. If the court continues the order for prayer for judgment continued, the order shall be continued for a specific period of time not to exceed 12 months. The court shall not continue a prayer for judgment continued order for more than one additional 12-month period. (2012-149, s. 11; 2012-194, s. 45(e).)

§ 15A-1331A. Forfeiture of licensing privileges after conviction of a felony.

(a)   The following definitions apply in this section:

(1)   Licensing agency. - Any department, division, agency, officer, board, or other unit of State or local government that issues licenses for licensing privileges.

(2)   Licensing privilege. - The privilege of an individual to be authorized to engage in an activity as evidenced by the following licenses: regular and commercial drivers licenses, occupational licenses, hunting licenses and permits, and fishing licenses and permits.

(3)   Occupational license. - A licensure, permission, certification, or similar authorization required by statute or rule to practice an occupation or business. The term does not include a tax license issued under Chapter 105 of the General Statutes, Article 7 of Chapter 153A of the General Statutes, or Article 9 of Chapter 160A of the General Statutes.

(b)   Upon conviction of a felony, an individual automatically forfeits the individual's licensing privileges for the full term of the period the individual is placed on probation by the sentencing court at the time of conviction for the offense, if:

(1)   The individual is offered a suspended sentence on condition the individual accepts probation and the individual refuses probation, or

(2) The individual's probation is revoked or suspended, and the judge makes findings in the judgment that the individual failed to make reasonable efforts to comply with the conditions of probation.

(c) Whenever an individual's licensing privileges are forfeited under this section, the judge shall make findings in the judgment of the licensing privileges held by the individual known to the court at that time, the drivers license number and social security number of the individual, and the beginning and ending date of the period of time of the forfeiture. The terms and conditions of the forfeiture shall be transmitted by the clerk of court to the Division of Motor Vehicles, in accordance with G.S. 20-24 and to the licensing agencies specified by the judge in the judgment. A licensing agency, upon receiving notice from the clerk of court, shall require the individual whose licensing privileges were forfeited to surrender the forfeited license issued by the agency and shall not reissue a license to that individual during the period of forfeiture as stated in the notice. Licensing agencies are authorized to establish procedures to implement this section.

(d) Notwithstanding any other provision of this section, the court may order that an individual whose licensing privileges are forfeited under this section be granted a limited driving privilege in accordance with the provisions of G.S. 20-179.3. (1994, Ex. Sess., c. 20, ss. 1, 5.)

§ 15A-1332. Presentence reports.

(a) Presentence Reports Generally. - To obtain a presentence report, the court may order either a presentence investigation as provided in subsection (b) or a presentence commitment for study as provided in subsection (c).

(b) Presentence Investigation. - The court may order a probation officer to make a presentence investigation of any defendant. The court may order the investigation only after conviction unless the defendant moves for an earlier presentence investigation. A motion for an earlier presentence investigation may be addressed only to the judge of the session of court for which the defendant's case is calendared or, if the case has not been calendared, to a resident superior court judge if the case is in the jurisdiction of the superior court or to the chief district court judge if the case is in the jurisdiction of the district court. When the court orders a presentence investigation, the probation officer must promptly investigate all circumstances relevant to sentencing and submit either a written report or an oral report either on the record or with defense counsel and the prosecutor present. The report may include sentence recommendations only if such recommendations are requested by the court.

(c) Presentence Commitment for Study. - When the court desires more detailed information as a basis for determining the sentence to be imposed than can be provided by a presentence investigation, the court may commit a defendant to the Division of Adult Correction of the Department of Public Safety for study for the shortest period necessary to complete the study, not to exceed 90 days, if that defendant has been charged with or convicted of any felony or a Class A1 or Class 1 misdemeanor crime or crimes for which he may be imprisoned for more than six months and if he consents. The period of commitment must end when the study is completed, and may not exceed 90 days. The Division must conduct a complete study of a defendant committed to it under this subsection, inquiring into such matters as the defendant's previous delinquency or criminal experience, his social background, his capabilities, his mental, emotional and physical health, and the availability of resources or programs appropriate to the defendant. Upon completion of the study or the end of the 90-day period, whichever occurs first, the Division of Adult Correction of the Department of Public Safety must release the defendant to the sheriff of the county in which his case is docketed. The Division must forward the study to the clerk in that county, including whatever recommendations the Division believes will be helpful to a proper resolution of the case. When a defendant is returned from a presentence commitment for study, the conditions of pretrial release which obtained for the defendant before the commitment continue until judgment is entered, unless the conditions are modified under the provisions of G.S. 15A-534(e). (1977, c. 711, s. 1; 1981, c. 377, s. 1; 1993, c. 538, s. 13; 1994, Ex. Sess., c. 24, s. 14(b); 1995, c. 507, s. 19.5(e); 2011-145, s. 19.1(h).)

§ 15A-1333. Availability of presentence report.

(a) Presentence Reports and Sentencing Services Information Not Public Records. - A written presentence report, the record of an oral presentence report, and information obtained in the preparation of a sentencing plan by a sentencing services program under Article 61 of Chapter 7A are not public records and may not be made available to any person except as provided in this section.

(b) Access to Reports. - The defendant, his counsel, the prosecutor, or the court may have access at any reasonable time to a written presentence report or to any record of an oral presentence report. Access to a sentencing plan and information obtained in the preparation of a sentencing plan shall be in accordance with the comprehensive sentencing services program plan developed pursuant to G.S. 7A-774.

(c) Expunging Reports. - On motion of the defendant, the court in its discretion may order a written presentence report, the record of an oral presentence report, or a sentencing plan expunged from the court record. (1977, c. 711, s. 1; 2000-67, s. 15.9(c).)

§ 15A-1334. The sentencing hearing.

(a) Time of Hearing. - Unless the defendant waives the hearing, the court must hold a hearing on the sentence. Either the defendant or the State may, upon a showing which the judge determines to be good cause, obtain a continuance of the sentencing hearing.

(b) Proceeding at Hearing. - The defendant at the hearing may make a statement in his own behalf. The defendant and prosecutor may present witnesses and arguments on facts relevant to the sentencing decision and may cross-examine the other party's witnesses. No person other than the defendant, his counsel, the prosecutor, and one making a presentence report may comment to the court on sentencing unless called as a witness by the defendant, the prosecutor, or the court. Formal rules of evidence do not apply at the hearing.

(c) Sentence Hearing in Other District. - The judge who orders a presentence report may, in his discretion, direct that the sentencing hearing be held before him in another county or another district court district as defined in G.S. 7A-133 or superior court district or set of districts as defined in G.S. 7A-41.1, as the case may be, during or after the session in which the defendant was convicted. If sentence is imposed in a county other than the one where the defendant was convicted, the clerk of the county where sentence is imposed must forward the records of the sentencing proceeding to the clerk of the county of conviction.

(d) Sentencing in Capital Cases. - Sentencing in capital cases is governed by Article 100 of this Chapter.

(e) Procedure Applicable when Certain Prior Convictions May Be Used. - The procedure in G.S. 15A-980 governs if the State seeks to use a prior conviction in a sentencing hearing. (1977, c. 711, s. 1; 1983, c. 513, s. 3; 1987 (Reg. Sess., 1988), c. 1037, s. 66.)

§ 15A-1335. Resentencing after appellate review.

When a conviction or sentence imposed in superior court has been set aside on direct review or collateral attack, the court may not impose a new sentence for the same offense, or for a different offense based on the same conduct, which is more severe than the prior sentence less the portion of the prior sentence previously served. This section shall not apply when a defendant, on direct review or collateral attack, succeeds in having a plea of guilty vacated. (1977, c. 711, s. 1; 2013-385, s. 3.)

§ 15A-1336. Compliance with criminal case firearm notification requirements of the federal Violence Against Women Act.

The Administrative Office of the Courts, in cooperation with the North Carolina Coalition Against Domestic Violence and the North Carolina Governor's Crime Commission, shall develop a form to comply with the criminal case firearm notification requirements of the Violence Against Women Act of 2005. (2007-294, s.2)

§ 15A-1337. Reserved for future codification purposes.

§ 15A-1338. Reserved for future codification purposes.

§ 15A-1339. Reserved for future codification purposes.

§ 15A-1340. Reserved for future codification purposes.

Article 81A.

Sentencing Persons Convicted of Felonies.

§§ 15A-1340.1 through 15A-1340.7: Repealed by Session Laws 1993, c. 538, s. 14.

§ 15A-1340.8. Reserved for future codification purposes.

§ 15A-1340.9. Reserved for future codification purposes.

Article 81B.

Structured Sentencing of Persons Convicted of Crimes.

Part 1. General Provisions.

§ 15A-1340.10. Applicability of structured sentencing.

This Article applies to criminal offenses in North Carolina, other than impaired driving under G.S. 20-138.1 and failure to comply with control measures under G.S. 130A-25, that occur on or after October 1, 1994. This Article does not apply to violent habitual felons sentenced under Article 2B of Chapter 14 of the General Statutes. (1993, c. 538, s. 1; 1994, Ex. Sess., c. 22, s. 35; c. 24, s. 14(a), (b); 1993 (Reg. Sess., 1994), c. 767, s. 17.)

§ 15A-1340.11. Definitions.

The following definitions apply in this Article:

(1)   Active punishment. - A sentence in a criminal case that requires an offender to serve a sentence of imprisonment and is not suspended. Special probation, as defined in G.S. 15A-1351, is not an active punishment.

(2)   Community punishment. - A sentence in a criminal case that does not include an active punishment or assignment to a drug treatment court, or special

probation as defined in G.S. 15A-1351(a). It may include any one or more of the conditions set forth in G.S. 15A-1343(a1).

(3) Repealed by Session Laws 2011-192, s. 1(h), effective December 1, 2011.

(4) Repealed by Session Laws 1997-57, s. 2.

(4a) House arrest with electronic monitoring. - Probation in which the offender is required to remain at his or her residence. The court, in the sentencing order, may authorize the offender to leave the offender's residence for employment, counseling, a course of study, vocational training, or other specific purposes and may modify that authorization. The probation officer may authorize the offender to leave the offender's residence for specific purposes not authorized in the court order upon approval of the probation officer's supervisor. The offender shall be required to wear a device which permits the supervising agency to monitor the offender's compliance with the condition.

(5) Repealed by Session Laws 2011-192, s. 1(i), effective December 1, 2011.

(6) Intermediate punishment. - A sentence in a criminal case that places an offender on supervised probation. It may include drug treatment court, special probation as defined in G.S. 15A-1351(a), and one or more of the conditions set forth in G.S. 15A-1343(a1).

(7) Prior conviction. - A person has a prior conviction when, on the date a criminal judgment is entered, the person being sentenced has been previously convicted of a crime:

a. In the district court, and the person has not given notice of appeal and the time for appeal has expired; or

b. In the superior court, regardless of whether the conviction is on appeal to the appellate division; or

c. In the courts of the United States, another state, the Armed Forces of the United States, or another country, regardless of whether the offense would be a crime if it occurred in North Carolina, regardless of whether the crime was committed before or after the effective date of this Article.

(8) Repealed by Session Laws 2011-192, s. 1(j), effective December 1, 2011. (1993, c. 538, s. 1; 1994, Ex. Sess., c. 14, s. 17; c. 24, s. 14(b); 1997-57, s. 2; 1997-80, s. 6; 1999-306, s. 2; 2004-128, s. 3; 2009-372, s. 5; 2009-547, s. 6; 2011-183, s. 17; 2011-192, s. 1(a), (b), (h)-(j).)

§ 15A-1340.12. Purposes of sentencing.

The primary purposes of sentencing a person convicted of a crime are to impose a punishment commensurate with the injury the offense has caused, taking into account factors that may diminish or increase the offender's culpability; to protect the public by restraining offenders; to assist the offender toward rehabilitation and restoration to the community as a lawful citizen; and to provide a general deterrent to criminal behavior. (1993, c. 538, s. 1; 1994, Ex. Sess., c. 24, s. 14(b).)

Part 2. Felony Sentencing.

§ 15A-1340.13. Procedure and incidents of sentence of imprisonment for felonies.

(a) Application to Felonies Only. - This Part applies to sentences imposed for felony convictions.

(b) Procedure Generally; Requirements of Judgment; Kinds of Sentences. - Before imposing a sentence, the court shall determine the prior record level for the offender pursuant to G.S. 15A-1340.14. The sentence shall contain a sentence disposition specified for the class of offense and prior record level, and its minimum term of imprisonment shall be within the range specified for the class of offense and prior record level, unless applicable statutes require or authorize another minimum sentence of imprisonment. The kinds of sentence dispositions are active punishment, intermediate punishment, and community punishment.

(c) Minimum and Maximum Term. - The judgment of the court shall contain a minimum term of imprisonment that is consistent with the class of offense for which the sentence is being imposed and with the prior record level for the offender. The maximum term of imprisonment applicable to each minimum term of imprisonment is, unless otherwise provided, as specified in G.S. 15A-1340.17. The maximum term shall be specified in the judgment of the court.

(d) Service of Minimum Required; Earned Time Authorization. - An offender sentenced to an active punishment shall serve the minimum term imposed, except as provided in G.S. 15A-1340.18. The maximum term may be reduced to, but not below, the minimum term by earned time credits awarded to an offender by the Division of Adult Correction of the Department of Public Safety or the custodian of the local confinement facility, pursuant to rules adopted in accordance with law.

(e) Deviation from Sentence Ranges for Aggravation and Mitigation; No Sentence Dispositional Deviation Allowed. - The court may deviate from the presumptive range of minimum sentences of imprisonment specified for a class of offense and prior record level if it finds, pursuant to G.S. 15A-1340.16, that aggravating or mitigating circumstances support such a deviation. The amount of the deviation is in the court's discretion, subject to the limits specified in the class of offense and prior record level for mitigated and aggravated punishment. Deviations for aggravated or mitigated punishment are allowed only in the ranges of minimum and maximum sentences of imprisonment, and not in the sentence dispositions specified for the class of offense and prior record level, unless a statute specifically authorizes a sentence dispositional deviation.

(f) Suspension of Sentence. - Unless otherwise provided, the court shall not suspend the sentence of imprisonment if the class of offense and prior record level do not permit community or intermediate punishment as a sentence disposition. The court shall suspend the sentence of imprisonment if the class of offense and prior record level require community or intermediate punishment as a sentence disposition. The court may suspend the sentence of imprisonment if the class of offense and prior record level authorize, but do not require, active punishment as a sentence disposition.

(g) Dispositional Deviation for Extraordinary Mitigation. - Except as provided in subsection (h) of this section, the court may impose an intermediate punishment for a class of offense and prior record level that requires the imposition of an active punishment if it finds in writing all of the following:

(1) That extraordinary mitigating factors of a kind significantly greater than in the normal case are present.

(2)   Those factors substantially outweigh any factors in aggravation.

(3)   It would be a manifest injustice to impose an active punishment in the case.

The court shall consider evidence of extraordinary mitigating factors, but the decision to find any such factors, or to impose an intermediate punishment is in the discretion of the court. The extraordinary mitigating factors which the court finds shall be specified in its judgment.

(h)   Exceptions When Extraordinary Mitigation Shall Not Be Used. - The court shall not impose an intermediate sanction pursuant to subsection (g) of this section if:

(1)   The offense is a Class A or Class B1 felony;

(2)   The offense is a drug trafficking offense under G.S. 90-95(h) or a drug trafficking conspiracy offense under G.S. 90-95(i); or

(3)   The defendant has five or more points as determined by G.S. 15A-1340.14. (1993, c. 538, s. 1; 1994, Ex. Sess., c. 14, ss. 18, 18.1, 19; c. 22, s. 9; c. 24, s. 14(b); 1995, c. 375, s. 1; 2011-145, s. 19.1(h); 2011-192, s. 5(d).)

§ 15A-1340.14. Prior record level for felony sentencing.

(a)   Generally. - The prior record level of a felony offender is determined by calculating the sum of the points assigned to each of the offender's prior convictions that the court, or with respect to subdivision (b)(7) of this section, the jury, finds to have been proved in accordance with this section.

(b)   Points. - Points are assigned as follows:

(1)   For each prior felony Class A conviction, 10 points.

(1a)   For each prior felony Class B1 conviction, 9 points.

(2)   For each prior felony Class B2, C, or D conviction, 6 points.

(3)   For each prior felony Class E, F, or G conviction, 4 points.

(4) For each prior felony Class H or I conviction, 2 points.

(5) For each prior misdemeanor conviction as defined in this subsection, 1 point. For purposes of this subsection, misdemeanor is defined as any Class A1 and Class 1 nontraffic misdemeanor offense, impaired driving (G.S. 20-138.1), impaired driving in a commercial vehicle (G.S. 20-138.2), and misdemeanor death by vehicle (G.S. 20-141.4(a2)), but not any other misdemeanor traffic offense under Chapter 20 of the General Statutes.

(6) If all the elements of the present offense are included in any prior offense for which the offender was convicted, whether or not the prior offense or offenses were used in determining prior record level, 1 point.

(7) If the offense was committed while the offender was on supervised or unsupervised probation, parole, or post-release supervision, or while the offender was serving a sentence of imprisonment, or while the offender was on escape from a correctional institution while serving a sentence of imprisonment, 1 point.

For purposes of determining prior record points under this subsection, a conviction for a first degree rape or a first degree sexual offense committed prior to the effective date of this subsection shall be treated as a felony Class B1 conviction, and a conviction for any other felony Class B offense committed prior to the effective date of this subsection shall be treated as a felony Class B2 conviction. G.S. 15A-1340.16(a5) specifies the procedure to be used to determine if a point exists under subdivision (7) of this subsection. The State must provide a defendant with written notice of its intent to prove the existence of the prior record point under subdivision (7) of this subsection as required by G.S. 15A-1340.16(a6).

(c) Prior Record Levels for Felony Sentencing. - The prior record levels for felony sentencing are:

(1) Level I - Not more than 1 point.

(2) Level II - At least 2, but not more than 5 points.

(3) Level III - At least 6, but not more than 9 points.

(4) Level IV - At least 10, but not more than 13 points.

(5) Level V - At least 14, but not more than 17 points.

(6) Level VI - At least 18 points.

In determining the prior record level, the classification of a prior offense is the classification assigned to that offense at the time the offense for which the offender is being sentenced is committed.

(d) Multiple Prior Convictions Obtained in One Court Week. - For purposes of determining the prior record level, if an offender is convicted of more than one offense in a single superior court during one calendar week, only the conviction for the offense with the highest point total is used. If an offender is convicted of more than one offense in a single session of district court, only one of the convictions is used.

(e) Classification of Prior Convictions From Other Jurisdictions. - Except as otherwise provided in this subsection, a conviction occurring in a jurisdiction other than North Carolina is classified as a Class I felony if the jurisdiction in which the offense occurred classifies the offense as a felony, or is classified as a Class 3 misdemeanor if the jurisdiction in which the offense occurred classifies the offense as a misdemeanor. If the offender proves by the preponderance of the evidence that an offense classified as a felony in the other jurisdiction is substantially similar to an offense that is a misdemeanor in North Carolina, the conviction is treated as that class of misdemeanor for assigning prior record level points. If the State proves by the preponderance of the evidence that an offense classified as either a misdemeanor or a felony in the other jurisdiction is substantially similar to an offense in North Carolina that is classified as a Class I felony or higher, the conviction is treated as that class of felony for assigning prior record level points. If the State proves by the preponderance of the evidence that an offense classified as a misdemeanor in the other jurisdiction is substantially similar to an offense classified as a Class A1 or Class 1 misdemeanor in North Carolina, the conviction is treated as a Class A1 or Class 1 misdemeanor for assigning prior record level points.

(f) Proof of Prior Convictions. - A prior conviction shall be proved by any of the following methods:

(1) Stipulation of the parties.

(2) An original or copy of the court record of the prior conviction.

(3) A copy of records maintained by the Division of Criminal Information, the Division of Motor Vehicles, or of the Administrative Office of the Courts.

(4) Any other method found by the court to be reliable.

The State bears the burden of proving, by a preponderance of the evidence, that a prior conviction exists and that the offender before the court is the same person as the offender named in the prior conviction. The original or a copy of the court records or a copy of the records maintained by the Division of Criminal Information, the Division of Motor Vehicles, or of the Administrative Office of the Courts, bearing the same name as that by which the offender is charged, is prima facie evidence that the offender named is the same person as the offender before the court, and that the facts set out in the record are true. For purposes of this subsection, "a copy" includes a paper writing containing a reproduction of a record maintained electronically on a computer or other data processing equipment, and a document produced by a facsimile machine. The prosecutor shall make all feasible efforts to obtain and present to the court the offender's full record. Evidence presented by either party at trial may be utilized to prove prior convictions. Suppression of prior convictions is pursuant to G.S. 15A-980. If a motion is made pursuant to that section during the sentencing stage of the criminal action, the court may grant a continuance of the sentencing hearing. If asked by the defendant in compliance with G.S. 15A-903, the prosecutor shall furnish the defendant's prior criminal record to the defendant within a reasonable time sufficient to allow the defendant to determine if the record available to the prosecutor is accurate. Upon request of a sentencing services program established pursuant to Article 61 of Chapter 7A of the General Statutes, the district attorney shall provide any information the district attorney has about the criminal record of a person for whom the program has been requested to provide a sentencing plan pursuant to G.S. 7A-773.1. (1993, c. 538, s. 1; 1994, Ex. Sess., c. 22, s. 10; c. 24, s. 14(b); 1993 (Reg. Sess., 1994), c. 767, ss. 11-13; 1995, c. 507, s. 19.5(f); 1995 (Reg. Sess., 1996), c. 742, s. 15; 1997-80, s. 7; 1997-486, s. 1; 1999-306, s. 3; 1999-408, s. 3; 2005-145, s. 2; 2009-555, s. 1.)

§ 15A-1340.15. Multiple convictions.

(a) Consecutive Sentences. - This Article does not prohibit the imposition of consecutive sentences. Unless otherwise specified by the court, all sentences of imprisonment run concurrently with any other sentences of imprisonment.

(b) Consolidation of Sentences. - If an offender is convicted of more than one offense at the same time, the court may consolidate the offenses for judgment and impose a single judgment for the consolidated offenses. The judgment shall contain a sentence disposition specified for the class of offense and prior record level of the most serious offense, and its minimum sentence of imprisonment shall be within the ranges specified for that class of offense and prior record level, unless applicable statutes require or authorize another minimum sentence of imprisonment. (1993, c. 538, s. 1; 1994, Ex. Sess., c. 24, s. 14(b).)

§ 15A-1340.16. Aggravated and mitigated sentences.

(a) Generally, Burden of Proof. - The court shall consider evidence of aggravating or mitigating factors present in the offense that make an aggravated or mitigated sentence appropriate, but the decision to depart from the presumptive range is in the discretion of the court. The State bears the burden of proving beyond a reasonable doubt that an aggravating factor exists, and the offender bears the burden of proving by a preponderance of the evidence that a mitigating factor exists.

(a1) Jury to Determine Aggravating Factors; Jury Procedure if Trial Bifurcated. - The defendant may admit to the existence of an aggravating factor, and the factor so admitted shall be treated as though it were found by a jury pursuant to the procedures in this subsection. Admissions of the existence of an aggravating factor must be consistent with the provisions of G.S. 15A-1022.1. If the defendant does not so admit, only a jury may determine if an aggravating factor is present in an offense. The jury impaneled for the trial of the felony may, in the same trial, also determine if one or more aggravating factors is present, unless the court determines that the interests of justice require that a separate sentencing proceeding be used to make that determination. If the court determines that a separate proceeding is required, the proceeding shall be conducted by the trial judge before the trial jury as soon as practicable after the guilty verdict is returned. If prior to the time that the trial jury begins its deliberations on the issue of whether one or more aggravating factors exist, any juror dies, becomes incapacitated or disqualified, or is discharged for any reason, an alternate juror shall become a part of the jury and serve in all respects as those selected on the regular trial panel. An alternate juror shall become a part of the jury in the order in which the juror was selected. If the trial jury is unable to reconvene for a hearing on the issue of whether one or more aggravating factors exist after having determined the guilt of the accused, the trial judge shall impanel a new jury to determine the issue. A jury selected to determine whether one or more aggravating factors exist shall be selected in the same manner as juries are selected for the trial of criminal cases.

(a2) Procedure if Defendant Admits Aggravating Factor Only. - If the defendant admits that an aggravating factor exists, but pleads not guilty to the underlying felony, a jury shall be impaneled to dispose of the felony charge. In that case, evidence that relates solely to the establishment of an aggravating factor shall not be admitted in the felony trial.

(a3) Procedure if Defendant Pleads Guilty to the Felony Only. - If the defendant pleads guilty to the felony, but contests the existence of one or more aggravating factors, a jury shall be impaneled to determine if the aggravating factor or factors exist.

(a4) Pleading of Aggravating Factors. - Aggravating factors set forth in subsection (d) of this section need not be included in an indictment or other charging instrument. Any aggravating factor alleged under subdivision (d)(20) of this section shall be included in an indictment or other charging instrument, as specified in G.S. 15A-924.

(a5) Procedure to Determine Prior Record Level Points Not Involving Prior Convictions. - If the State seeks to establish the existence of a prior record level point under G.S. 15A-1340.14(b)(7), the jury shall determine whether the point should be assessed using the procedures specified in subsections (a1) through (a3) of this section. The State need not allege in an indictment or other pleading that it intends to establish the point.

(a6) Notice of Intent to Use Aggravating Factors or Prior Record Level Points. - The State must provide a defendant with written notice of its intent to prove the existence of one or more aggravating factors under subsection (d) of this section or a prior record level point under G.S. 15A-1340.14(b)(7) at least 30 days before trial or the entry of a guilty or no contest plea. A defendant may waive the right to receive such notice. The notice shall list all the aggravating factors the State seeks to establish.

(b) When Aggravated or Mitigated Sentence Allowed. - If the jury, or with respect to an aggravating factor under G.S. 15A-1340.16(d)(12a) or (18a), the court, finds that aggravating factors exist or the court finds that mitigating factors exist, the court may depart from the presumptive range of sentences specified in

G.S. 15A-1340.17(c)(2). If aggravating factors are present and the court determines they are sufficient to outweigh any mitigating factors that are present, it may impose a sentence that is permitted by the aggravated range described in G.S. 15A-1340.17(c)(4). If the court finds that mitigating factors are present and are sufficient to outweigh any aggravating factors that are present, it may impose a sentence that is permitted by the mitigated range described in G.S. 15A-1340.17(c)(3).

(c) Written Findings; When Required. - The court shall make findings of the aggravating and mitigating factors present in the offense only if, in its discretion, it departs from the presumptive range of sentences specified in G.S. 15A-1340.17(c)(2). If the jury finds factors in aggravation, the court shall ensure that those findings are entered in the court's determination of sentencing factors form or any comparable document used to record the findings of sentencing factors. Findings shall be in writing. The requirement to make findings in order to depart from the presumptive range applies regardless of whether the sentence of imprisonment is activated or suspended.

(d) Aggravating Factors. - The following are aggravating factors:

(1) The defendant induced others to participate in the commission of the offense or occupied a position of leadership or dominance of other participants.

(2) The defendant joined with more than one other person in committing the offense and was not charged with committing a conspiracy.

(2a) The offense was committed for the benefit of, or at the direction of, any criminal street gang, with the specific intent to promote, further, or assist in any criminal conduct by gang members, and the defendant was not charged with committing a conspiracy. A "criminal street gang" means any ongoing organization, association, or group of three or more persons, whether formal or informal, having as one of its primary activities the commission of felony or violent misdemeanor offenses, or delinquent acts that would be felonies or violent misdemeanors if committed by an adult, and having a common name or common identifying sign, colors, or symbols.

(3) The offense was committed for the purpose of avoiding or preventing a lawful arrest or effecting an escape from custody.

(4) The defendant was hired or paid to commit the offense.

(5) The offense was committed to disrupt or hinder the lawful exercise of any governmental function or the enforcement of laws.

(6) The offense was committed against or proximately caused serious injury to a present or former law enforcement officer, employee of the Division of Adult Correction of the Department of Public Safety, jailer, fireman, emergency medical technician, ambulance attendant, social worker, justice or judge, clerk or assistant or deputy clerk of court, magistrate, prosecutor, juror, or witness against the defendant, while engaged in the performance of that person's official duties or because of the exercise of that person's official duties.

(6a) The offense was committed against or proximately caused serious harm as defined in G.S. 14-163.1 or death to a law enforcement agency animal, an assistance animal, or a search and rescue animal as defined in G.S. 14-163.1, while engaged in the performance of the animal's official duties.

(7) The offense was especially heinous, atrocious, or cruel.

(8) The defendant knowingly created a great risk of death to more than one person by means of a weapon or device which would normally be hazardous to the lives of more than one person.

(9) The defendant held public elected or appointed office or public employment at the time of the offense and the offense directly related to the conduct of the office or employment.

(9a) The defendant is a firefighter or rescue squad worker, and the offense is directly related to service as a firefighter or rescue squad worker.

(10) The defendant was armed with or used a deadly weapon at the time of the crime.

(11) The victim was very young, or very old, or mentally or physically infirm, or handicapped.

(12) The defendant committed the offense while on pretrial release on another charge.

(12a) The defendant has, during the 10-year period prior to the commission of the offense for which the defendant is being sentenced, been found by a court of this State to be in willful violation of the conditions of probation imposed pursuant to a suspended sentence or been found by the Post-Release Supervision and Parole Commission to be in willful violation of a condition of parole or post-release supervision imposed pursuant to release from incarceration.

(13)   The defendant involved a person under the age of 16 in the commission of the crime.

(14)   The offense involved an attempted or actual taking of property of great monetary value or damage causing great monetary loss, or the offense involved an unusually large quantity of contraband.

(15)   The defendant took advantage of a position of trust or confidence, including a domestic relationship, to commit the offense.

(16)   The offense involved the sale or delivery of a controlled substance to a minor.

(16a)   The offense is the manufacture of methamphetamine and was committed where a person under the age of 18 lives, was present, or was otherwise endangered by exposure to the drug, its ingredients, its by-products, or its waste.

(16b)   The offense is the manufacture of methamphetamine and was committed in a dwelling that is one of four or more contiguous dwellings.

(17)   The offense for which the defendant stands convicted was committed against a victim because of the victim's race, color, religion, nationality, or country of origin.

(18)   The defendant does not support the defendant's family.

(18a)   The defendant has previously been adjudicated delinquent for an offense that would be a Class A, B1, B2, C, D, or E felony if committed by an adult.

(19)   The serious injury inflicted upon the victim is permanent and debilitating.

(19a)   The offense is a violation of G.S. 14-43.11 (human trafficking), G.S. 14-43.12 (involuntary servitude), or G.S. 14-43.13 (sexual servitude) and involved multiple victims.

(19b) The offense is a violation of G.S. 14-43.11 (human trafficking), G.S. 14-43.12 (involuntary servitude), or G.S. 14-43.13 (sexual servitude), and the victim suffered serious injury as a result of the offense.

(20) Any other aggravating factor reasonably related to the purposes of sentencing.

Evidence necessary to prove an element of the offense shall not be used to prove any factor in aggravation, and the same item of evidence shall not be used to prove more than one factor in aggravation. Evidence necessary to establish that an enhanced sentence is required under G.S. 15A-1340.16A may not be used to prove any factor in aggravation.

The judge shall not consider as an aggravating factor the fact that the defendant exercised the right to a jury trial.

Notwithstanding the provisions of subsection (a1) of this section, the determination that an aggravating factor under G.S. 15A-1340.16(d)(18a) is present in a case shall be made by the court, and not by the jury. That determination shall be made in the sentencing hearing.

(e) Mitigating Factors. - The following are mitigating factors:

(1) The defendant committed the offense under duress, coercion, threat, or compulsion that was insufficient to constitute a defense but significantly reduced the defendant's culpability.

(2) The defendant was a passive participant or played a minor role in the commission of the offense.

(3) The defendant was suffering from a mental or physical condition that was insufficient to constitute a defense but significantly reduced the defendant's culpability for the offense.

(4) The defendant's age, immaturity, or limited mental capacity at the time of commission of the offense significantly reduced the defendant's culpability for the offense.

(5) The defendant has made substantial or full restitution to the victim.

(6)   The victim was more than 16 years of age and was a voluntary participant in the defendant's conduct or consented to it.

(7)   The defendant aided in the apprehension of another felon or testified truthfully on behalf of the prosecution in another prosecution of a felony.

(8)   The defendant acted under strong provocation, or the relationship between the defendant and the victim was otherwise extenuating.

(9)   The defendant could not reasonably foresee that the defendant's conduct would cause or threaten serious bodily harm or fear, or the defendant exercised caution to avoid such consequences.

(10)   The defendant reasonably believed that the defendant's conduct was legal.

(11)   Prior to arrest or at an early stage of the criminal process, the defendant voluntarily acknowledged wrongdoing in connection with the offense to a law enforcement officer.

(12)   The defendant has been a person of good character or has had a good reputation in the community in which the defendant lives.

(13)   The defendant is a minor and has reliable supervision available.

(14)   The defendant has been honorably discharged from the Armed Forces of the United States.

(15)   The defendant has accepted responsibility for the defendant's criminal conduct.

(16)   The defendant has entered and is currently involved in or has successfully completed a drug treatment program or an alcohol treatment program subsequent to arrest and prior to trial.

(17)   The defendant supports the defendant's family.

(18)   The defendant has a support system in the community.

(19)   The defendant has a positive employment history or is gainfully employed.

(20) The defendant has a good treatment prognosis, and a workable treatment plan is available.

(21) Any other mitigating factor reasonably related to the purposes of sentences.

(f) [Notice to State Treasurer of Finding. -] If the court determines that an aggravating factor under subdivision (9) of subsection (d) of this section has been proven, the court shall notify the State Treasurer of the fact of the conviction as well as the finding of the aggravating factor. The indictment charging the defendant with the underlying offense must include notice that the State seeks to prove the defendant acted in accordance with subdivision (9) of subsection (d) of this section and that the State will seek to prove that as an aggravating factor. (1993, c. 538, s. 1; 1994, Ex. Sess., c. 7, s. 6; c. 22, s. 22; c. 24, s. 14(b); 1995, c. 509, s. 13; 1997-443, ss. 19.25(w), 19.25(ee); 2003-378, s. 6; 2004-178, s. 2; 2004-186, s. 8.1; 2005-101, s. 1; 2005-145, s. 1; 2005-434, s. 4; 2007-80, s. 2; 2008-129, ss. 1, 2; 2009-460, s. 2; 2011-145, s. 19.1(h); 2011-183, s. 18; 2012-193, s. 9, 10; 2013-284, s. 2(b); 2013-368, s. 14.)

§ 15A-1340.16A. Enhanced sentence if defendant is convicted of a Class A, B1, B2, C, D, or E felony and the defendant used, displayed, or threatened to use or display a firearm or deadly weapon during the commission of the felony.

(a), (b) Repealed by Session Laws 2003-378, s. 2, effective August 1, 2003.

(c) If a person is convicted of a felony and it is found as provided in this section that: (i) the person committed the felony by using, displaying, or threatening the use or display of a firearm or deadly weapon and (ii) the person actually possessed the firearm or deadly weapon about his or her person, then the person shall have the minimum term of imprisonment to which the person is sentenced for that felony increased as follows:

(1) If the felony is a Class A, B1, B2, C, D, or E felony, the minimum term of imprisonment to which the person is sentenced for that felony shall be increased by 72 months. The maximum term of imprisonment shall be the maximum term that corresponds to the minimum term after it is increased by 72 months, as specified in G.S. 15A-1340.17(e) and (e1).

(2) If the felony is a Class F or G felony, the minimum term of imprisonment to which the person is sentenced for that felony shall be increased by 36 months. The maximum term of imprisonment shall be the maximum term that

corresponds to the minimum term after it is increased by 36 months, as specified in G.S. 15A-1340.17(d).

(3)   If the felony is a Class H or I felony, the minimum term of imprisonment to which the person is sentenced for that felony shall be increased by 12 months. The maximum term of imprisonment shall be the maximum term that corresponds to the minimum term after it is increased by 12 months, as specified in G.S. 15A-1340.17(d).

(d)   An indictment or information for the felony shall allege in that indictment or information the facts set out in subsection (c) of this section. The pleading is sufficient if it alleges that the defendant committed the felony by using, displaying, or threatening the use or display of a firearm or deadly weapon and the defendant actually possessed the firearm or deadly weapon about the defendant's person. One pleading is sufficient for all felonies that are tried at a single trial.

(e)   The State shall prove the issues set out in subsection (c) of this section beyond a reasonable doubt during the same trial in which the defendant is tried for the felony unless the defendant pleads guilty or no contest to the issues. If the defendant pleads guilty or no contest to the felony but pleads not guilty to the issues set out in subsection (c) of this section, then a jury shall be impaneled to determine the issues.

(f)   Subsection (c) of this section does not apply if the evidence of the use, display, or threatened use or display of the firearm or deadly weapon is needed to prove an element of the felony or if the person is not sentenced to an active term of imprisonment. (1994, Ex. Sess., c. 22, s. 20; 2003-378, s. 2; 2008-214, s. 5; 2013-369, s. 5.)

§ 15A-1340.16B. Life imprisonment without parole for a second or subsequent conviction of a Class B1 felony if the victim was 13 years of age or younger and there are no mitigating factors.

(a)   If a person is convicted of a Class B1 felony and it is found as provided in this section that: (i) the person committed the felony against a victim who was 13 years of age or younger at the time of the offense and (ii) the person has one or more prior convictions of a Class B1 felony, then the person shall be sentenced to life imprisonment without parole.

(b), (c) Repealed by Session Laws 2003-378, s. 3, effective August 1, 2003.

(d) An indictment or information for the Class B1 felony shall allege in that indictment or information or in a separate indictment or information the facts set out in subsection (a) of this section. The pleading is sufficient if it alleges that the defendant committed the felony against a victim who was 13 years of age or younger at the time of the felony and that the defendant had one or more prior convictions of a Class B1 felony. One pleading is sufficient for all Class B1 felonies that are tried at a single trial.

(e) The State shall prove the issues set out in subsection (a) of this section beyond a reasonable doubt during the same trial in which the defendant is tried for the felony unless the defendant pleads guilty or no contest to the issues. The issues shall be presented in the same manner as provided in G.S. 15A-928(c). If the defendant pleads guilty or no contest to the felony but pleads not guilty to the issues set out in subsection (a) of this section, then a jury shall be impaneled to determine the issues.

(f) Subsection (a) of this section does not apply if there are mitigating factors present under G.S. 15A-1340.16(e). (1998-212, s. 17.16(a); 2003-378, s. 3.)

§ 15A-1340.16C. Enhanced sentence if defendant is convicted of a felony and the defendant was wearing or had in his or her immediate possession a bullet-proof vest during the commission of the felony.

(a) If a person is convicted of a felony and it is found as provided in this section that the person wore or had in his or her immediate possession a bullet-proof vest at the time of the felony, then the person is guilty of a felony that is one class higher than the underlying felony for which the person was convicted.

(b) Repealed by Session Laws 2003-378, s. 4, effective August 1, 2003.

(b1) This section does not apply to law enforcement officers, unless the State proves beyond a reasonable doubt, pursuant to subsection (d) of this section, both of the following:

(1) That the law enforcement officer was not performing or attempting to perform a law enforcement function.

(2) That the law enforcement officer knowingly wore or had in his or her immediate possession a bulletproof vest at the time of the commission of the felony for the purpose of aiding the law enforcement officer in the commission of the felony.

(c) An indictment or information for the felony shall allege in that indictment or information or in a separate indictment or information the facts set out in subsection (a) of this section. The pleading is sufficient if it alleges that the defendant committed the felony while wearing or having in the defendant's immediate possession a bulletproof vest. One pleading is sufficient for all felonies that are tried at a single trial.

(d) The State shall prove the issue set out in subsection (a) of this section beyond a reasonable doubt during the same trial in which the defendant is tried for the felony unless the defendant pleads guilty or no contest to that issue. If the defendant pleads guilty or no contest to the felony but pleads not guilty to the issue set out in subsection (a) of this section, then a jury shall be impaneled to determine that issue.

(e) Subsection (a) of this section does not apply if the evidence that the person wore or had in the person's immediate possession a bulletproof vest is needed to prove an element of the felony. (1999-263, s. 1; 2003-378, s. 4.)

§ 15A-1340.16D. Manufacturing methamphetamine; enhanced sentence.

(a) If a person is convicted of the offense of manufacture of methamphetamine under G.S. 90-95(b)(1a) and it is found as provided in this section that a law enforcement officer, probation officer, parole officer, emergency medical services employee, or a firefighter suffered serious injury while discharging or attempting to discharge his or her official duties and that the injury was directly caused by one of the hazards associated with the manufacture of methamphetamine, then the person shall have the minimum term of imprisonment to which the person is sentenced for that felony increased by 24 months. The maximum term of imprisonment shall be the maximum term that corresponds to the minimum term after it is increased by 24 months, as specified in G.S. 15A-1340.17(e) and (e1).

(a1)   If a person is convicted of the offense of manufacture of methamphetamine under G.S. 90-95(b)(1a) and it is found as provided in this section that:

(1)   A minor under 18 years of age resided on the property used for the manufacture of methamphetamine, or was present at a location where methamphetamine was being manufactured, then the person shall have the minimum term of imprisonment to which the person is sentenced for that felony increased by 24 months. The maximum term of imprisonment shall be the maximum term that corresponds to the minimum term after it is increased by 24 months, as specified in G.S. 15A-1340.17(e) and (e1).

(2)   A disabled or elder adult resided on the property used for the manufacture of methamphetamine, or was present at a location where methamphetamine was being manufactured, then the person shall have the minimum term of imprisonment to which the person is sentenced for that felony increased by 24 months. The maximum term of imprisonment shall be the maximum term that corresponds to the minimum term after it is increased by 24 months, as specified in G.S. 15A-1340.17(e) and (e1).

(3)   A minor and a disabled or elder adult resided on the property, or were present at a location where methamphetamine was being manufactured, then the person shall have the minimum term of imprisonment to which the person is sentenced for that felony increased by 48 months. The maximum term of imprisonment shall be the maximum term that corresponds to the minimum term after it is increased by 48 months, as specified in G.S. 15A-1340.17(e) and (e1).

(a2)   For the purposes of this section, the terms "disabled adult" and "elder adult" shall be defined as set forth in G.S. 14-32.3(d).

(a3)   The penalties set forth in this section are cumulative. The minimum sentence shall be increased by the sum of the number of months for convictions under subsections (a) and (a1) of this section, and the maximum term of imprisonment shall be the maximum term that corresponds to the total number of months, as specified in G.S. 15A-1340.17(e) and (e1).

(b)   An indictment or information for the offense of manufacture of methamphetamine under G.S. 90-95(b)(1a) shall allege in that indictment or information the facts set out in subsection (a) or (a1) of this section. The pleading is sufficient if it alleges any or all of the following:

(1) The defendant committed the offense of manufacture of methamphetamine and that as a result of the offense a law enforcement officer, probation officer, parole officer, emergency medical services employee, or firefighter suffered serious injury while discharging or attempting to discharge his or her official duties.

(2) The defendant committed the offense of manufacture of methamphetamine and that a minor resided on the property used for manufacturing the methamphetamine, or was present at a location where methamphetamine was being manufactured.

(3) The defendant committed the offense of manufacture of methamphetamine and that a disabled or elder adult resided on the property used for manufacturing the methamphetamine, or was present at a location where methamphetamine was being manufactured.

(4) The defendant committed the offense of manufacture of methamphetamine and that a minor and a disabled or elder adult resided on the property used for manufacturing the methamphetamine, or were present at a location where methamphetamine was being manufactured.

One pleading is sufficient for all felonies that are tried at a single trial.

(c) The State shall prove the issue or issues set out in subsection (b) of this section beyond a reasonable doubt during the same trial in which the defendant is tried for the offense of manufacture of methamphetamine unless the defendant pleads guilty or no contest to the issue. If the defendant pleads guilty or no contest to the offense of manufacture of methamphetamine but pleads not guilty to the issue or issues set out in subsection (b) of this section, then a jury shall be impaneled to determine the issue.

(d) This section does not apply if the offense is packaging or repackaging methamphetamine, or labeling or relabeling the methamphetamine container. (2004-178, s. 8; 2013-124, s. 2.)

§ 15A-1340.17. Punishment limits for each class of offense and prior record level.

(a) Offense Classification; Default Classifications. - The offense classification is as specified in the offense for which the sentence is being imposed. If the offense is a felony for which there is no classification, it is a Class I felony.

(b) Fines. - Any judgment that includes a sentence of imprisonment may also include a fine. If a community punishment is authorized, the judgment may consist of a fine only. Additionally, when the defendant is other than an individual, the judgment may consist of a fine only. Unless otherwise provided, the amount of the fine is in the discretion of the court.

(c) Punishments for Each Class of Offense and Prior Record Level; Punishment Chart Described. - The authorized punishment for each class of offense and prior record level is as specified in the chart below. Prior record levels are indicated by the Roman numerals placed horizontally on the top of the chart. Classes of offense are indicated by the letters placed vertically on the left side of the chart. Each cell on the chart contains the following components:

(1) A sentence disposition or dispositions: "C" indicates that a community punishment is authorized; "I" indicates that an intermediate punishment is authorized; "A" indicates that an active punishment is authorized; and "Life Imprisonment Without Parole" indicates that the defendant shall be imprisoned for the remainder of the prisoner's natural life.

(2) A presumptive range of minimum durations, if the sentence of imprisonment is neither aggravated or mitigated; any minimum term of imprisonment in that range is permitted unless the court finds pursuant to G.S. 15A-1340.16 that an aggravated or mitigated sentence is appropriate. The presumptive range is the middle of the three ranges in the cell.

(3) A mitigated range of minimum durations if the court finds pursuant to G.S. 15A-1340.16 that a mitigated sentence of imprisonment is justified; in such a case, any minimum term of imprisonment in the mitigated range is permitted. The mitigated range is the lower of the three ranges in the cell.

(4) An aggravated range of minimum durations if the court finds pursuant to G.S. 15A-1340.16 that an aggravated sentence of imprisonment is justified; in such a case, any minimum term of imprisonment in the aggravated range is permitted. The aggravated range is the higher of the three ranges in the cell.

PRIOR RECORD LEVEL

	I 0-1 Pt	II 2-5 Pts	III 6-9 Pts	IV 10-13 Pts	V 14-17 Pts	VI 18+ Pts
A	Life Imprisonment With Parole or Without Parole, or Death, as Established by Statute					
	A DISPOSITION	A	A	A	A	A
	240-300 Aggravated Without Parole	276-345	317-397	365-456	Life Imprisonment	
B1	192-240 PRESUMPTIVE	221-276	254-317	292-365	336-420	386-483
	144-192 Mitigated	166-221	190-254	219-292	252-336	290-386
	A DISPOSITION	A	A	A	A	A
	157-196 Aggravated	180-225	207-258	238-297	273-342	314-393
B2	125-157 PRESUMPTIVE	144-180	165-207	190-238	219-273	251-314
	94-125 Mitigated	108-144	124-165	143-190	164-219	189-251
	A DISPOSITION	A	A	A	A	A
	73-92 Aggravated	83-104	96-120	110-138	127-159	146-182
C	58-73 PRESUMPTIVE	67-83	77-96	88-110	101-127	117-146

Mitigated	44-58	50-67	58-77	66-88	76-101	87-117
DISPOSITION	A	A	A	A	A	A
Aggravated	64-80	73-92	84-105	97-121	111-139	128-160
D PRESUMPTIVE	51-64	59-73	67-84	78-97	89-111	103-128
Mitigated	38-51	44-59	51-67	58-78	67-89	77-103
DISPOSITION	I/A	I/A	A	A	A	A
Aggravated	25-31	29-36	33-41	38-48	44-55	50-63
E PRESUMPTIVE	20-25	23-29	26-33	30-38	35-44	40-50
Mitigated	15-20	17-23	20-26	23-30	26-35	30-40
DISPOSITION	I/A	I/A	I/A	A	A	A
Aggravated	16-20	19-23	21-27	25-31	28-36	33-41
F PRESUMPTIVE	13-16	15-19	17-21	20-25	23-28	26-33
Mitigated	10-13	11-15	13-17	15-20	17-23	20-26
DISPOSITION	I/A	I/A	I/A	I/A	A	A

Class		I	II	III	IV	V	VI
G	Aggravated	13-16	14-18	17-21	19-24	22-27	25-31
G	PRESUMPTIVE	10-13	12-14	13-17	15-19	17-22	20-25
G	Mitigated	8-10	9-12	10-13	11-15	13-17	15-20
G	DISPOSITION	C/I/A	I/A	I/A	I/A	I/A	A
H	Aggravated	6-8	8-10	10-12	11-14	15-19	20-25
H	PRESUMPTIVE	5-6	6-8	8-10	9-11	12-15	16-20
H	Mitigated	4-5	4-6	6-8	7-9	9-12	12-16
H	DISPOSITION	C	C/I	I	I/A	I/A	I/A
I	Aggravated	6-8	6-8	6-8	8-10	9-11	10-12
I	PRESUMPTIVE	4-6	4-6	5-6	6-8	7-9	8-10
I	Mitigated	3-4	3-4	4-5	4-6	5-7	6-8

(d) Maximum Sentences Specified for Class F through Class I Felonies. - Unless provided otherwise in a statute establishing a punishment for a specific crime, for each minimum term of imprisonment in the chart in subsection (c) of this section, expressed in months, the corresponding maximum term of imprisonment, also expressed in months, is as specified in the table below for Class F through Class I felonies. The first figure in each cell in the table is the minimum term and the second is the maximum term.

3-13	4-14	5-15	6-17	7-18	8-19	9-20	10-21
11-23	12-24	13-25	14-26	15-27	16-29	17-30	18-31
19-32	20-33	21-35	22-36	23-37	24-38	25-39	26-41
27-42	28-43	29-44	30-45	31-47	32-48	33-49	34-50
35-51	36-53	37-54	38-55	39-56	40-57	41-59	42-60
43-61	44-62	45-63	46-65	47-66	48-67	49-68	

(e) Maximum Sentences Specified for Class B1 through Class E Felonies for Minimum Terms up to 339 Months. Unless provided otherwise in a statute establishing a punishment for a specific crime, for each minimum term of imprisonment in the chart in subsection (c) of this section, expressed in months, the corresponding maximum term of imprisonment, also expressed in months, is as specified in the table below for Class B1 through Class E felonies. The first figure in each cell of the table is the minimum term and the second is the maximum term.

15-30	16-32	17-33	18-34	19-35	20-36	21-38	
	22-39						
23-40	24-41	25-42	26-44	27-45	28-46	29-47	
	30-48						
31-50	32-51	33-52	34-53	35-54	36-56	37-57	
	38-58						
39-59	40-60	41-62	42-63	43-64	44-65	45-66	
	46-68						
47-69	48-70	49-71	50-72	51-74	52-75	53-76	
	54-77						
55-78	56-80	57-81	58-82	59-83	60-84	61-86	
	62-87						
63-88	64-89	65-90	66-92	67-93	68-94	69-95	
	70-96						

71-98   72-99   73-100   74-101   75-102   76-104   77-105   78-106

79-107   80-108   81-110   82-111   83-112   84-113   85-114   86-116

87-117   88-118   89-119   90-120   91-122   92-123   93-124   94-125

95-126   96-128   97-129   98-130   99-131   100-132   101-134   102-135

103-136 104-137 105-138   106-140   107-141   108-142   109-143   110-144

111-146 112-147 113-148   114-149   115-150   116-152   117-153   118-154

119-155 120-156 121-158   122-159   123-160   124-161   125-162   126-164

127-165 128-166 129-167   130-168   131-170   132-171   133-172   134-173

135-174 136-176 137-177   138-178   139-179   140-180   141-182   142-183

143-184 144-185 145-186   146-188   147-189   148-190   149-191   150-192

151-194 152-195 153-196   154-197   155-198   156-200   157-201   158-202

159-203 160-204 161-206   162-207   163-208   164-209   165-210   166-212

167-213 168-214 169-215   170-216   171-218   172-219   173-220   174-221

175-222 176-224 177-225   178-226   179-227   180-228   181-230   182-231

183-232   184-233   185-234   186-236   187-237   188-238   189-239   190-240

191-242   192-243   193-244   194-245   195-246   196-248   197-249   198-250

199-251   200-252   201-254   202-255   203-256   204-257   205-258   206-260

207-261   208-262   209-263   210-264   211-266   212-267   213-268   214-269

215-270   216-272   217-273   218-274   219-275   220-276   221-278   222-279

223-280   224-281   225-282   226-284   227-285   228-286   229-287   230-288

231-290   232-291   233-292   234-293   235-294   236-296   237-297   238-298

239-299   240-300   241-302   242-303   243-304   244-305   245-306   246-308

247-309   248-310   249-311   250-312   251-314   252-315   253-316   254-317

255-318   256-320   257-321   258-322   259-323   260-324   261-326   262-327

263-328   264-329   265-330   266-332   267-333   268-334   269-335   270-336

271-338   272-339   273-340   274-341   275-342   276-344   277-345   278-346

279-347   280-348   281-350   282-351   283-352   284-353   285-354   286-356

287-357   288-358   289-359   290-360   291-362   292-363   293-364   294-365

295-366   296-368   297-369   298-370   299-371   300-372   301-374
           302-375

303-376   304-377   305-378   306-380   307-381   308-382   309-383
           310-384

311-386   312-387   313-388   314-389   315-390   316-392   317-393
           318-394

319-395   320-396   321-398   322-399   323-400   324-401   325-402
           326-404

327-405   328-406   329-407   330-408   331-410   332-411   333-412
           334-413

335-414   336-416   337-417   338-418   339-419.

(e1) Maximum Sentences Specified for Class B1 through Class E Felonies for Minimum Terms of 340 Months or More. - Unless provided otherwise in a statute establishing a punishment for a specific crime, when the minimum sentence is 340 months or more, the corresponding maximum term of imprisonment shall be equal to the sum of the minimum term of imprisonment and twenty percent (20%) of the minimum term of imprisonment, rounded to the next highest month, plus 12 additional months.

(f) Maximum Sentences Specified for Class B1 Through Class E Sex Offenses. - Unless provided otherwise in a statute establishing a punishment for a specific crime, for offenders sentenced for a Class B1 through E felony that is a reportable conviction subject to the registration requirement of Article 27A of Chapter 14 of the General Statutes, the maximum term of imprisonment shall be equal to the sum of the minimum term of imprisonment and twenty percent (20%) of the minimum term of imprisonment, rounded to the next highest month, plus 60 additional months. (1993, c. 538, s. 1; 1994, Ex. Sess., c. 14, ss. 20, 21; c. 22, s. 7; c. 24, s. 14(b); 1995, c. 507, s. 19.5(l); 1997-80, s. 3; 2009-555, s. 2; 2009-556, s. 1; 2011-192, s. 2(e)-(g); 2011-307, s. 1; 2011-412, s. 2.4(a); 2013-101, s. 6; 2013-410, s. 3(b).)

§ 15A-1340.18. Advanced supervised release.

(a) Definitions. - For the purposes of this section, the following definitions apply:

(1) "Advanced supervised release" or "ASR" means release from prison and placement on post-release supervision under this section if an eligible defendant is sentenced to active time.

(2) "Eligible defendant" means a defendant convicted and sentenced based upon any of the following felony classes and prior record levels:

a. Class D, Prior Record Level I-III.

b. Class E, Prior Record Level I-IV.

c. Class F, Prior Record Level I-V.

d. Class G, Prior Record Level I-VI.

e. Class H, Prior Record Level I-VI.

(3) "Risk reduction incentive" is a sentencing condition which, upon successful completion during incarceration, results in a prisoner being placed on ASR.

(b) The Division of Adult Correction of the Department of Public Safety is authorized to create risk reduction incentives consisting of treatment, education, and rehabilitative programs. The incentives shall be designed to reduce the likelihood that the prisoner who receives the incentive will reoffend.

(c) When imposing an active sentence for an eligible defendant, the court, in its discretion and without objection from the prosecutor, may order that the Department of Correction admit the defendant to the ASR program. The Department of Correction shall admit to the ASR program only those defendants for which ASR is ordered in the sentencing judgment.

(d) The court shall impose a sentence calculated pursuant to Article 81B of the General Statutes. The ASR date shall be the shortest mitigated sentence for the offense at the offender's prior record level. If the court utilizes the mitigated range in sentencing the defendant, then the ASR date shall be eighty percent (80%) of the minimum sentence imposed.

(e) The defendant shall be notified at sentencing that if the defendant completes the risk reduction incentives as identified by the Department, then he or she will be released on the ASR date, as determined by the Department pursuant to the provisions of subsection (d) of this section. If the Department determines that the defendant is unable to complete the incentives by the ASR date, through no fault of the defendant, then the defendant shall be released at the ASR date.

(f) Termination from the risk reduction incentive program shall result in the nullification of the ASR date, and the defendant's release date shall be calculated based upon the adjudged sentence. A prisoner who has completed the risk reduction incentives prior to the ASR date may have the ASR date nullified due to noncompliance with Division rules or regulations.

(g) A defendant released on the ASR date is subject to post-release supervision under this Article. Notwithstanding the provisions in G.S. 15A-1368.3(c), if the defendant has been returned to prison for three, three-month periods of confinement, a subsequent violation shall result in the defendant returning to prison to serve the time remaining on the maximum imposed term, and is ineligible for further post-release supervision regardless of the amount of time remaining to be served.

(h) The Division shall adopt policies and procedures for the assessment to occur at diagnostic processing, for documentation of the inmate's progress, and for termination from the incentive program due to a lack of progress or a pattern of noncompliance in the program or with other Division rules or regulations. (2011-145, s. 19.1(h); 2011-192, s. 5(c); 2011-412, ss. 2.7, 2.8.)

§ 15A-1340.19. Reserved for future codification purposes.

Part 2A. Sentencing for Minors Subject to Life Imprisonment Without Parole.

§ 15A-1340.19A. Applicability.

Notwithstanding the provisions of G.S. 14-17, a defendant who is convicted of first degree murder, and who was under the age of 18 at the time of the offense, shall be sentenced in accordance with this Part. For the purposes of this Part, "life imprisonment with parole" shall mean that the defendant shall serve a minimum of 25 years imprisonment prior to becoming eligible for parole. (2012-148, s. 1.)

§ 15A-1340.19B. Penalty determination.

(a)   In determining a sentence under this Part, the court shall do one of the following:

(1)   If the sole basis for conviction of a count or each count of first degree murder was the felony murder rule, then the court shall sentence the defendant to life imprisonment with parole.

(2)   If the court does not sentence the defendant pursuant to subdivision (1) of this subsection, then the court shall conduct a hearing to determine whether the defendant should be sentenced to life imprisonment without parole, as set forth in G.S. 14-17, or a lesser sentence of life imprisonment with parole.

(b)   The hearing under subdivision (2) of subsection (a) of this section shall be conducted by the trial judge as soon as practicable after the guilty verdict is returned. The State and the defendant shall not be required to resubmit evidence presented during the guilt determination phase of the case. Evidence, including evidence in rebuttal, may be presented as to any matter that the court deems relevant to sentencing, and any evidence which the court deems to have probative value may be received.

(c)   The defendant or the defendant's counsel may submit mitigating circumstances to the court, including, but not limited to, the following factors:

(1)   Age at the time of the offense.

(2)   Immaturity.

(3)   Ability to appreciate the risks and consequences of the conduct.

(4)   Intellectual capacity.

(5)   Prior record.

(6) Mental health.

(7) Familial or peer pressure exerted upon the defendant.

(8) Likelihood that the defendant would benefit from rehabilitation in confinement.

(9) Any other mitigating factor or circumstance.

(d) The State and the defendant or the defendant's counsel shall be permitted to present argument for or against the sentence of life imprisonment with parole. The defendant or the defendant's counsel shall have the right to the last argument.

(e) The provisions of Article 58 of Chapter 15A of the General Statutes apply to proceedings under this Part. (2012-148, s. 1.)

§ 15A-1340.19C. Sentencing; assignment for resentencing.

(a) The court shall consider any mitigating factors in determining whether, based upon all the circumstances of the offense and the particular circumstances of the defendant, the defendant should be sentenced to life imprisonment with parole instead of life imprisonment without parole. The order adjudging the sentence shall include findings on the absence or presence of any mitigating factors and such other findings as the court deems appropriate to include in the order.

(b) All motions for appropriate relief filed in superior court seeking resentencing under the provisions of this Part may be heard and determined in the trial division by any judge (i) who is empowered to act in criminal matters in the superior court district or set of districts as defined in G.S. 7A-41.1, in which the judgment was entered and (ii) who is assigned pursuant to this section to review the motion for appropriate relief and take the appropriate administrative action to dispense with the motion.

(c) The judge who presided at the trial of the defendant is empowered to act upon the motion for appropriate relief even though the judge is in another district or even though the judge's commission has expired; however, if the judge who presided at the trial is still unavailable to act, the senior resident superior court judge shall assign a judge who is empowered to act under subsection (b) of this section.

(d)   All motions for appropriate relief filed in superior court seeking resentencing under the provisions of this Part shall, when filed, be referred to the senior resident superior court judge, who shall assign the motion as provided by this section for review and administrative action, including, as may be appropriate, dismissal, calendaring for hearing, entry of a scheduling order for subsequent events in the case, or other appropriate actions. (2012-148, s. 1.)

§ 15A-1340.19D. Incidents of parole.

(a)   Except as otherwise provided in this section, a defendant sentenced to life imprisonment with parole shall be subject to the conditions and procedures set forth in Article 85 of Chapter 15A of the General Statutes, including the notification requirement in G.S. 15A-1371(b)(3).

(b)   The term of parole for a person released from imprisonment from a sentence of life imprisonment with parole shall be five years and may not be terminated earlier by the Post-Release Supervision and Parole Commission.

(c)   A defendant sentenced to life imprisonment with parole who is paroled, and then violates a condition of parole and is returned to prison to serve the life sentence, shall not be eligible for parole for five years from the date of the return to confinement.

(d)   Life imprisonment with parole under this Part means that unless the defendant receives parole, the defendant shall remain imprisoned for the defendant's natural life. (2012-148, s. 1.)

Part 3. Misdemeanor Sentencing.

§ 15A-1340.20. Procedure and incidents of sentence of imprisonment for misdemeanors.

(a) Application to Misdemeanors Only. - This Part applies to sentences imposed for misdemeanor convictions.

(b) Procedure Generally; Term of Imprisonment. - A sentence imposed for a misdemeanor shall contain a sentence disposition specified for the class of offense and prior conviction level, and any sentence of imprisonment shall be within the range specified for the class of offense and prior conviction level, unless applicable statutes require otherwise. The kinds of sentence dispositions are active punishment, intermediate punishment, and community punishment. Except for the work and earned time credits authorized by G.S. 162-60, or earned time credits authorized by G.S. 15A-1355(c), if applicable, an offender whose sentence of imprisonment is activated shall serve each day of the term imposed.

(c) Suspension of Sentence. - Unless otherwise provided, the court shall suspend a sentence of imprisonment if the class of offense and prior conviction level requires community or intermediate punishment as a sentence disposition.

(c1) Active Punishment Exception. - The court may impose an active punishment for a class of offense and prior conviction level that does not otherwise authorize the imposition of an active punishment if the term of imprisonment is equal to or less than the total amount of time the offender has already spent committed to or in confinement in any State or local correctional, mental, or other institution as a result of the charge that culminated in the sentence.

(d) Earned Time Authorization. - An offender sentenced to a term of imprisonment that is activated is eligible to receive earned time credit for misdemeanant offenders awarded by the Division of Adult Correction of the Department of Public Safety or the custodian of a local confinement facility, pursuant to rules adopted in accordance with law and pursuant to G.S. 162-60. These rules and statute combined shall not award misdemeanant offenders more than four days of earned time credit per month of incarceration. (1993, c. 538, s. 1; 1994, Ex. Sess., c. 24, s. 14(b); 1993 (Reg. Sess., 1994), c. 767, s. 1; 1997-79, s. 1; 2011-145, s. 19.1(h).)

§ 15A-1340.21. Prior conviction level for misdemeanor sentencing.

(a) Generally. - The prior conviction level of a misdemeanor offender is determined by calculating the number of the offender's prior convictions that the court finds to have been proven in accordance with this section.

(b) Prior Conviction Levels for Misdemeanor Sentencing. - The prior conviction levels for misdemeanor sentencing are:

(1) Level I - 0 prior convictions.

(2) Level II - At least 1, but not more than 4 prior convictions.

(3) Level III - At least 5 prior convictions.

In determining the prior conviction level, a prior offense may be included if it is either a felony or a misdemeanor at the time the offense for which the offender is being sentenced is committed.

(c) Proof of Prior Convictions. - A prior conviction shall be proved by any of the following methods:

(1) Stipulation of the parties.

(2) An original or copy of the court record of the prior conviction.

(3) A copy of records maintained by the Division of Criminal Information, the Division of Motor Vehicles, or of the Administrative Office of the Courts.

(4) Any other method found by the court to be reliable.

The State bears the burden of proving, by a preponderance of the evidence, that a prior conviction exists and that the offender before the court is the same person as the offender named in the prior conviction. The original or a copy of the court records or a copy of the records maintained by the Division of Criminal Information, the Division of Motor Vehicles, or of the Administrative Office of the Courts, bearing the same name as that by which the offender is charged, is prima facie evidence that the offender named is the same person as the offender before the court, and that the facts set out in the record are true. For purposes of this subsection, "copy" includes a paper writing containing a reproduction of a record maintained electronically on a computer or other data processing equipment, and a document produced by a facsimile machine. Evidence presented by either party at trial may be utilized to prove prior convictions. Suppression of prior convictions is pursuant to G.S. 15A-980. If a motion is made pursuant to that section during the sentencing stage of the criminal action, the court may grant a continuance of the sentencing hearing.

(d) Multiple Prior Convictions Obtained in One Court Week. - For purposes of this section, if an offender is convicted of more than one offense in a single session of district court, or in a single week of superior court or of a court in another jurisdiction, only one of the convictions may be used to determine the prior conviction level. (1993, c. 538, s. 1; 1994, Ex. Sess., c. 24, s. 14(b); 1993 (Reg. Sess., 1994), c. 767, s. 13.1; 1997-80, s. 8.)

§ 15A-1340.22. Multiple convictions.

(a) Limits on Consecutive Sentences. - If the court elects to impose consecutive sentences for two or more misdemeanors and the most serious misdemeanor is classified in Class A1, Class 1, or Class 2, the cumulative length of the sentences of imprisonment shall not exceed twice the maximum sentence authorized for the class and prior conviction level of the most serious offense. Consecutive sentences shall not be imposed if all convictions are for Class 3 misdemeanors.

(b) Consolidation of Sentences. - If an offender is convicted of more than one offense at the same session of court, the court may consolidate the offenses for judgment and impose a single judgment for the consolidated offenses. Any sentence imposed shall be consistent with the appropriate prior conviction level of the most serious offense. (1993, c. 538, s. 1; 1994, Ex. Sess., c. 24, s. 14(b); 1995 (Reg. Sess., 1996), c. 742, s. 16.)

§ 15A-1340.23. Punishment limits for each class of offense and prior conviction level.

(a) Offense Classification; Default Classifications. - The offense classification is as specified in the offense for which the sentence is being imposed. If the offense is a misdemeanor for which there is no classification, it is as classified in G.S. 14-3.

(b) Fines. - Any judgment that includes a sentence of imprisonment may also include a fine. Additionally, when the defendant is other than an individual, the judgment may consist of a fine only. If a community punishment is authorized, the judgment may consist of a fine only. Unless otherwise provided for a specific offense, the maximum fine that may be imposed is two hundred dollars ($200.00) for a Class 3 misdemeanor and one thousand dollars ($1,000) for a Class 2 misdemeanor. The amount of the fine for a Class 1 misdemeanor and a Class A1 misdemeanor is in the discretion of the court.

(c) Punishment for Each Class of Offense and Prior Conviction Level; Punishment Chart Described. - Unless otherwise provided for a specific offense, the authorized punishment for each class of offense and prior conviction level is as specified in the chart below. Prior conviction levels are indicated by the Roman numerals placed horizontally on the top of the chart. Classes of offenses are indicated by the Arabic numbers placed vertically on the left side of the chart. Each grid on the chart contains the following components:

(1) A sentence disposition or dispositions: "C" indicates that a community punishment is authorized; "I" indicates that an intermediate punishment is authorized; and "A" indicates that an active punishment is authorized; and

(2) A range of durations for the sentence of imprisonment: any sentence within the duration specified is permitted.

PRIOR CONVICTION LEVELS

MISDEMEANOR

OFFENSE CLASS	LEVEL I	LEVEL II	LEVEL III
	No Prior Convictions	One to Four Prior Convictions	Five or More Prior Convictions

A1 days C/I/A	1-60 days C/I/A	1-75 days C/I/A	1-150
1 days C/I/A	1-45 days C	1-45 days C/I/A	1-120
2 days C/I/A	1-30 days C	1-45 days C/I	1-60
3 days C/I/A.	1-10 days C		1-20
		1-15 days C	
		if one to three prior convictions	
		1-15 days C/I if four prior convictions	

(d)   Fine Only for Certain Class 3 Misdemeanors. - Unless otherwise provided for a specific offense, the judgment for a person convicted of a Class 3 misdemeanor who has no more than three prior convictions shall consist only of a fine. (1993, c. 538, s. 1; 1994, Ex. Sess., c. 24, s. 14(b); 1995, c. 507, s. 19.5(g); 2013-360, s. 18B.13(a).)

§§ 15A-1340.24 through 15A-1340.33. Reserved for future codification purposes.

Article 81C.

Restitution

§ 15A-1340.34. Restitution generally.

(a) When sentencing a defendant convicted of a criminal offense, the court shall determine whether the defendant shall be ordered to make restitution to any victim of the offense in question. For purposes of this Article, the term "victim" means a person directly and proximately harmed as a result of the defendant's commission of the criminal offense.

(b) If the defendant is being sentenced for an offense for which the victim is entitled to restitution under Article 46 of this Chapter, the court shall, in addition to any penalty authorized by law, require that the defendant make restitution to the victim or the victim's estate for any injuries or damages arising directly and proximately out of the offense committed by the defendant. If the defendant is placed on probation or post-release supervision, any restitution ordered under this subsection shall be a condition of probation as provided in G.S. 15A-1343(d) or a condition of post-release supervision as provided in G.S. 148-57.1.

(c) When subsection (b) of this section does not apply, the court may, in addition to any other penalty authorized by law, require that the defendant make restitution to the victim or the victim's estate for any injuries or damages arising directly and proximately out of the offense committed by the defendant. (1998-212, s. 19.4(d).)

§ 15A-1340.35. Basis for restitution.

(a) In determining the amount of restitution, the court shall consider the following:

(1) In the case of an offense resulting in bodily injury to a victim:

a. The cost of necessary medical and related professional services and devices or equipment relating to physical, psychiatric, and psychological care required by the victim;

b. The cost of necessary physical and occupational therapy and rehabilitation required by the victim; and

c. Income lost by the victim as a result of the offense.

(2) In the case of an offense resulting in the damage, loss, or destruction of property of a victim of the offense:

a. Return of the property to the owner of the property or someone designated by the owner; or

b. If return of the property under sub-subdivision (2)a. of this subsection is impossible, impracticable, or inadequate:

1. The value of the property on the date of the damage, loss, or destruction; or

2. The value of the property on the date of sentencing, less the value of any part of the property that is returned.

(3) Any measure of restitution specifically provided by law for the offense committed by the defendant.

(4) In the case of an offense resulting in bodily injury that results in the death of the victim, the cost of the victim's necessary funeral and related services, in addition to the items set out in subdivisions (1), (2), and (3) of this subsection.

(b) The court may require that the victim or the victim's estate provide admissible evidence that documents the costs claimed by the victim or the victim's estate under this section. Any such documentation shall be shared with the defendant before the sentencing hearing. (1998-212, s. 19.4(d).)

§ 15A-1340.36. Determination of restitution.

(a) In determining the amount of restitution to be made, the court shall take into consideration the resources of the defendant including all real and personal property owned by the defendant and the income derived from the property, the defendant's ability to earn, the defendant's obligation to support dependents, and any other matters that pertain to the defendant's ability to make restitution, but the court is not required to make findings of fact or conclusions of law on these matters. The amount of restitution must be limited to that supported by the record, and the court may order partial restitution when it appears that the damage or loss caused by the offense is greater than that which the defendant is able to pay. If the court orders partial restitution, the court shall state on the record the reasons for such an order.

(b) The court may require the defendant to make full restitution no later than a certain date or, if the circumstances warrant, may allow the defendant to make restitution in installments over a specified time period.

(c) When an active sentence is imposed, the court shall consider whether it should recommend to the Secretary of Public Safety that restitution be made by the defendant out of any earnings gained by the defendant if the defendant is granted work-release privileges, as provided in G.S. 148-33.2. The court shall also consider whether it should recommend to the Post-Release Supervision and Parole Commission that restitution by the defendant be made a condition of any parole or post-release supervision granted the defendant, as provided in G.S. 148-57.1. (1998-212, s. 19.4(d); 2011-145, s. 19.1(i).)

§ 15A-1340.37. Effect of restitution order; beneficiaries.

(a) An order providing for restitution does not abridge the right of a victim or the victim's estate to bring a civil action against the defendant for damages arising out of the offense committed by the defendant. Any amount paid by the defendant under the terms of a restitution order under this Article shall be credited against any judgment rendered against the defendant in favor of the same victim in a civil action arising out of the criminal offense committed by the defendant.

(b) The court may order the defendant to make restitution to a person other than the victim, or to any organization, corporation, or association, including the Crime Victims Compensation Fund, that provided assistance to the victim following the commission of the offense by the defendant and is subrogated to the rights of the victim. Restitution shall be made to the victim or the victim's estate before it is made to any other person, organization, corporation, or association under this subsection.

(c) No government agency shall benefit by way of restitution except for particular damage or loss to it over and above its normal operating costs and except that the State may receive restitution for the total amount of a judgment authorized by G.S. 7A-455(b).

(d) No third party shall benefit by way of restitution as a result of the liability of that third party to pay indemnity to an aggrieved party for the damage or loss caused by the defendant, but the liability of a third party to pay indemnity to an aggrieved party or any payment of indemnity actually made by a third party to an aggrieved party does not prohibit or limit in any way the power of the court to require the defendant to make complete and full restitution to the aggrieved party for the total amount of the damage or loss caused by the defendant. (1998-212, s. 19.4(d).)

§ 15A-1340.38. Enforcement of certain orders for restitution.

(a) In addition to the provisions of G.S. 15A-1340.36, when an order for restitution under G.S. 15A-1340.34(b) requires the defendant to pay restitution in an amount in excess of two hundred fifty dollars ($250.00) to a victim, the order may be enforced in the same manner as a civil judgment, subject to the provisions of this section.

(b) The order for restitution under G.S. 15A-1340.34(b) shall be docketed and indexed in the county of the original conviction in the same manner as a civil judgment pursuant to G.S. 1-233, et seq., and may be docketed in any other county pursuant to G.S. 1-234. The judgment may be collected in the same manner as a civil judgment unless the order to pay restitution is a condition of probation. If the order to pay restitution is a condition of probation, the judgment may only be executed upon in accordance with subsection (c) of this section.

(c) If the defendant is ordered to pay restitution under G.S. 15A-1340.34(b) as a condition of probation, a judgment docketed under this section may be collected in the same manner as a civil judgment. However, the docketed judgment for restitution may not be executed upon the property of the defendant until the date of notification to the clerk of superior court in the county of the original conviction that the judge presiding at the probation termination or revocation hearing has made a finding that restitution in a sum certain remains due and payable, that the defendant's probation has been terminated or revoked, and that the remaining balance of restitution owing may be collected by execution on the judgment. The clerk shall then enter upon the judgment docket the amount that remains due and payable on the judgment, together with amounts equal to the standard fees for docketing, copying, certifying, and mailing, as appropriate, and shall collect any other fees or charges incurred as in the enforcement of other civil judgments, including accrued interest. However, no interest shall accrue on the judgment until the entry of an order terminating or revoking probation and finding the amount remaining due and payable, at which time interest shall begin to accrue at the legal rate pursuant to G.S. 24-5. The interest shall be applicable to the amount determined at the termination or revocation hearing to be then due and payable. The clerk shall notify the victim by first-class mail at the victim's last known address that the judgment may be executed upon, together with the amount of the judgment. Until the clerk receives notification of termination or revocation of probation and the amount that remains due and payable on the order of restitution, the clerk shall not be required to update the judgment docket to reflect partial payments on the order of restitution as a condition of probation. The stay of execution under this subsection shall not apply to property of the defendant after the transfer or conveyance of the property to another person. When the criminal order of restitution has been paid in full, the civil judgment indexed under this section shall be deemed satisfied and the judgment shall be cancelled. Payment satisfying the civil judgment shall also be credited against the order of restitution.

(d) An appeal of the conviction upon which the order of restitution is based shall stay execution on the judgment until the appeal is completed. If the conviction is overturned, the judgment shall be cancelled. (1998-212, s. 19.4(d).)

§ 15A-1340.39: Reserved for future codification purposes.

§ 15A-1340.40: Reserved for future codification purposes.

§ 15A-1340.41: Reserved for future codification purposes.

§ 15A-1340.42: Reserved for future codification purposes.

§ 15A-1340.43: Reserved for future codification purposes.

§ 15A-1340.44: Reserved for future codification purposes.

§ 15A-1340.45: Reserved for future codification purposes.

§ 15A-1340.46: Reserved for future codification purposes.

§ 15A-1340.47: Reserved for future codification purposes.

§ 15A-1340.48: Reserved for future codification purposes.

§ 15A-1340.49: Reserved for future codification purposes.

Article 81D.

Permanent No Contact Order Against Convicted Sex Offender.

§ 15A-1340.50. Permanent no contact order prohibiting future contact by convicted sex offender with crime victim.

(a) The following definitions apply in this Article:

(1) Permanent no contact order. - A permanent injunction that prohibits any contact by a defendant with the victim of the sex offense for which the defendant is convicted. The duration of the injunction is the lifetime of the defendant.

(2) Sex offense. - Any criminal offense that requires registration under Article 27A of Chapter 14 of the General Statutes.

(3) Victim. - The person against whom the sex offense was committed.

(b) When sentencing a defendant convicted of a sex offense, the judge, at the request of the district attorney, shall determine whether to issue a permanent no contact order. The judge shall order the defendant to show cause why a permanent no contact order shall not be issued and shall hold a show cause hearing as part of the sentencing procedures for the defendant.

(c) The victim shall have a right to be heard at the show cause hearing.

(d) The judge sentencing the defendant is the trier of fact regarding the show cause hearing.

(e) At the conclusion of the show cause hearing the judge shall enter a finding for or against the defendant. If the judge determines that reasonable grounds exist for the victim to fear any future contact with the defendant, the judge shall issue the permanent no contact order. The judge shall enter written findings of fact and the grounds on which the permanent no contact order is issued. The no contact order shall be incorporated into the judgment imposing the sentence on the defendant for the conviction of the sex offense.

(f) The court may grant one or more of the following forms of relief in a permanent no contact order under this Article:

(1) Order the defendant not to threaten, visit, assault, molest, or otherwise interfere with the victim.

(2) Order the defendant not to follow the victim, including at the victim's workplace.

(3) Order the defendant not to harass the victim.

(4) Order the defendant not to abuse or injure the victim.

(5) Order the defendant not to contact the victim by telephone, written communication, or electronic means.

(6) Order the defendant to refrain from entering or remaining present at the victim's residence, school, place of employment, or other specified places at times when the victim is present.

(7) Order other relief deemed necessary and appropriate by the court.

(g) A permanent no contact order entered pursuant to this Article shall be enforced by all North Carolina law enforcement agencies without further order of the court. A law enforcement officer shall arrest and take a person into custody, with or without a warrant or other process, if the officer has probable cause to believe that the person knowingly has violated a permanent no contact order. A person who knowingly violates a permanent no contact order is guilty of a Class A1 misdemeanor.

(h) At any time after the issuance of the order, the State, at the request of the victim, or the defendant may make a motion to rescind the permanent no contact order. If the court determines that reasonable grounds for the victim to fear any future contact with the defendant no longer exist, the court may rescind the permanent no contact order.

(i) The remedy provided by this Article is not exclusive but is in addition to other remedies provided under law. (2009-380, s. 1)

Article 82.

Probation.

§ 15A-1341. Probation generally.

(a) Use of Probation. - Unless specifically prohibited, a person who has been convicted of any criminal offense may be placed on probation as provided by this Article if the class of offense of which the person is convicted and the person's prior record or conviction level under Article 81B of this Chapter authorizes a community or intermediate punishment as a type of sentence disposition or if the person is convicted of impaired driving under G.S. 20-138.1.

(a1) Deferred Prosecution. - A person who has been charged with a Class H or I felony or a misdemeanor may be placed on probation as provided in this Article on motion of the defendant and the prosecutor if the court finds each of the following facts:

(1) Prosecution has been deferred by the prosecutor pursuant to written agreement with the defendant, with the approval of the court, for the purpose of allowing the defendant to demonstrate his good conduct.

(2) Each known victim of the crime has been notified of the motion for probation by subpoena or certified mail and has been given an opportunity to be heard.

(3) The defendant has not been convicted of any felony or of any misdemeanor involving moral turpitude.

(4) The defendant has not previously been placed on probation and so states under oath.

(5) The defendant is unlikely to commit another offense other than a Class 3 misdemeanor.

(a2) Deferred Prosecution for Purpose of Drug Treatment Court Program. - A defendant eligible for a Drug Treatment Court Program pursuant to Article 62 of Chapter 7A of the General Statutes may be placed on probation if the court finds that prosecution has been deferred by the prosecutor, with the approval of the court, pursuant to a written agreement with the defendant, for the purpose of allowing the defendant to participate in and successfully complete the Drug Treatment Court Program.

(a3) Deferred Prosecution for Prostitution. - A defendant whose prosecution is deferred pursuant to G.S. 14-204(c) may be placed on probation as provided in this Article.

(b) Supervised and Unsupervised Probation. - The court may place a person on supervised or unsupervised probation. A person on unsupervised probation is subject to all incidents of probation except supervision by or assignment to a probation officer.

(c) Repealed by Session Laws 1995, c. 429, s. 1.

(d) Search of Sex Offender Registration Information Required When Placing a Defendant on Probation. - When the court places a defendant on probation, the probation officer assigned to the defendant shall conduct a search of the defendant's name or other identifying information against the registration information regarding sex offenders compiled by the Division of Criminal Statistics of the Department of Justice in accordance with Article 27A of Chapter 14 of the General Statutes. The probation officer may conduct the search using the Internet site maintained by the Division of Criminal Statistics.

(e) Review of Defendant's Juvenile Record. - The probation officer assigned to a defendant may examine and obtain copies of the defendant's juvenile record in a manner consistent with G.S. 7B-3000(b) and (e1). (1977, c. 711, s. 1; 1977, 2nd Sess., c. 1147, ss. 4A, 5; 1981, c. 377, ss. 2, 3; 1993, c. 538, s. 15; 1994, Ex. Sess., c. 24, s. 14(b); 1995, c. 429, s. 1; 1999-298, s. 1; 2006-247, s. 14; 2009-372, s. 4; 2013-368, s. 7.)

§ 15A-1342. Incidents of probation.

(a) Period. - The court may place a convicted offender on probation for the appropriate period as specified in G.S. 15A-1343.2(d), not to exceed a maximum of five years. The court may place a defendant as to whom prosecution has been deferred on probation for a maximum of two years. The probation remains conditional and subject to revocation during the period of probation imposed, unless terminated as provided in subsection (b) or G.S. 15A-1341(c).

Extension. - In addition to G.S. 15A-1344, the court with the consent of the defendant may extend the period of probation beyond the original period (i) for the purpose of allowing the defendant to complete a program of restitution, or (ii) to allow the defendant to continue medical or psychiatric treatment ordered as a condition of the probation. The period of extension shall not exceed three years beyond the original period of probation. The special extension authorized herein may be ordered only in the last six months of the original period of probation. Any probationary judgment form provided to a defendant on supervised probation shall state that probation may be extended pursuant to this subsection.

(a1) Supervision of Defendants on Deferred Prosecution. - The Section of Community Corrections of the Division of Adult Correction of the Department of Public Safety may be ordered by the court to supervise an offender's compliance with the terms of a deferred prosecution agreement entered into under G.S. 15A-1341(a1) or (a3). Violations of the terms of the agreement shall be reported to the court as provided in this Article and to the district attorney in the district in which the agreement was entered.

(b) Early Termination. - The court may terminate a period of probation and discharge the defendant at any time earlier than that provided in subsection (a) if warranted by the conduct of the defendant and the ends of justice.

(c) Conditions; Suspended Sentence. - When the court places a convicted offender on probation, it must determine conditions of probation as provided in G.S. 15A-1343. In addition, it must impose a suspended sentence of imprisonment, determined as provided in Article 83, Imprisonment, which may be activated upon violation of conditions of probation.

(d) Mandatory Review of Probation. - Each probation officer must bring the cases of each probationer assigned to him before a court with jurisdiction to review the probation when the probationer has served three years of a probationary period greater than three years. The probation officer must give reasonable notice to the probationer, and the probationer may appear. The court must review the case file of a probationer so brought before it and determine whether to terminate his probation.

(e) Out-of-State Supervision. - Supervised probationers are subject to out-of-State supervision under the provisions of Article 4B of Chapter 148 of the General Statutes.

(f) Appeal from Judgment of Probation. - A defendant may seek post-trial relief from a judgment which includes probation notwithstanding the authority of the court to modify or revoke the probation.

(g) Invalid Conditions; Timing of Objection. - The regular conditions of probation imposed pursuant to G.S. 15A-1343(b) are in every circumstance valid conditions of probation. A court may not revoke probation for violation of an invalid condition imposed pursuant to G.S. 15A-1343(b1). The failure of a defendant to object to a condition of probation imposed pursuant to G.S. 15A-1343(b1) at the time such a condition is imposed does not constitute a waiver of the right to object at a later time to the condition.

(h) Limitation on Jurisdiction to Alter or Revoke Unsupervised Probation. - In the judgment placing a person on unsupervised probation, the judge may limit jurisdiction to alter or revoke the sentence under G.S. 15A-1344. When jurisdiction to alter or revoke is limited, the effect is as provided in G.S. 15A-1344(b).

(i) Immunity from Prosecution upon Compliance. - Upon the expiration or early termination as provided in subsection (b) of a period of probation imposed after deferral of prosecution and before conviction, the defendant shall be immune from prosecution of the charges deferred.

(j) Immunity for Injury to Defendant Performing Community Service. - Immunity from liability for injury to a defendant performing community service shall be as set forth in G.S. 143B-708(d). (1977, c. 711, s. 1; 1977, 2nd Sess., c. 1147, ss. 6, 7; 1981, c. 377, ss. 4-6; 1983, c. 435, s. 5.1; c. 561, s. 7; 1985 (Reg. Sess., 1986), c. 960, s. 1; 1993, c. 84, s. 1; 1993 (Reg. Sess., 1994), c. 767, s. 6; 1995, c. 330, s. 1; 2008-129, s. 3; 2009-372, s. 10; 2010-96, s. 5; 2011-145, s. 19.1(h), (k), (ee); 2013-368, s. 8.)

§ 15A-1343. Conditions of probation.

(a) In General. - The court may impose conditions of probation reasonably necessary to insure that the defendant will lead a law-abiding life or to assist him to do so.

(a1) Community and Intermediate Probation Conditions. - In addition to any conditions a court may be authorized to impose pursuant to G.S. 15A-1343(b1), the court may include any one or more of the following conditions as part of a community or intermediate punishment:

(1)   House arrest with electronic monitoring.

(2)   Perform community service and pay the fee prescribed by law for this supervision.

(3)   Submission to a period or periods of confinement in a local confinement facility for a total of no more than six days per month during any three separate months during the period of probation. The six days per month confinement provided for in this subdivision may only be imposed as two-day or three-day consecutive periods. When a defendant is on probation for multiple judgments, confinement periods imposed under this subdivision shall run concurrently and may total no more than six days per month.

(4)   Substance abuse assessment, monitoring, or treatment.

(4a)   Abstain from alcohol consumption and submit to continuous alcohol monitoring when alcohol dependency or chronic abuse has been identified by a substance abuse assessment.

(5)   Participation in an educational or vocational skills development program, including an evidence-based program.

(6)   Submission to satellite-based monitoring, pursuant to Part 5 of Article 27A of Chapter 14 of the General Statutes, if the defendant is described by G.S. 14-208.40(a)(2).

(b)   Regular Conditions. - As regular conditions of probation, a defendant must:

(1)   Commit no criminal offense in any jurisdiction.

(2)   Remain within the jurisdiction of the court unless granted written permission to leave by the court or his probation officer.

(3)   Report as directed by the court or his probation officer to the officer at reasonable times and places and in a reasonable manner, permit the officer to visit him at reasonable times, answer all reasonable inquiries by the officer and

obtain prior approval from the officer for, and notify the officer of, any change in address or employment.

(3a) Not abscond by willfully avoiding supervision or by willfully making the defendant's whereabouts unknown to the supervising probation officer, if the defendant is placed on supervised probation.

(4) Satisfy child support and other family obligations as required by the court. If the court requires the payment of child support, the amount of the payments shall be determined as provided in G.S. 50-13.4(c).

(5) Possess no firearm, explosive device or other deadly weapon listed in G.S. 14-269 without the written permission of the court.

(6) Pay a supervision fee as specified in subsection (c1).

(7) Remain gainfully and suitably employed or faithfully pursue a course of study or of vocational training that will equip him for suitable employment. A defendant pursuing a course of study or of vocational training shall abide by all of the rules of the institution providing the education or training, and the probation officer shall forward a copy of the probation judgment to that institution and request to be notified of any violations of institutional rules by the defendant.

(8) Notify the probation officer if he fails to obtain or retain satisfactory employment.

(9) Pay the costs of court, any fine ordered by the court, and make restitution or reparation as provided in subsection (d).

(10) Pay the State of North Carolina for the costs of appointed counsel, public defender, or appellate defender to represent him in the case(s) for which he was placed on probation.

(11) Repealed by Session Laws 2011-62, s. 1, as amended by Session Laws 2011-412, s. 2.2, effective December 1, 2011, and applicable to offenses committed on or after December 1, 2011.

(12) Attend and complete an abuser treatment program if (i) the court finds the defendant is responsible for acts of domestic violence and (ii) there is a program, approved by the Domestic Violence Commission, reasonably available

to the defendant, unless the court finds that such would not be in the best interests of justice. A defendant attending an abuser treatment program shall abide by all of the rules of the program.

a. If the defendant is placed on supervised probation, the following procedures apply:

1. The probation officer shall forward a copy of the judgment, including all conditions of probation, to the abuser treatment program.

2. The program shall notify the probation officer if the defendant fails to participate in the program or if the defendant is discharged from the program for violating any of the program rules.

3. If the defendant fails to participate in the program or is discharged from the program for failure to comply with the program or its rules, the probation officer shall file a violation report with the court and notify the district attorney of such noncompliance.

b. If the defendant is placed on unsupervised probation, the following procedures apply:

1. The defendant shall be required to notify the district attorney and the abuser treatment program of their choice of program within 10 days of the judgment if the program has not previously been selected.

2. The district attorney shall forward a copy of the judgment, including all conditions of probation, to the abuser treatment program.

3. If the defendant fails to participate in the program or is discharged from the program for failure to comply with the program or its rules, the program shall notify the district attorney of such noncompliance.

(13) Submit at reasonable times to warrantless searches by a probation officer of the probationer's person and of the probationer's vehicle and premises while the probationer is present, for purposes directly related to the probation supervision, but the probationer may not be required to submit to any other search that would otherwise be unlawful.

(14) Submit to warrantless searches by a law enforcement officer of the probationer's person and of the probationer's vehicle, upon a reasonable

suspicion that the probationer is engaged in criminal activity or is in possession of a firearm, explosive device, or other deadly weapon listed in G.S. 14-269 without written permission of the court.

(15)   Not use, possess, or control any illegal drug or controlled substance unless it has been prescribed for him or her by a licensed physician and is in the original container with the prescription number affixed on it; not knowingly associate with any known or previously convicted users, possessors, or sellers of any such illegal drugs or controlled substances; and not knowingly be present at or frequent any place where such illegal drugs or controlled substances are sold, kept, or used.

(16)   Supply a breath, urine, or blood specimen for analysis of the possible presence of prohibited drugs or alcohol when instructed by the defendant's probation officer for purposes directly related to the probation supervision. If the results of the analysis are positive, the probationer may be required to reimburse the Division of Adult Correction of the Department of Public Safety for the actual costs of drug or alcohol screening and testing.

In addition to these regular conditions of probation, a defendant required to serve an active term of imprisonment as a condition of special probation pursuant to G.S. 15A-1344(e) or G.S. 15A-1351(a) shall, as additional regular conditions of probation, obey the rules and regulations of the Division of Adult Correction of the Department of Public Safety governing the conduct of inmates while imprisoned and report to a probation officer in the State of North Carolina within 72 hours of his discharge from the active term of imprisonment.

Regular conditions of probation apply to each defendant placed on supervised probation unless the presiding judge specifically exempts the defendant from one or more of the conditions in open court and in the judgment of the court. It is not necessary for the presiding judge to state each regular condition of probation in open court, but the conditions must be set forth in the judgment of the court.

Defendants placed on unsupervised probation are subject to the provisions of this subsection, except that defendants placed on unsupervised probation are not subject to the regular conditions contained in subdivisions (2), (3), (6), (8), (13), (14), and (15) of this subsection.

(b1)   Special Conditions. - In addition to the regular conditions of probation specified in subsection (b), the court may, as a condition of probation, require that during the probation the defendant comply with one or more of the following special conditions:

(1) Undergo available medical or psychiatric treatment and remain in a specified institution if required for that purpose. Notwithstanding the provisions of G.S. 15A-1344(e) or any other provision of law, the defendant may be required to participate in such treatment for its duration regardless of the length of the suspended sentence imposed.

(2) Attend or reside in a facility providing rehabilitation, counseling, treatment, social skills, or employment training, instruction, recreation, or residence for persons on probation.

(2a) Repealed by Session Laws 2002, ch. 126, s. 17.18, effective August 15, 2002.

(2b) Participate in and successfully complete a Drug Treatment Court Program pursuant to Article 62 of Chapter 7A of the General Statutes.

(2c) Abstain from alcohol consumption and submit to continuous alcohol monitoring when alcohol dependency or chronic abuse has been identified by a substance abuse assessment.

(3) Submit to imprisonment required for special probation under G.S. 15A-1351(a) or G.S. 15A-1344(e).

(3a) Repealed by Session Laws 1997-57, s. 3.

(3b) Repealed by Session Laws 2011-192, s. 1(g), effective December 1, 2011.

(3c) Remain at his or her residence. The court, in the sentencing order, may authorize the offender to leave the offender's residence for employment, counseling, a course of study, vocational training, or other specific purposes and may modify that authorization. The probation officer may authorize the offender to leave the offender's residence for specific purposes not authorized in the court order upon approval of the probation officer's supervisor. The offender shall be required to wear a device which permits the supervising agency to monitor the offender's compliance with the condition electronically and to pay a fee for the device as specified in subsection (c2) of this section.

(4) Surrender his or her driver's license to the clerk of superior court, and not operate a motor vehicle for a period specified by the court.

(5) Compensate the Department of Environment and Natural Resources or the North Carolina Wildlife Resources Commission, as the case may be, for the replacement costs of any marine and estuarine resources or any wildlife resources which were taken, injured, removed, harmfully altered, damaged or destroyed as a result of a criminal offense of which the defendant was convicted. If any investigation is required by officers or agents of the Department of Environment and Natural Resources or the Wildlife Resources Commission in determining the extent of the destruction of resources involved, the court may include compensation of the agency for investigative costs as a condition of probation. The court may also include, as a condition of probation, compensation of an agency for any reward paid for information leading to the arrest and conviction of the offender. This subdivision does not apply in any case governed by G.S. 143-215.3(a)(7).

(6) Perform community or reparation service under the supervision of the Section of Community Corrections of the Division of Adult Correction and pay the fee required by G.S. 143B-708.

(7), (8) Repealed by Session Laws 2009-372, s. 9(b), effective December 1, 2009, and applicable to offenses committed on or after that date.

(8a) Purchase the least expensive annual statewide license or combination of licenses to hunt, trap, or fish listed in G.S. 113-270.2, 113-270.3, 113-270.5, 113-271, 113-272, and 113-272.2 that would be required to engage lawfully in the specific activity or activities in which the defendant was engaged and which constitute the basis of the offense or offenses of which he was convicted.

(9) If the offense is one in which there is evidence of physical, mental or sexual abuse of a minor, the court should encourage the minor and the minor's parents or custodians to participate in rehabilitative treatment and may order the defendant to pay the cost of such treatment.

(9a) Repealed by Session Laws 2004-186, s. 1.1, effective December 1, 2004, and applicable to offenses committed on or after that date.

(9b) Any or all of the following conditions relating to street gangs as defined in G.S. 14-50.16(b):

a. Not knowingly associate with any known street gang members and not knowingly be present at or frequent any place or location where street gangs gather or where street gang activity is known to occur.

b. Not wear clothes, jewelry, signs, symbols, or any paraphernalia readily identifiable as associated with or used by a street gang.

c. Not initiate or participate in any contact with any individual who was or may be a witness against or victim of the defendant or the defendant's street gang.

(9c) Participate in any Project Safe Neighborhood activities as directed by the probation officer.

(10) Satisfy any other conditions determined by the court to be reasonably related to his rehabilitation.

(b2) Special Conditions of Probation for Sex Offenders and Persons Convicted of Offenses Involving Physical, Mental, or Sexual Abuse of a Minor. - As special conditions of probation, a defendant who has been convicted of an offense which is a reportable conviction as defined in G.S. 14-208.6(4), or which involves the physical, mental, or sexual abuse of a minor, must:

(1) Register as required by G.S. 14-208.7 if the offense is a reportable conviction as defined by G.S. 14-208.6(4).

(2) Participate in such evaluation and treatment as is necessary to complete a prescribed course of psychiatric, psychological, or other rehabilitative treatment as ordered by the court.

(3) Not communicate with, be in the presence of, or found in or on the premises of the victim of the offense.

(4) Not reside in a household with any minor child if the offense is one in which there is evidence of sexual abuse of a minor.

(5) Not reside in a household with any minor child if the offense is one in which there is evidence of physical or mental abuse of a minor, unless the court expressly finds that it is unlikely that the defendant's harmful or abusive conduct will recur and that it would be in the minor child's best interest to allow the probationer to reside in the same household with a minor child.

(6) Satisfy any other conditions determined by the court to be reasonably related to his rehabilitation.

(7) Submit to satellite-based monitoring pursuant to Part 5 of Article 27A of Chapter 14 of the General Statutes, if the defendant is described by G.S. 14-208.40(a)(1).

(8) Submit to satellite-based monitoring pursuant to Part 5 of Article 27A of Chapter 14 of the General Statutes, if the defendant is in the category described by G.S. 14-208.40(a)(2), and the Division of Adult Correction of the Department of Public Safety, based on the Division's risk assessment program, recommends that the defendant submit to the highest possible level of supervision and monitoring.

(9) Submit at reasonable times to warrantless searches by a probation officer of the probationer's person and of the probationer's vehicle and premises while the probationer is present, for purposes specified by the court and reasonably related to the probation supervision, but the probationer may not be required to submit to any other search that would otherwise be unlawful. For purposes of this subdivision, warrantless searches of the probationer's computer or other electronic mechanism which may contain electronic data shall be considered reasonably related to the probation supervision. Whenever the warrantless search consists of testing for the presence of illegal drugs, the probationer may also be required to reimburse the Division of Adult Correction of the Department of Public Safety for the actual cost of drug screening and drug testing, if the results are positive.

Defendants subject to the provisions of this subsection shall not be placed on unsupervised probation.

(b3) Screening and Assessing for Chemical Dependency. - A defendant ordered to submit to a period of residential treatment in the Drug Alcohol Recovery Treatment program (DART) or the Black Mountain Substance Abuse Treatment Center for Women operated by the Division of Adult Correction of the Department of Public Safety must undergo a screening to determine chemical dependency. If the screening indicates the defendant is chemically dependent, the court shall order an assessment to determine the appropriate level of treatment. The assessment may be conducted either before or after the court imposes the condition, but participation in the program shall be based on the results of the assessment.

(b4) Intermediate Conditions. - The following conditions of probation apply to each defendant subject to intermediate punishment:

(1) If required in the discretion of the defendant's probation officer, perform community service under the supervision of the Section of Community Corrections of the Division of Adult Correction and pay the fee required by G.S. 143B-708.

(2) Not use, possess, or control alcohol.

(3) Remain within the county of residence unless granted written permission to leave by the court or the defendant's probation officer.

(4) Participate in any evaluation, counseling, treatment, or educational program as directed by the probation officer, keeping all appointments and abiding by the rules, regulations, and direction of each program.

These conditions apply to each defendant subject to intermediate punishment unless the court specifically exempts the defendant from one or more of the conditions in its judgment or order. It is not necessary for the presiding judge to state each of these conditions in open court, but the conditions must be set forth in the judgment or order of the court.

(c) Statement of Conditions. - A defendant released on supervised probation must be given a written statement explicitly setting forth the conditions on which he is being released. If any modification of the terms of that probation is subsequently made, he must be given a written statement setting forth the modifications.

(c1) Supervision Fee. - Any person placed on supervised probation pursuant to subsection (a) of this section shall pay a supervision fee of forty dollars ($40.00) per month, unless exempted by the court. The court may exempt a person from paying the fee only for good cause and upon motion of the person placed on supervised probation. No person shall be required to pay more than one supervision fee per month. The court may require that the fee be paid in advance or in a lump sum or sums, and a probation officer may require payment by such methods if he is authorized by subsection (g) to determine the payment schedule. Supervision fees must be paid to the clerk of court for the county in which the judgment was entered or the deferred prosecution agreement was filed. Fees collected under this subsection shall be transmitted to the State for deposit into the State's General Fund.

(c2) Electronic Monitoring Device Fees. - Any person placed on house arrest with electronic monitoring under subsection (a1) or (b1) of this section shall pay a fee of ninety dollars ($90.00) for the electronic monitoring device and a daily fee in an amount that reflects the actual cost of providing the electronic monitoring. The court may exempt a person from paying the fees only for good cause and upon motion of the person placed on house arrest with electronic monitoring. The court may require that the fees be paid in advance or in a lump sum or sums, and a probation officer may require payment by those methods if the officer is authorized by subsection (g) of this section to determine the payment schedule. The fees must be paid to the clerk of court for the county in which the judgment was entered or the deferred prosecution agreement was filed. Fees collected under this subsection for the electronic monitoring device shall be transmitted to the State for deposit into the State's General Fund. The daily fees collected under this subsection shall be remitted to the Department of Public Safety to cover the costs of providing the electronic monitoring.

(d) Restitution as a Condition of Probation. - As a condition of probation, a defendant may be required to make restitution or reparation to an aggrieved party or parties who shall be named by the court for the damage or loss caused by the defendant arising out of the offense or offenses committed by the defendant. When restitution or reparation is a condition imposed, the court shall take into consideration the factors set out in G.S. 15A-1340.35 and G.S. 15A-1340.36. As used herein, "reparation" shall include but not be limited to the performing of community services, volunteer work, or doing such other acts or things as shall aid the defendant in his rehabilitation. As used herein "aggrieved party" includes individuals, firms, corporations, associations, other organizations, and government agencies, whether federal, State or local, including the Crime Victims Compensation Fund established by G.S. 15B-23. A government agency may benefit by way of reparation even though the agency was not a party to the crime provided that when reparation is ordered, community service work shall be rendered only after approval has been granted by the owner or person in charge of the property or premises where the work will be done.

(e) Costs of Court and Appointed Counsel. - Unless the court finds there are extenuating circumstances, any person placed upon supervised or unsupervised probation under the terms set forth by the court shall, as a condition of probation, be required to pay all court costs and all fees and costs for appointed counsel, public defender, or counsel employed by or under contract with the Office of Indigent Defense Services in the case in which the person was convicted. The fees and costs for appointed counsel, public defender, or other counsel services shall be determined in accordance with rules adopted by the Office of Indigent Defense Services. The court shall determine the amount of those costs and fees to be repaid and the method of payment.

(f) Repealed by Session Laws 1983, c. 561, s. 5.

(g) Probation Officer May Determine Payment Schedules and May Transfer Low-Risk Misdemeanants to Unsupervised Probation. - If a person placed on supervised probation is required as a condition of that probation to pay any moneys to the clerk of superior court, the court may delegate to a probation officer the responsibility to determine the payment schedule. The court may also authorize the probation officer to transfer the person to unsupervised probation after all the moneys are paid to the clerk. If the probation officer transfers a person to unsupervised probation, he must notify the clerk of that action. In addition, a probation officer may transfer a misdemeanant from supervised to unsupervised probation if the misdemeanant is not subject to any special conditions and was placed on probation solely for the collection of court-ordered payments, and the risk assessment shows the misdemeanant to be a low-risk offender; however, such a transfer to unsupervised probation does not relieve the misdemeanant of the obligation to continue making court-ordered payments under the terms of the misdemeanant's probation. (1977, c. 711, s. 1; 1977, 2nd Sess., c. 1147, ss. 8-10; 1979, c. 662, s. 1; c. 801, s. 3; c. 830, s. 12; 1981, c. 530, ss. 1, 2; 1983, c. 135, s. 1; c. 561, ss. 1-6; c. 567, s. 2; c. 712, s. 1; 1983 (Reg. Sess., 1984), c. 972, ss. 1, 2; 1985, c. 474, ss. 1, 7, 8; 1985 (Reg. Sess., 1986), c. 859, ss. 1, 2; 1987, c. 282, s. 33; c. 397, s. 1; c. 579, ss. 1, 2; c. 598, s. 1; c. 819, s. 32; c. 830, s. 17; 1989, c. 529, s. 5; c. 727, s. 218(4); 1989 (Reg. Sess., 1990), c. 1010, s. 1; c. 1034, s. 1; 1991 (Reg. Sess., 1992), c. 1000, s. 1; 1993, c. 538, s. 16; 1994, Ex. Sess., c. 9, s. 1; c. 24, s. 14(b); 1996, 2nd Ex. Sess., c. 18, s. 20.14(c); 1997-57, s. 3; 1997-443, ss. 11A.119(a), 19.11(a); 1998-212, ss. 17.21(a), 19.4(f); 1999-298, s. 2; 2000-125, s. 8; 2000-144, s. 31; 2002-105, s. 3; 2002-126, ss. 17.18(a), 29A.2(a); 2003-141, s. 1; 2004-186, s. 1.1; 2005-250, s. 4; 2005-276, ss. 17.29, 43.1(f), 43.2(a); 2006-247, s. 15(b); 2007-213, s. 7; 2009-275, s. 1; 2009-372, s. 9(a)-(c); 2009-547, s. 7; 2010-31, s. 19.3(a); 2010-96, s. 28(a), (b); 2011-62, ss. 1, 2; 2011-145, s. 19.1(h), (k); 2011-192, s. 1(c), (g), 4(a); 2011-254, ss. 1, 2; 2011-412, ss. 2.1, 2.2, 2.3(a), 2.5; 2012-39, s. 1; 2012-146, ss. 3-5; 2012-188, s. 3; 2013-101, s. 1; 2013-123, s. 1; 2013-360, s. 16C.16(a); 2013-363, ss. 6.7(a), (c); 2013-380, s. 2.)

§ 15A-1343.1: Repealed by Session Laws 2002-126, s. 17.18, effective August 15, 2002.

§ 15A-1343.2. Special probation rules for persons sentenced under Article 81B.

(a) Applicability. - This section applies only to persons sentenced under Article 81B of this Chapter.

(b) Purposes of Probation for Community and Intermediate Punishments. - The Division of Adult Correction of the Department of Public Safety shall develop a plan to handle offenders sentenced to community and intermediate punishments. The probation program designed to handle these offenders shall have the following principal purposes: to hold offenders accountable for making restitution, to ensure compliance with the court's judgment, to effectively rehabilitate offenders by directing them to specialized treatment or education programs, and to protect the public safety.

(b1) Departmental Risk Assessment by Validated Instrument Required. - As part of the probation program developed by the Division of Adult Correction of the Department of Public Safety pursuant to subsection (b) of this section, the Division of Adult Correction of the Department of Public Safety shall use a validated instrument to assess each probationer for risk of reoffending and shall place a probationer in a supervision level based on the probationer's risk of reoffending and criminogenic needs.

(c) Probation Caseload Goals. - It is the goal of the General Assembly that, subject to the availability of funds, caseloads for probation officers supervising persons who are determined to be high or moderate risk of rearrest as determined by the Division's validated risk assessment should not exceed an average of 60 offenders per officer.

(d) Lengths of Probation Terms Under Structured Sentencing. - Unless the court makes specific findings that longer or shorter periods of probation are necessary, the length of the original period of probation for offenders sentenced under Article 81B shall be as follows:

(1) For misdemeanants sentenced to community punishment, not less than six nor more than 18 months;

(2) For misdemeanants sentenced to intermediate punishment, not less than 12 nor more than 24 months;

(3) For felons sentenced to community punishment, not less than 12 nor more than 30 months; and

(4) For felons sentenced to intermediate punishment, not less than 18 nor more than 36 months.

If the court finds at the time of sentencing that a longer period of probation is necessary, that period may not exceed a maximum of five years, as specified in G.S. 15A-1342 and G.S. 15A-1351.

Extension. - The court may with the consent of the offender extend the original period of the probation if necessary to complete a program of restitution or to complete medical or psychiatric treatment ordered as a condition of probation. This extension may be for no more than three years, and may only be ordered in the last six months of the original period of probation.

(e) Delegation to Probation Officer in Community Punishment. - Unless the presiding judge specifically finds in the judgment of the court that delegation is not appropriate, the Section of Community Corrections of the Division of Adult Correction of the Department of Public Safety may require an offender sentenced to community punishment to do any of the following:

(1) Perform up to 20 hours of community service, and pay the fee prescribed by law for this supervision.

(2) Report to the offender's probation officer on a frequency to be determined by the officer.

(3) Submit to substance abuse assessment, monitoring or treatment.

(4) Submit to house arrest with electronic monitoring.

(5) Submit to a period or periods of confinement in a local confinement facility for a total of no more than six days per month during any three separate months during the period of probation. The six days per month confinement provided for in this subdivision may only be imposed as two-day or three-day consecutive periods. When a defendant is on probation for multiple judgments,

confinement periods imposed under this subdivision shall run concurrently and may total no more than six days per month.

(6)   Submit to a curfew which requires the offender to remain in a specified place for a specified period each day and wear a device that permits the offender's compliance with the condition to be monitored electronically.

(7)   Participate in an educational or vocational skills development program, including an evidence-based program.

If the Section imposes any of the above requirements, then it may subsequently reduce or remove those same requirements.

The probation officer may exercise authority delegated to him or her by the court pursuant to subsection (e) of this section after administrative review and approval by a Chief Probation Officer. The offender may file a motion with the court to review the action taken by the probation officer. The offender shall be given notice of the right to seek such a court review. However, the offender shall have no right of review if he or she has signed a written waiver of rights as required by this subsection. The Section may exercise any authority delegated to it under this subsection only if it first determines that the offender has failed to comply with one or more of the conditions of probation imposed by the court or the offender is determined to be high risk based on the results of the risk assessment in G.S. 15A-1343.2, except that the condition at subdivision (5) of this subsection may not be imposed unless the Section determines that the offender failed to comply with one or more of the conditions imposed by the court. Nothing in this section shall be construed to limit the availability of the procedures authorized under G.S. 15A-1345.

The Division shall adopt guidelines and procedures to implement the requirements of this section, which shall include a supervisor's approval prior to exercise of the delegation of authority authorized by this section. Prior to imposing confinement pursuant to subdivision (5) of this subsection, the probationer must first be presented with a violation report, with the alleged violations noted and advised of the right (i) to a hearing before the court on the alleged violation, with the right to present relevant oral and written evidence; (ii) to have counsel at the hearing, and that one will be appointed if the probationer is indigent; (iii) to request witnesses who have relevant information concerning the alleged violations; and (iv) to examine any witnesses or evidence. The probationer may be confined for the period designated on the violation report upon the execution of a waiver of rights signed by the probationer and by two officers acting as witnesses. Those two witnesses shall be the probation officer and another officer to be designated by the Chief of the Community Corrections Section in written Division policy.

(f) Delegation to Probation Officer in Intermediate Punishments. - Unless the presiding judge specifically finds in the judgment of the court that delegation is not appropriate, the Section of Community Corrections of the Division of Adult Correction of the Department of Public Safety may require an offender sentenced to intermediate punishment to do any of the following:

(1) Perform up to 50 hours of community service, and pay the fee prescribed by law for this supervision.

(2) Submit to a curfew which requires the offender to remain in a specified place for a specified period each day and wear a device that permits the offender's compliance with the condition to be monitored electronically.

(3) Submit to substance abuse assessment, monitoring or treatment, including continuous alcohol monitoring when abstinence from alcohol consumption has been specified as a term of probation.

(4) Participate in an educational or vocational skills development program, including an evidence-based program.

(5) Submit to satellite-based monitoring pursuant to Part 5 of Article 27A of Chapter 14 of the General Statutes, if the defendant is described by G.S. 14-208.40(a)(2).

(6) Submit to a period or periods of confinement in a local confinement facility for a total of no more than six days per month during any three separate months during the period of probation. The six days per month confinement provided for in this subdivision may only be imposed as two-day or three-day consecutive periods. When a defendant is on probation for multiple judgments, confinement periods imposed under this subdivision shall run concurrently and may total no more than six days per month.

(7) Submit to house arrest with electronic monitoring.

(8) Report to the offender's probation officer on a frequency to be determined by the officer.

If the Section imposes any of the above requirements, then it may subsequently reduce or remove those same requirements.

The probation officer may exercise authority delegated to him or her by the court pursuant to subsection (f) of this section after administrative review and approval by a Chief Probation Officer. The offender may file a motion with the court to review the action taken by the probation officer. The offender shall be given notice of the right to seek such a court review. However, the offender shall have no right of review if he or she has signed a written waiver of rights as required by this subsection. The Section may exercise any authority delegated to it under this subsection only if it first determines that the offender has failed to comply with one or more of the conditions of probation imposed by the court or the offender is determined to be high risk based on the results of the risk assessment in G.S. 15A-1343.2, except that the condition at subdivision (6) of this subsection may not be imposed unless the Section determines that the offender failed to comply with one or more of the conditions imposed by the court. Nothing in this section shall be construed to limit the availability of the procedures authorized under G.S. 15A-1345.

The Division shall adopt guidelines and procedures to implement the requirements of this section, which shall include a supervisor's approval prior to exercise of the delegation of authority authorized by this section. Prior to imposing confinement pursuant to subdivision (6) of this subsection, the probationer must first be presented with a violation report, with the alleged violations noted and advised of the right (i) to a hearing before the court on the alleged violation, with the right to present relevant oral and written evidence; (ii) to have counsel at the hearing, and that one will be appointed if the probationer is indigent; (iii) to request witnesses who have relevant information concerning the alleged violations; and (iv) to examine any witnesses or evidence. The probationer may be confined for the period designated on the violation report upon the execution of a waiver of rights signed by the probationer and by two officers acting as witnesses. Those two witnesses shall be the probation officer and another officer to be designated by the Chief of the Community Corrections Section in written Division policy.

(f1)   Mandatory Condition of Satellite-Based Monitoring for Some Sex Offenders. - Notwithstanding any other provision of this section, the court shall impose satellite-based monitoring pursuant to Part 5 of Article 27A of Chapter 14 of the General Statutes as a condition of probation on any offender who is described by G.S. 14-208.40(a)(1).

(g) Repealed by Session Laws 1993 (Reg. Sess., 1994), c. 19, s. 3.

(h) Definitions. - For purposes of this section, the definitions in G.S. 15A-1340.11 apply. (1993, c. 538, s. 17.1; 1994, Ex. Sess., c. 14, s. 22; c. 19, s. 3; c. 24, s. 14(b); 1993 (Reg. Sess., 1994), c. 767, s. 8; 1997-57, s. 4; 2001-487, s. 47(b); 2006-247, ss. 15(c), 15(d); 2011-145, s. 19.1(h), (k); 2011-192, s. 1(d)-(f), (k); 2011-412, s. 2.3(b), (c); 2012-146, s. 6; 2012-188, s. 1(a), (b).)

§ 15A-1343.3. Division of Adult Correction of the Department of Public Safety to establish regulations for continuous alcohol monitoring systems; payment of fees; authority to terminate monitoring.

(a) The Division of Adult Correction of the Department of Public Safety shall establish regulations for continuous alcohol monitoring systems that are authorized for use by the courts as evidence that an offender on probation has abstained from the use of alcohol for a specified period of time. A "continuous alcohol monitoring system" is a device that is worn by a person that can detect, monitor, record, and report the amount of alcohol within the wearer's system over a continuous 24-hour daily basis. The regulations shall include the procedures for supervision of the offender, collection and monitoring of the results, and the transmission of the data to the court for consideration by the court. All courts, including those using continuous alcohol monitoring systems prior to July 4, 2007, shall comply with the regulations established by the Division pursuant to this section.

The Secretary, or the Secretary's designee, shall approve continuous alcohol monitoring systems for use by the courts prior to their use by a court as evidence of alcohol abstinence, or their use as a condition of probation. The Secretary shall not unreasonably withhold approval of a continuous alcohol monitoring system and shall consult with the Division of Purchase and Contract in the Department of Administration to ensure that potential vendors are not discriminated against.

(b) Any fees or costs paid by an offender on probation in order to comply with continuous alcohol monitoring shall be paid directly to the monitoring provider. A monitoring provider shall not terminate the provision of continuous alcohol monitoring for nonpayment of fees unless authorized by the court. (2007-165, s. 6; 2011-145, s. 19.1(h); 2012-146, s. 7.)

§ 15A-1344. Response to violations; alteration and revocation.

(a) Authority to Alter or Revoke. - Except as provided in subsection (a1) or (b), probation may be reduced, terminated, continued, extended, modified, or revoked by any judge entitled to sit in the court which imposed probation and who is resident or presiding in the district court district as defined in G.S. 7A-133 or superior court district or set of districts as defined in G.S. 7A-41.1, as the case may be, where the sentence of probation was imposed, where the probationer violates probation, or where the probationer resides. Upon a finding that an offender sentenced to community punishment under Article 81B has violated one or more conditions of probation, the court's authority to modify the probation judgment includes the authority to require the offender to comply with conditions of probation that would otherwise make the sentence an intermediate punishment. The court may only revoke probation for a violation of a condition of probation under G.S. 15A-1343(b)(1) or G.S. 15A-1343(b)(3a), except as provided in G.S. 15A-1344(d2). Imprisonment may be imposed pursuant to G.S. 15A-1344(d2) for a violation of a requirement other than G.S. 15A-1343(b)(1) or G.S. 15A-1343(b)(3a). The district attorney of the prosecutorial district as defined in G.S. 7A-60 in which probation was imposed must be given reasonable notice of any hearing to affect probation substantially.

(a1) Authority to Supervise Probation in Drug Treatment Court. - Jurisdiction to supervise, modify, and revoke probation imposed in cases in which the offender is required to participate in a drug treatment court or a therapeutic court is as provided in G.S. 7A-272(e) and G.S. 7A-271(f). Proceedings to modify or revoke probation in these cases must be held in the county in which the drug treatment court or therapeutic court is located.

(b) Limits on Jurisdiction to Alter or Revoke Unsupervised Probation. - If the sentencing judge has entered an order to limit jurisdiction to consider a sentence of unsupervised probation under G.S. 15A-1342(h), a sentence of unsupervised probation may be reduced, terminated, continued, extended, modified, or revoked only by the sentencing judge or, if the sentencing judge is no longer on the bench, by a presiding judge in the court where the defendant was sentenced.

(b1) Service of Notice of Hearing on Violation of Unsupervised Probation. -

(1) Notice of a hearing in response to a violation of unsupervised probation shall be given either by personal delivery to the person to be notified or by depositing the notice in the United States mail in an envelope with postage

prepaid, addressed to the person at the last known address available to the preparer of the notice and reasonably believed to provide actual notice to the offender. The notice shall be mailed at least 10 days prior to any hearing and shall state the nature of the violation.

(2)   If notice is given by depositing the notice in the United States mail, pursuant to subdivision (1) of this subsection, and the defendant does not appear at the hearing, the court may do either of the following:

a.   Terminate the probation and enter appropriate orders for the enforcement of any outstanding monetary obligations as otherwise provided by law.

b.   Provide for other notice to the person as authorized by this Chapter for further proceedings and action authorized by Article 82 of Chapter 15A of the General Statutes for a violation of a condition of probation.

If the person is present at the hearing, the court may take any further action authorized by Article 82 of Chapter 15A of the General Statutes for a violation of a condition of probation.

(c)   Procedure on Altering or Revoking Probation; Returning Probationer to District Where Sentenced. - When a judge reduces, terminates, extends, modifies, or revokes probation outside the county where the judgment was entered, the clerk must send a copy of the order and any other records to the court where probation was originally imposed. A court on its own motion may return the probationer to the district court district as defined in G.S. 7A-133 or superior court district or set of districts as defined in G.S. 7A-41.1, as the case may be, where probation was imposed or where the probationer resides for reduction, termination, continuation, extension, modification, or revocation of probation. In cases where the probation is revoked in a county other than the county of original conviction the clerk in that county must issue a commitment order and must file the order revoking probation and the commitment order, which will constitute sufficient permanent record of the proceeding in that court, and must send a certified copy of the order revoking probation, the commitment order, and all other records pertaining thereto to the county of original conviction to be filed with the original records. The clerk in the county other than the county of original conviction must issue the formal commitment to the Division of Adult Correction of the Department of Public Safety.

(d) Extension and Modification; Response to Violations. - At any time prior to the expiration or termination of the probation period or in accordance with subsection (f) of this section, the court may after notice and hearing and for good cause shown extend the period of probation up to the maximum allowed under G.S. 15A-1342(a) and may modify the conditions of probation. A hearing extending or modifying probation may be held in the absence of a defendant who fails to appear for the hearing after a reasonable effort to notify the defendant. If a probationer violates a condition of probation at any time prior to the expiration or termination of the period of probation, the court, in accordance with the provisions of G.S. 15A-1345, may continue the defendant on probation, with or without modifying the conditions, may place the defendant on special probation as provided in subsection (e), or, if continuation, modification, or special probation is not appropriate, may revoke the probation and activate the suspended sentence imposed at the time of initial sentencing, if any, or may order that charges as to which prosecution has been deferred be brought to trial; provided that probation may not be revoked solely for conviction of a Class 3 misdemeanor. The court, before activating a sentence to imprisonment established when the defendant was placed on probation, may reduce the sentence, but the reduction shall be consistent with subsection (d1) of this section. A sentence activated upon revocation of probation commences on the day probation is revoked and runs concurrently with any other period of probation, parole, or imprisonment to which the defendant is subject during that period unless the revoking judge specifies that it is to run consecutively with the other period.

(d1) Reduction of Initial Sentence. - If the court elects to reduce the sentence of imprisonment for a felony, it shall not deviate from the range of minimum durations established in Article 81B of this Chapter for the class of offense and prior record level used in determining the initial sentence. If the presumptive range is used for the initial suspended sentence, the reduced sentence shall be within the presumptive range. If the mitigated range is used for the initial suspended sentence, the reduced sentence shall be within the mitigated range. If the aggravated range is used for the initial suspended sentence, the reduced sentence shall be within the aggravated range. If the court elects to reduce the sentence for a misdemeanor, it shall not deviate from the range of durations established in Article 81B for the class of offense and prior conviction level used in determining the initial sentence.

(d2) Confinement in Response to Violation. - When a defendant under supervision for a felony conviction has violated a condition of probation other than G.S. 15A-1343(b)(1) or G.S. 15A-1343(b)(3a), the court may impose a period of confinement of 90 consecutive days. The court may not revoke probation unless the defendant has previously received a total of two periods of confinement under this subsection. A defendant may receive only two periods of confinement under this subsection. If the time remaining on the maximum imposed sentence on a defendant under supervision for a felony conviction is 90 days or less, then the term of confinement is for the remaining period of the sentence. Confinement under this section shall be credited pursuant to G.S. 15-196.1.

When a defendant under supervision for a misdemeanor conviction has violated a condition of probation other than G.S. 15A-1343(b)(1) or G.S. 15A-1343(b)(3a), the court may impose a period of confinement of up to 90 consecutive days. The court may not revoke probation unless the defendant has previously received a total of two periods of confinement under this subsection. A defendant may receive only two periods of confinement under this subsection. Confinement under this section shall be credited pursuant to G.S. 15-196.1.

If a defendant is arrested for violation of a condition of probation and is lawfully confined to await a hearing for the violation, then the judge shall first credit any confinement time spent awaiting the hearing to any confinement imposed under this subsection; any excess time shall be credited to the activated sentence. The period of confinement imposed under this subsection on a defendant who is on probation for multiple offenses shall run concurrently on all cases related to the violation. Confinement shall be immediate unless otherwise specified by the court.

A defendant shall serve any confinement imposed under this subsection in the correctional facility where the defendant would have served an active sentence.

(e) Special Probation in Response to Violation. - When a defendant has violated a condition of probation, the court may modify the probation to place the defendant on special probation as provided in this subsection. In placing the defendant on special probation, the court may continue or modify the conditions of probation and in addition require that the defendant submit to a period or periods of imprisonment, either continuous or noncontinuous, at whatever time or intervals within the period of probation the court determines. In addition to any other conditions of probation which the court may impose, the court shall impose, when imposing a period or periods of imprisonment as a condition of special probation, the condition that the defendant obey the rules and regulations of the Division of Adult Correction of the Department of Public Safety governing conduct of inmates, and this condition shall apply to the defendant whether or not the court imposes it as a part of the written order. If imprisonment is for continuous periods, the confinement may be in either the custody of the Division of Adult Correction of the Department of Public Safety or a local confinement facility. Noncontinuous periods of imprisonment under special probation may only be served in a designated local confinement or treatment facility. Except for probationary sentences for impaired driving under G.S. 20-138.1, the total of all periods of confinement imposed as an incident of special probation, but not including an activated suspended sentence, may not exceed one-fourth the maximum sentence of imprisonment imposed for the offense. For probationary sentences for impaired driving under G.S. 20-138.1, the total of all periods of confinement imposed as an incident of special probation, but not including an activated suspended sentence, shall not exceed one-fourth the maximum penalty allowed by law. No confinement other than an activated suspended sentence may be required beyond the period of probation or beyond two years of the time the special probation is imposed, whichever comes first.

(e1) Criminal Contempt in Response to Violation. - If a defendant willfully violates a condition of probation, the court may hold the defendant in criminal contempt as provided in Article 1 of Chapter 5A of the General Statutes. A finding of criminal contempt by the court shall not revoke the probation. If the offender serves a sentence for contempt in a local confinement facility, the Division of Adult Correction of the Department of Public Safety shall pay for the confinement at the standard rate set by the General Assembly pursuant to G.S. 148-32.1(a) regardless of whether the offender would be eligible under the terms of that subsection.

(e2) Mandatory Satellite-Based Monitoring Required for Extension of Probation in Response to Violation by Certain Sex Offenders. - If a defendant who is in the category described by G.S. 14-208.40(a)(1) or G.S. 14-208.40(a)(2) violates probation and if the court extends the probation as a result of the violation, then the court shall order satellite-based monitoring pursuant to Part 5 of Article 27A of Chapter 14 of the General Statutes as a condition of the extended probation.

(f) Extension, Modification, or Revocation after Period of Probation. - The court may extend, modify, or revoke probation after the expiration of the period of probation if all of the following apply:

(1) Before the expiration of the period of probation the State has filed a written violation report with the clerk indicating its intent to conduct a hearing on one or more violations of one or more conditions of probation.

(2) The court finds that the probationer did violate one or more conditions of probation prior to the expiration of the period of probation.

(3) The court finds for good cause shown and stated that the probation should be extended, modified, or revoked.

(4) If the court opts to extend the period of probation, the court may extend the period of probation up to the maximum allowed under G.S. 15A-1342(a).

(g) Repealed by Session Laws 2011-62, s. 3, as amended by Session Laws 2011-412, s. 2.2, effective December 1, 2011, and applicable to persons placed on probation on or after December 1, 2011. (1977, c. 711, s. 1; 1977, 2nd Sess., c. 1147, ss. 11, 11A, 13A; 1979, c. 749, ss. 1-3; 1981, c. 377, s. 7; 1983, c. 536; 1987, (Reg. Sess., 1988), c. 1037, ss. 67, 68; 1993, c. 538, s. 18; 1994, Ex. Sess., c. 19, s. 2; c. 24, s. 14(b); 1993 (Reg. Sess., 1994), c. 767, s. 9; c. 769, s. 21.7(a); 1998-212, s. 17.21(c); 2003-151, s. 1; 2006-247, s. 15(e); 2008-129, s. 4; 2008-187, s. 46; 2009-372, s. 11(a), (b); 2009-411, s. 1; 2009-452, ss. 3, 4; 2009-516, ss. 9, 10(a), (b); 2010-96, s. 26(c); 2010-97, s. 13; 2011-62, s. 3; 2011-145, s. 19.1(h); 2011-192, s. 4(b), (c); 2011-412, ss. 2.2, 2.3(d), 2.5; 2012-83, s. 28; 2012-188, s. 2; 2012-194, s. 7; 2013-101, s. 4.)

§ 15A-1344.1. Procedure to insure payment of child support.

(a) When the court requires, as a condition of supervised or unsupervised probation, that a defendant support his children, the court may order at any time that support payments be made to the State Child Support Collection and Disbursement Unit for remittance to the party entitled to receive the payments. For child support orders initially entered on or after January 1, 1994, the immediate income withholding provisions of G.S. 110-136.5(c1) apply. If child support is to be paid through income withholding, the payments shall be made in accordance with G.S. 110-139(f).

(b) After entry of such an order by the court, the clerk of court shall maintain records listing the amount of payments, the date payments are required to be made, and the names and addresses of the parties affected by the order.

(c) The parties affected by the order shall inform the clerk of court and the State Child Support Collection and Disbursement Unit of any change of address or of other condition that may affect the administration of the order. The court may provide in the order that a defendant failing to inform the court and the State Child Support Collection and Disbursement Unit of a change of address within reasonable period of time may be held in violation of probation.

(d) When a defendant in a non-IV-D case, as defined in G.S. 110-129, fails to make required payments of child support and is in arrears, upon notification by the State Child Support Collection and Disbursement Unit the clerk of superior court may mail by regular mail to the last known address of the defendant a notice of delinquency that sets out the amount of child support currently due and that demands immediate payment of the amount. Failure to receive the delinquency notice is not a defense in any probation violation hearing or other proceeding thereafter. If the arrearage is not paid in full within 21 days after the mailing of the delinquency notice, or is not paid within 30 days after the defendant becomes delinquent if the clerk has elected not to send a delinquency notice, the clerk shall certify the amount due to the district attorney and probation officer, who shall initiate proceedings for revocation of probation pursuant to Article 82 of Chapter 15A or make a motion in the criminal case for income withholding pursuant to G.S. 110-136.5 or both.

When a defendant in a IV-D case, as defined in G.S. 110-129, fails to make required payments of child support and is in arrears, at the request of the IV-D obligee the clerk shall certify the amount due to the district attorney and probation officer, who shall initiate proceedings for revocation of probation pursuant to Article 82 of Chapter 15A or make a motion in the criminal case for income withholding pursuant to G.S. 110-136.5 or both. (1983, c. 567, s. 1; 1983 (Reg. Sess., 1984), c. 1100, ss. 1, 2; 1985 (Reg. Sess., 1986), c. 949, s. 7; 1993, c. 517, s. 4; 1999-293, ss. 10, 23.)

§ 15A-1345. Arrest and hearing on probation violation.

(a) Arrest for Violation of Probation. - A probationer is subject to arrest for violation of conditions of probation by a law-enforcement officer or probation officer upon either an order for arrest issued by the court or upon the written request of a probation officer, accompanied by a written statement signed by the probation officer that the probationer has violated specified conditions of his probation. However, a probation revocation hearing under subsection (e) may be held without first arresting the probationer.

(a1) Suspension of Public Assistance Benefits for Probation Violators Who Avoid Arrest. - The court may order the suspension of any public assistance benefits that are being received by a probationer for whom the court has issued an order for arrest for violation of the conditions of probation but who is absconding or otherwise willfully avoiding arrest. The suspension of benefits shall continue until such time as the probationer surrenders to or is otherwise brought under the jurisdiction of the court. For purposes of this section, the term "public assistance benefits" includes unemployment benefits, Medicaid or other medical assistance benefits, Work First Family Assistance, food and nutrition benefits, any other programs of public assistance under Article 2 of Chapter 108A of the General Statutes, and any other financial assistance of any kind being paid to the probationer from State or federal funds. Nothing in this subsection shall be construed to suspend, or in any way affect the eligibility for, any public assistance benefits that are being received by or for the benefit of a family member of a probation violator.

(b) Bail Following Arrest for Probation Violation. - If at any time during the period of probation the probationer is arrested for a violation of any of the conditions of probation, he must be taken without unnecessary delay before a judicial official to have conditions of release pending a revocation hearing set in the same manner as provided in G.S. 15A-534.

(b1) If the probationer is arrested for a violation of any of the conditions of probation and (i) has a pending charge for a felony offense or (ii) has been convicted of an offense at any time that requires registration under Article 27A of Chapter 14 of the General Statutes or an offense that would have required registration but for the effective date of the law establishing the Sex Offender and Public Protection Registration Program, the judicial official shall determine whether the probationer poses a danger to the public prior to imposing conditions of release and must record that determination in writing.

(1) If the judicial official determines that the probationer poses a danger to the public, the probationer shall be denied release pending a revocation hearing.

(2) If the judicial official finds that the defendant does not pose a danger to the public, then conditions of release shall be imposed as otherwise provided in Article 26 of this Chapter.

(3) If there is insufficient information to determine whether the defendant poses a danger to the public, then the defendant shall be retained in custody for

not more than seven days from the date of the arrest in order for the judicial official, or a subsequent reviewing judicial official, to obtain sufficient information to determine whether the defendant poses a danger to the public.

(4)   If the defendant has been held seven days from the date of arrest pursuant to subdivision (3) of this subsection, and the court has been unable to obtain sufficient information to determine whether the defendant poses a danger to the public, then the defendant shall be brought before any judicial official, who shall record that fact in writing and shall impose conditions of pretrial release as otherwise provided in this section.

(c)   When Preliminary Hearing on Probation Violation Required. - Unless the hearing required by subsection (e) is first held or the probationer waives the hearing, a preliminary hearing on probation violation must be held within seven working days of an arrest of a probationer to determine whether there is probable cause to believe that he violated a condition of probation. Otherwise, the probationer must be released seven working days after his arrest to continue on probation pending a hearing, unless the probationer has been denied release pursuant to subdivision (1) of subsection (b1) of this section, in which case the probationer shall be held until the revocation hearing date.

(d)   Procedure for Preliminary Hearing on Probation Violation. - The preliminary hearing on probation violation must be conducted by a judge who is sitting in the county where the probationer was arrested or where the alleged violation occurred. If no judge is sitting in the county where the hearing would otherwise be held, the hearing may be held anywhere in the district court district as defined in G.S. 7A-133 or superior court district or set of districts as defined in G.S. 7A-41.1, as the case may be. The State must give the probationer notice of the hearing and its purpose, including a statement of the violations alleged. At the hearing the probationer may appear and speak in his own behalf, may present relevant information, and may, on request, personally question adverse informants unless the court finds good cause for not allowing confrontation. Formal rules of evidence do not apply at the hearing. If probable cause is found or if the probable cause hearing is waived, the probationer may be held for a revocation hearing, subject to release under the provisions of subsection (b). If the hearing is held and probable cause is not found, the probationer must be released to continue on probation.

(e)   Revocation Hearing. - Before revoking or extending probation, the court must, unless the probationer waives the hearing, hold a hearing to determine whether to revoke or extend probation and must make findings to support the decision and a summary record of the proceedings. The State must give the probationer notice of the hearing and its purpose, including a statement of the violations alleged. The notice, unless waived by the probationer, must be given at least 24 hours before the hearing. At the hearing, evidence against the probationer must be disclosed to him, and the probationer may appear and speak in his own behalf, may present relevant information, and may confront and cross-examine adverse witnesses unless the court finds good cause for not allowing confrontation. The probationer is entitled to be represented by counsel at the hearing and, if indigent, to have counsel appointed in accordance with rules adopted by the Office of Indigent Defense Services. Formal rules of evidence do not apply at the hearing, but the record or recollection of evidence or testimony introduced at the preliminary hearing on probation violation are inadmissible as evidence at the revocation hearing. When the violation alleged is the nonpayment of fine or costs, the issues and procedures at the hearing include those specified in G.S. 15A-1364 for response to nonpayment of fine. (1977, c. 711, s. 1; 1977, 2nd Sess., c. 1147, ss. 12, 13; 1979, c. 749, s. 4; 1979, 2nd Sess., c. 1316, s. 39; 1987 (Reg. Sess., 1988), c. 1037, s. 69; 2008-117, s. 19; 2009-412, s. 2; 2011-326, s. 12(c); 2012-170, s. 1.)

§ 15A-1346. Commencement of probation; multiple sentence.

(a) Commencement of Probation. - Except as provided in subsection (b), a period of probation commences on the day it is imposed and runs concurrently with any other period of probation, parole, or imprisonment to which the defendant is subject during that period.

(b) Consecutive and Concurrent Sentences. - If a period of probation is being imposed at the same time a period of imprisonment is being imposed or if it is being imposed on a person already subject to an undischarged term of imprisonment, the period of probation may run either concurrently or consecutively with the term of imprisonment, as determined by the court. If not specified, it runs concurrently. (1977, c. 711, s. 1.)

§ 15A-1347. Appeal from revocation of probation or imposition of special probation upon violation; consequences of waiver of hearing.

(a) Except as provided in subsection (b) of this section, when a district court judge, as a result of a finding of a violation of probation, activates a sentence or imposes special probation, the defendant may appeal to the superior court for a de novo revocation hearing. At the hearing the probationer has all rights and the court has all authority they have in a revocation hearing held before the superior court in the first instance. Appeals from lower courts to the superior courts from judgments revoking probation may be heard in term or out of term, in the county or out of the county by the resident superior court judge of the district or the superior court judge assigned to hold the courts of the district, or a judge of the superior court commissioned to hold court in the district, or a special superior court judge residing in the district. When the defendant appeals to the superior court because a district court has found he violated probation and has activated his sentence or imposed special probation, and the superior court, after a de novo revocation hearing, orders that the defendant continue on probation under the same or modified conditions, the superior court is considered the court that originally imposed probation with regard to future revocation proceedings and other purposes of this Article. When a superior court judge, as a result of a finding of a violation of probation, activates a sentence or imposes special probation, either in the first instance or upon a de novo hearing after appeal from a district court, the defendant may appeal under G.S. 7A-27.

(b) If a defendant waives a revocation hearing, the finding of a violation of probation, activation of sentence, or imposition of special probation may not be appealed to the superior court. (1977, c. 711, s. 1; 1977, 2nd Sess., c. 1147, s. 14; 2013-385, s. 2.)

§§ 15A-1348 through 15A-1350: Reserved for future codification purposes.

Article 83.

Imprisonment.

§ 15A-1351. Sentence of imprisonment; incidents; special probation.

(a) The judge may sentence to special probation a defendant convicted of a criminal offense other than impaired driving under G.S. 20-138.1, if based on the defendant's prior record or conviction level as found pursuant to Article 81B of this Chapter, an intermediate punishment is authorized for the class of offense of which the defendant has been convicted. A defendant convicted of impaired driving under G.S. 20-138.1 may also be sentenced to special probation. Under a sentence of special probation, the court may suspend the term of imprisonment and place the defendant on probation as provided in Article 82, Probation, and in addition require that the defendant submit to a period or periods of imprisonment in the custody of the Division of Adult Correction of the Department of Public Safety or a designated local confinement or treatment facility at whatever time or intervals within the period of probation, consecutive or nonconsecutive, the court determines. In addition to any other conditions of probation which the court may impose, the court shall impose, when imposing a period or periods of imprisonment as a condition of special probation, the condition that the defendant obey the Rules and Regulations of the Division of Adult Correction of the Department of Public Safety governing conduct of inmates, and this condition shall apply to the defendant whether or not the court imposes it as a part of the written order. If imprisonment is for continuous periods, the confinement may be in the custody of either the Division of Adult Correction of the Department of Public Safety or a local confinement facility. Noncontinuous periods of imprisonment under special probation may only be served in a designated local confinement or treatment facility. Except for probationary sentences of impaired driving under G.S. 20-138.1, the total of all periods of confinement imposed as an incident of special probation, but not including an activated suspended sentence, may not exceed one-fourth the maximum sentence of imprisonment imposed for the offense, and no confinement other than an activated suspended sentence may be required beyond two years of conviction. For probationary sentences for impaired driving under G.S. 20-138.1, the total of all periods of confinement imposed as an incident of special probation, but not including an activated suspended sentence, shall not exceed one-fourth the maximum penalty allowed by law. In imposing a sentence of special probation, the judge may credit any time spent committed or confined, as a result of the charge, to either the suspended sentence or to the imprisonment required for special probation. The original period of probation, including the period of imprisonment required for special probation, shall be as specified in G.S. 15A-1343.2(d), but may not exceed a maximum of five years, except as provided by G.S. 15A-1342(a). The court may revoke, modify, or terminate special probation as otherwise provided for probationary sentences.

(b) Sentencing of a person convicted of a felony or of a misdemeanor other than impaired driving under G.S. 20-138.1 that occurred on or after the effective date of Article 81B is subject to that Article. For persons convicted of impaired driving under G.S. 20-138.1, a sentence to imprisonment must impose a maximum term and may impose a minimum term. The impaired driving judgment may state the minimum term or may state that a term constitutes both the minimum and maximum terms. If the impaired driving judgment states no minimum term, the defendant becomes eligible for parole in accordance with G.S. 15A-1371(a).

(c) Repealed by Session Laws 1979, c. 749, s. 7.

(d), (e) Repealed by Session Laws 1993, c. 538, s. 19.

(f) Work Release. - When sentencing a person convicted of a felony, the sentencing court may recommend that the sentenced offender be granted work release as authorized in G.S. 148-33.1. When sentencing a person convicted of a misdemeanor, the sentencing court may recommend or, with the consent of the person sentenced, order that the sentenced offender be granted work release as authorized in G.S. 148-33.1.

(g) Credit. - Credit towards a sentence to imprisonment is as provided in Article 19A of Chapter 15 of the General Statutes.

(h) Repealed by Session Laws 2003-141, s. 2, effective December 1, 2003. (1977, c. 711, s. 1; 1977, 2nd Sess., c. 1147, ss. 15-17; 1979, c. 749, ss. 5-7; c. 760, s. 4; 1985 (Reg. Sess., 1986), c. 1014, s. 201(a); 1987, c. 738, s. 111(e); 1993, c. 84, s. 2; c. 538, s. 19; 1994, Ex. Sess., c. 24, s. 14(b); 1993 (Reg. Sess., 1994), c. 767, ss. 7, 10; 1998-212, s. 17.21(b); 2003-141, s. 2; 2003-151, s. 2; 2011-145, s. 19.1(h).)

§ 15A-1352. Commitment to Division of Adult Correction of the Department of Public Safety or local confinement facility.

(a) A person sentenced to imprisonment for a misdemeanor under this Article or for nonpayment of a fine under Article 84 of this Chapter shall be committed for the term designated by the court to the custody of the Division of Adult Correction of the Department of Public Safety or to a local confinement facility. If the sentence imposed for a misdemeanor is for a period of 90 days or less, the commitment must be to a facility other than one maintained by the Division of Adult Correction of the Department of Public Safety, except as provided in G.S. 148-32.1(b). If the sentence or sentences imposed require confinement for more than 180 days, the commitment must be to the custody of the Division of Adult Correction of the Department of Public Safety.

If a person is sentenced to imprisonment for a misdemeanor under this Article or for nonpayment of a fine under Article 84 of this Chapter, the sentencing judge shall make a finding of fact as to whether the person would be suitable for placement in a county satellite jail/work release unit operated pursuant to G.S. 153A-230.3. If the sentencing judge makes a finding of fact that the person would be suitable for placement in a county satellite jail/work release unit and the person meets the requirements listed in G.S. 153A-230.3(a)(1), then the custodian of the local confinement facility may transfer the misdemeanant to a county satellite jail/work release unit.

(b) A person sentenced to imprisonment for a felony under this Article shall be committed for the term designated by the court to the custody of the Division of Adult Correction of the Department of Public Safety.

(c) A person sentenced to imprisonment for nonpayment of a fine under Article 84, Fines, shall be committed for the term designated by the court:

(1) To the custody of the Division of Adult Correction of the Department of Public Safety if the person was fined for conviction of a felony;

(2) To the custody of the Division of Adult Correction of the Department of Public Safety or to a local confinement facility if the person was fined for conviction of a misdemeanor, provided that (i) if the sentence imposed is for a period of 90 days or less, the commitment shall be to a facility other than one maintained by the Division of Adult Correction of the Department of Public Safety, except as provided in G.S. 148-32.1(b) and (ii) if the sentence or sentences imposed require confinement for more than 180 days, the commitment must be to the custody of the Division of Adult Correction of the Department of Public Safety.

(d) Notwithstanding any other provision of law, when the sentencing court, with the consent of the person sentenced, orders that a person convicted of a misdemeanor be granted work release, the court may commit the person to a specific prison facility or local confinement facility or satellite jail/work release unit within the county of the sentencing court in order to facilitate the work release arrangement. When appropriate to facilitate the work release arrangement, the sentencing court may, with the consent of the sheriff or board of commissioners, commit the person to a specific local confinement facility or satellite jail/work release unit in another county, or, with the consent of the Division of Adult Correction of the Department of Public Safety, commit the person to a specific prison facility in another county. The Division of Adult Correction of the Department of Public Safety may transfer a prisoner committed to a specific prison facility to a different facility when necessary to alleviate overcrowding or for other administrative purposes.

(e) A person sentenced for a misdemeanor who has a sentence imposed that requires confinement for a period of more than 90 days and up to 180 days, except for those serving sentences for an impaired driving offense under G.S. 20-138.1 under this Article or for nonpayment of a fine under Article 84 of this Chapter, shall be committed for the term designated by the court to confinement pursuant to the Statewide Misdemeanant Confinement Program established by G.S. 148-32.1. (1977, c. 711, s. 1; 1977, 2nd Sess., c. 1147, s. 18; 1979, c. 456, s. 1; c. 787, ss. 1, 2; 1985 (Reg. Sess., 1986), c. 1014, s. 201(b); 1987, c. 207, s. 3; 1989, c. 761, s. 6; 1991, Ex. Sess., c. 486, s. 1; c. 8, s. 1; 1993, c. 538, s. 37; 1994, Ex. Sess., c. 24, s. 14(b); 2011-145, s. 19.1(h); 2011-192, s. 7(b)-(c).)

§ 15A-1353. Order of commitment when imprisonment imposed; release pending appeal.

(a) When a sentence includes a term or terms of imprisonment, the court must issue an order of commitment setting forth the judgment. Unless otherwise specified in the order of commitment, the date of the order is the date service of the sentence is to begin.

If a female defendant is convicted of a nonviolent crime and the court is provided medical evidence from a licensed physician that the defendant is pregnant or the court otherwise determines that the defendant is pregnant, the court may specify in the order that the date of service of the sentence is not to begin until at least six weeks after the birth of the child or other termination of the pregnancy unless the defendant requests to serve her term as the court would otherwise order. The court may impose reasonable conditions upon defendant during such waiting period to insure that defendant will return to begin service of the sentence.

If the court sentences a defendant pursuant to G.S. 15A-1351(a), the period during which that defendant is awaiting imprisonment shall be considered part of the probationary sentence and such defendant shall be subject to all incidents and conditions of probation.

(b)   There must be included in the commitment, or in a separate order referred to in the commitment, any provisions with regard to release under Article 26, Bail, if an appeal is taken, and the conditions of the release. If the commitment has been entered before appeal or the setting of the conditions for release, appropriate copies of those documents must be forwarded to the agency having custody of the defendant.

(c)   Unless a later time is directed in the order of commitment, or the defendant has been released from custody pursuant to Article 26, Bail, or the defendant is appealing from a judgment of the district court to the superior court for a trial de novo, the sheriff must cause the defendant to be placed in the custody of the agency specified in the judgment on the day service of sentence is to begin or as soon thereafter as practicable.

(d)   A certified copy of the order of commitment, together with any separate order providing for release of the defendant pending appeal, must be delivered to the custodian of the confinement facility.

(e)   When a defendant has been committed pursuant to this section:

(1)   If appeal has been entered and conditions of release have been set as provided in Article 26, Bail, the agency having custody of the defendant may effect his release in the manner provided in G.S. 15A-537; or

(2)   If appeal is entered and the conditions of release are not set until after the order of commitment has been issued, and the defendant has been placed in the custody of the agency directed therein, appropriate copies of the conditions of release must be certified by the clerk and forwarded to the agency, which then may effect his release in the manner provided in G.S. 15A-537.

(f)   When the sentencing court, with the consent of the person sentenced, orders that a person convicted of a misdemeanor be granted work release, the following provisions must be included in the commitment, or in a separate order referred to in the commitment:

(1)   The date work release is to begin;

(2) The prison or local confinement facility to which the offender is to be committed;

(3) A provision that work release terminates the date the offender loses his job or violates the conditions of the work-release plan established by the Division of Adult Correction of the Department of Public Safety; and

(4) A determination whether the earnings of the offender are to be disbursed by the Division of Adult Correction of the Department of Public Safety or the clerk of the sentencing court in the manner that the court in its order directs. (1977, c. 711, s. 1; 1979, c. 758, s. 1; 1983, c. 389; 1985 (Reg. Sess., 1986), c. 1014, s. 201(c); 2011-145, s. 19.1(h).)

§ 15A-1354. Concurrent and consecutive terms of imprisonment.

(a) Authority of Court. - When multiple sentences of imprisonment are imposed on a person at the same time or when a term of imprisonment is imposed on a person who is already subject to an undischarged term of imprisonment, including a term of imprisonment in another jurisdiction, the sentences may run either concurrently or consecutively, as determined by the court. If not specified or not required by statute to run consecutively, sentences shall run concurrently.

(b) Effect of Consecutive Terms. - In determining the effect of consecutive sentences imposed under authority of this Article and the manner in which they will be served, the Division of Adult Correction of the Department of Public Safety must treat the defendant as though he has been committed for a single term with the following incidents:

(1) The maximum prison sentence consists of the total of the maximum terms of the consecutive sentences, less 12 months for each of the second and subsequent sentences imposed for Class B through Class E felonies, or less 60 months for each second or subsequent Class B1 through E felony for which the sentence was established pursuant to G.S. 15A-1340.17(f), and less nine months for each of the second and subsequent sentences imposed for Class F through Class I felonies; and

(2) The minimum term consists of the total of the minimum terms of the consecutive sentences. (1977, c. 711, s. 1; 1979, c. 760, s. 4; 1979, 2nd Sess.,

c. 1316, s. 40; 1985, c. 21; 1994, Ex. Sess., c. 14, s. 23; 2011-145, s. 19.1(h); 2011-192, s. 2(i); 2011-307, s. 3.)

§ 15A-1355. Calculation of terms of imprisonment.

(a) Commencement of Sentence. - The commencement date of a sentence of imprisonment under authority of this Article is as provided in G.S. 15A-1353(a), except when the sentence is a consecutive sentence. When it is a consecutive sentence, it commences to run when the State has custody of the defendant following completion of the prior sentence.

(b) Repealed by Session Laws 1977, 2nd Sess., c. 1147, s. 19.

(c) Earned Time; Credit for Good Behavior for Impaired Drivers. - Persons convicted of felonies or misdemeanors under Article 81B of this Chapter may, consistent with rules of the Division of Adult Correction of the Department of Public Safety, earn credit which may be used to reduce their maximum terms of imprisonment as provided in G.S. 15A-1340.13(d) for felony sentences and in G.S. 15A-1340.20(d) for misdemeanor sentences.

For sentences of imprisonment imposed for convictions of impaired driving under G.S. 20-138.1, the Division of Adult Correction of the Department of Public Safety may give credit toward service of the maximum term and any minimum term of imprisonment and toward eligibility for parole for allowances of time as provided in rules and regulations made under G.S. 148-11 and 148-13.

(d) Earned Time Credit for Medically and Physically Unfit Inmates. - Inmates in the custody of the Division of Adult Correction of the Department of Public Safety who suffer from medical conditions or physical disabilities that prevent their assignment to work release or other rehabilitative activities may, consistent with rules of the Division of Adult Correction of the Department of Public Safety, earn credit based upon good behavior or other criteria determined by the Division that may be used to reduce their maximum term of imprisonment as provided in G.S. 15A-1340.13(d) for felony sentences and in G.S. 15A-1340.20(d) for misdemeanor sentences. (1977, c. 711, s. 1; 1977, 2nd Sess., c. 1147, s. 19; 1979, c. 749, s. 8; c. 760, s. 4; 1981, c. 571; c. 1127, s. 84; 1983, c. 560, § 1; 1993, c. 538, s. 20; 1994, Ex. Sess., c. 24, s. 14(b); 2001-424, s. 25.1(a); 2002-126, s. 17.19(d); 2002-159, s. 77; 2011-145, s. 19.1(h).)

§§ 15A-1356 through 15A-1360. Reserved for future codification purposes.

Article 84.

Fines.

§ 15A-1361. Authorized fines and penalties.

A person who has been convicted of a criminal offense may be ordered to pay a fine as provided by law. A person who has been found responsible for an infraction may be ordered to pay a penalty as provided by law. Unless the context clearly requires otherwise, references in this Article to fines also include penalties. (1977, c. 711, s. 1; 1985, c. 764, s. 6.)

§ 15A-1362. Imposition of fines.

(a)   General Criteria. - In determining the method of payment of a fine, the court should consider the burden that payment will impose in view of the financial resources of the defendant.

(b)   Installment or Delayed Payments. - When a defendant is ordered to pay a fine, the court may provide for the payment to be made within a specified period of time or in specified installments. If no such provision is made a part of the sentence, the fine is payable forthwith.

(c)   Nonpayment. - When a defendant is ordered, other than as a condition of probation, to pay a fine, costs, or both, the court may impose at the same time a sentence to be served in the event that the fine is not paid. The court also may impose an order that the defendant appear, if he fails to make the required payment, at a specified time to show cause why he should not be imprisoned. (1977, c. 711, s. 1.)

§ 15A-1363. Remission of a fine or costs.

A defendant who has been required to pay a fine or costs, including a requirement to pay fine or costs as a condition of probation, or a prosecutor, may at any time petition the sentencing court for a remission or revocation of the fine or costs or any unpaid portion of it. If it appears to the satisfaction of the court that the circumstances which warranted the imposition of the fine or costs no longer exist, that it would otherwise be unjust to require payment, or that the proper administration of justice requires resolution of the case, the court may remit or revoke the fine or costs or the unpaid portion in whole or in part or may modify the method of payment. (1977, c. 711, s. 1.)

§ 15A-1364. Response to nonpayment.

(a) Response to Default. - When a defendant who has been required to pay a fine or costs or both defaults in payment or in any installment, the court, upon the motion of the prosecutor or upon its own motion, may require the defendant to appear and show cause why he should not be imprisoned or may rely upon a conditional show cause order entered under G.S. 15A-1362(c). If the defendant fails to appear, an order for his arrest may be issued.

(b) Imprisonment; Criteria. - Following a requirement to show cause under subsection (a), unless the defendant shows inability to comply and that his nonpayment was not attributable to a failure on his part to make a good faith effort to obtain the necessary funds for payment, the court may order the suspended sentence, if any, activated, or, if the law provides no term of imprisonment for the offense for which the defendant was convicted or if no suspended sentence was imposed, the court may order the defendant imprisoned for a term not to exceed 30 days. The court, before activating a sentence of imprisonment, may reduce the sentence. The court may provide in its order that payment or satisfaction at any time of the fine and costs imposed by the court will entitle the defendant to his release from the imprisonment or, after entering the order, may at any time reduce the sentence for good cause shown, including payment or satisfaction of the fine.

(c) Modification of Fine or Costs. - If it appears that the default in the payment of a fine or costs is not attributable to failure on the defendant's part to make a good faith effort to obtain the necessary funds for payment, the court may enter an order:

(1) Allowing the defendant additional time for payment; or

(2) Reducing the amount of the fine or costs or of each installment; or

(3) Revoking the fine or costs or the unpaid portion in whole or in part.

(d) Organizations. - When an organization is required to pay a fine or costs or both, it is the duty of the person or persons authorized to make disbursement of the assets of the organization to make payment from assets of the organization, and a failure to do so constitutes contempt of court. (1977, c. 711, s. 1.)

§ 15A-1365. Judgment for fines docketed; lien and execution.

When a defendant has defaulted in payment of a fine or costs, the judge may order that the judgment be docketed. Upon being docketed, the judgment becomes a lien on the real estate of the defendant in the same manner as do judgments in civil actions. Executions on docketed judgments may be stayed only when an appeal is taken and security is given as required in civil cases. If the judgment is affirmed on appeal to the appellate division, the clerk of the superior court, on receipt of the certificate from the appellate division, must issue execution on the judgment. The clerk may not issue an execution, however, if the fine or costs were imposed for an offense other than trafficking in controlled substances or conspiring to traffic in controlled substances under G.S. 90-95(h) and (i), respectively, and the defendant elects to serve the suspended sentence, if any, or serve a term of 30 days, if no suspended sentence was imposed. (1977, c. 711, s. 1; 1985, c. 411.)

§ 15A-1366. Reserved for future codification purposes.

§ 15A-1367. Reserved for future codification purposes.

Article 84A.

Post-Release Supervision.

§ 15A-1368. Definitions and administration.

(a) The following words have the listed meaning in this Article:

(1) Post-release supervision or supervision. - The time for which a sentenced prisoner is released from prison before the termination of his maximum prison term, controlled by the rules and conditions of this Article. Purposes of post-release supervision include all or any of the following: to monitor and control the prisoner in the community, to assist the prisoner in reintegrating into society, to collect restitution and other court indebtedness from the prisoner, and to continue the prisoner's treatment or education.

(2) Supervisee. - A person released from incarceration and in the custody of the Division of Adult Correction of the Department of Public Safety and Post-Release Supervision and Parole Commission on post-release supervision.

(3) Commission. - The Post-Release Supervision and Parole Commission, whose general authority is described in G.S. 143B-720.

(4) Minimum imposed term. - The minimum term of imprisonment imposed on an individual prisoner by a court judgment, as described in G.S. 15A-1340.13(c). When a prisoner is serving consecutive imprisonment terms, the minimum imposed term, for purposes of this Article, is the sum of all minimum terms imposed in the court judgment.

(5) Maximum imposed term. - The maximum term of imprisonment imposed on an individual prisoner by a court judgment, as described in G.S. 15A-1340.13(c). When a prisoner is serving consecutive prison terms, the maximum imposed term, for purposes of this Article, is the sum of all maximum terms imposed in the court judgment or judgments, less 12 months for each of the second and subsequent sentences imposed for Class B through Class E felonies, or less 60 months for each second or subsequent Class B1 through E felony for which the sentence was established pursuant to G.S. 15A-1340.17(f), and less nine months for each of the second and subsequent sentences imposed for Class F through Class I felonies.

(b) Administration. - The Post-Release Supervision and Parole Commission, as authorized in Chapter 143 of the General Statutes, shall administer post-release supervision as provided in this Article. (1993, c. 538, s.

20.1; 1994, Ex. Sess., c. 14, ss. 24, 25; c. 24, s. 14(b); 1997-237, s. 2; 2011-145, s. 19.1(h); 2011-192, s. 2(h); 2011-307, s. 4.)

§ 15A-1368.1. Applicability of Article 84A.

This Article applies to all felons sentenced to an active punishment under Article 81B of this Chapter or G.S. 90-95(h), but does not apply to felons in Class A and Class B1 sentenced to life imprisonment without parole. Prisoners subject to Articles 85 and 85A of this Chapter are excluded from this Article's coverage. (1993, c. 538, s. 20.1; 1994, Ex. Sess., c. 14, s. 26; c. 22, s. 8; c. 24, s. 14(b); 2011-192, s. 2(a); 2012-188, s. 6.)

§ 15A-1368.2. Post-release supervision eligibility and procedure.

(a) Except as otherwise provided in this subsection, a prisoner to whom this Article applies shall be released from prison for post-release supervision on the date equivalent to his maximum imposed prison term less 12 months in the case of Class B1 through E felons and less nine months in the case of Class F through I felons, less any earned time awarded by the Division of Adult Correction of the Department of Public Safety or the custodian of a local confinement facility under G.S. 15A-1340.13(d). A prisoner whose maximum sentence is established pursuant to G.S. 15A-1340.17(f) shall be released from prison for post-release supervision on the date equivalent to his or her maximum imposed prison term less 60 months, less any earned time awarded by the Division of Adult Correction of the Department of Public Safety or the custodian of a local confinement facility under G.S. 15A-1340.13(d). If a prisoner has not been awarded any earned time, the prisoner shall be released for post-release supervision on the date equivalent to his maximum prison term less 12 months for Class B1 through E felons and less nine months for Class F through I felons.

(b) A prisoner shall not refuse post-release supervision. Willful refusal to accept post-release supervision or to comply with the terms of post-release supervision by a prisoner whose offense requiring post-release supervision is a reportable conviction subject to the registration requirement of Article 27A of Chapter 14 of the General Statutes, is punishable as contempt of court under G.S. 5A-11 and may result in imprisonment under G.S. 5A-12. Furthermore, any period of time during which a prisoner whose offense requiring post-release supervision is a reportable conviction subject to the registration requirement of

Article 27A of Chapter 14 of the General Statutes is not in fact released pursuant to subsection (a) of this section due to the prisoner's resistance to that release shall toll the running of the period of supervised release imposed by subsection (c) of this section. For purposes of this subsection and the provisions of G.S. 5A-11, "willful refusal to accept post-release supervision or to comply with the terms of post-release supervision" includes, but is not limited to, knowingly violating the terms of post-release supervision in order to be returned to prison to serve out the remainder of the prisoner's sentence. Notwithstanding any other provision of law, a prisoner punished for the offense of contempt of court under this subsection is not eligible for credit for time served against the sentence for which the prisoner is subject to post-release supervision. Punishment by contempt for willful refusal to accept post-release supervision or to comply with the terms of post-release supervision does not preclude the application of any other sanction provided by law for the same conduct.

(c) A supervisee's period of post-release supervision shall be for a period of 12 months in the case of Class B1 through E felons and nine months in the case of Class F through I felons, unless the offense is an offense for which registration is required pursuant to Article 27A of Chapter 14 of the General Statutes. For offenses subject to the registration requirement of Article 27A of Chapter 14 of the General Statutes, the period of post-release supervision is five years. The conditions of post-release supervision are as authorized in G.S. 15A-1368.5.

(c1) Notwithstanding subsection (c) of this section, a person required to submit to satellite-based monitoring pursuant to G.S. 15A-1368.4(b1)(6) shall continue to participate in satellite-based monitoring beyond the period of post-release supervision until the Commission releases the person from that requirement pursuant to G.S. 14-208.43.

(d) A supervisee's period of post-release supervision may be reduced while the supervisee is under supervision by earned time awarded by the Division of Adult Correction of the Department of Public Safety, pursuant to rules adopted in accordance with law. A supervisee is eligible to receive earned time credit toward the period of supervision for compliance with reintegrative conditions described in G.S. 15A-1368.5.

(e) Repealed by Session Laws 1997-237, s. 7.

(f) When a supervisee completes the period of post-release supervision, the sentence or sentences from which the supervisee was placed on post-release supervision are terminated. (1993, c. 538, s. 20.1; 1994, Ex. Sess., c. 24, s. 14(b); 1993 (Reg. Sess., 1994), c. 767, s. 4; 1996, 2nd Ex. Sess., c. 18, s. 20.14(a); 1997-237, s. 7; 2006-247, s. 15(f); 2011-145, s. 19.1(h); 2011-192, s. 2(b); 2011-307, ss. 2, 5.)

§ 15A-1368.3. Incidents of post-release supervision.

(a) Conditionality. - Post-release supervision is conditional and subject to revocation.

(b) Modification. - The Commission may for good cause shown modify the conditions of post-release supervision at any time before the termination of the supervision period.

(c) Effect of Violation. - If the supervisee violates a condition, described in G.S. 15A-1368.4, at any time before the termination of the supervision period, the Commission may continue the supervisee on the existing supervision, with or without modifying the conditions, or if continuation or modification is not appropriate, may revoke post-release supervision as provided in G.S. 15A-1368.6 and reimprison the supervisee for a term consistent with the following requirements:

(1) Supervisees who were convicted of an offense for which registration is required under Article 27A of Chapter 14 of the General Statutes and supervisees whose supervision is revoked for a violation of the required controlling condition under G.S. 15A-1368.4(b) or for absconding in violation of G.S. 15A-1368.4(e)(7a) will be returned to prison up to the time remaining on their maximum imposed terms. All other supervisees will be returned to prison for three months and may be returned for three months on each of two subsequent violations, after which supervisees who were Class B1 through E felons may be returned to prison up to the time remaining on their maximum imposed terms. Reimprisonment for a violation under this subdivision tolls the running of the period of supervised release, except that a supervisee shall not be rereleased on post-release supervision if the supervisee has served all the time remaining on the supervisee's maximum imposed term.

(2) The supervisee shall not receive any credit for days on post-release supervision against the maximum term of imprisonment imposed by the court under G.S. 15A-1340.13.

(3) Pursuant to Article 19A of Chapter 15, the Division of Adult Correction of the Department of Public Safety shall award a prisoner credit against any term of reimprisonment for all time spent in custody as a result of revocation proceedings under G.S. 15A-1368.6.

(4) The prisoner is eligible to receive earned time credit against the maximum prison term as provided in G.S. 15A-1340.13(d) for time served in prison after the revocation.

(d) Re-Release After Revocation of Post-Release Supervision. - A prisoner who has been reimprisoned prior to completing a post-release supervision period may again be released on post-release supervision by the Commission subject to the provisions which govern initial release.

(e) Timing of Revocation. - The Commission may revoke post-release supervision for violation of a condition during the period of supervision. The Commission may also revoke post-release supervision following a period of supervision if:

(1) Before the expiration of the period of post-release supervision, the Commission has recorded its intent to conduct a revocation hearing; and

(2) The Commission finds that every reasonable effort has been made to notify the supervisee and conduct the hearing earlier. Prima facie evidence of reasonable effort to notify is the issuance of a temporary or conditional revocation order, as provided in G.S. 15A-1376, that goes unserved. (1993, c. 538, s. 20.1; 1994, Ex. Sess., c. 14, s. 27; c. 24, s. 14(b); 1993 (Reg. Sess., 1994), c. 767, s. 5; 2011-145, s. 19.1(h); 2011-192, s. 2(d); 2012-188, s. 4.)

§ 15A-1368.4. Conditions of post-release supervision.

(a) In General. - Conditions of post-release supervision may be reintegrative in nature or designed to control the supervisee's behavior and to enforce compliance with law or judicial order. A supervisee may have his supervision period revoked for any violation of a controlling condition or for repeated violation of a reintegrative condition. Compliance with reintegrative conditions may entitle a supervisee to earned time credits as described in G.S. 15A-1368.2(d).

(b) Required Condition. - The Commission shall provide as an express condition of every release that the supervisee not commit another crime during the period for which the supervisee remains subject to revocation. A supervisee's failure to comply with this controlling condition is a supervision violation for which the supervisee may face revocation as provided in G.S. 15A-1368.3.

(b1) Additional Required Conditions for Sex Offenders and Persons Convicted of Offenses Involving Physical, Mental, or Sexual Abuse of a Minor. - In addition to the required condition set forth in subsection (b) of this section, for a supervisee who has been convicted of an offense which is a reportable conviction as defined in G.S. 14-208.6(4), or which involves the physical, mental, or sexual abuse of a minor, controlling conditions, violations of which may result in revocation of post-release supervision, are:

(1) Register as required by G.S. 14-208.7 if the offense is a reportable conviction as defined by G.S. 14-208.6(4).

(2) Participate in such evaluation and treatment as is necessary to complete a prescribed course of psychiatric, psychological, or other rehabilitative treatment as ordered by the Commission.

(3) Not communicate with, be in the presence of, or found in or on the premises of the victim of the offense.

(4) Not reside in a household with any minor child if the offense is one in which there is evidence of sexual abuse of a minor.

(5) Not reside in a household with any minor child if the offense is one in which there is evidence of physical or mental abuse of a minor, unless a court of competent jurisdiction expressly finds that it is unlikely that the defendant's harmful or abusive conduct will recur and that it would be in the child's best interest to allow the supervisee to reside in the same household with a minor child.

(6) Submit to satellite-based monitoring pursuant to Part 5 of Article 27A of Chapter 14 of the General Statutes, if the offense is a reportable conviction as defined by G.S. 14-208.6(4) and the supervisee is in the category described by G.S. 14-208.40(a)(1).

(7) Submit to satellite-based monitoring pursuant to Part 5 of Article 27A of Chapter 14 of the General Statutes, if the offense is a reportable conviction as defined by G.S. 14-208.6(4) and the supervisee is in the category described by G.S. 14-208.40(a)(2).

(8) Submit at reasonable times to warrantless searches by a post-release supervision officer of the supervisee's person and of the supervisee's vehicle and premises while the supervisee is present, for purposes reasonably related to the post-release supervision, but the supervisee may not be required to submit to any other search that would otherwise be unlawful. For purposes of this subdivision, warrantless searches of the supervisee's computer or other electronic mechanism which may contain electronic data shall be considered reasonably related to the post-release supervision. Whenever the warrantless search consists of testing for the presence of illegal drugs, the supervisee may also be required to reimburse the Division of Adult Correction of the Department of Public Safety for the actual cost of drug screening and drug testing, if the results are positive.

(c) Discretionary Conditions. - The Commission, in consultation with the Section of Community Corrections of the Division of Adult Correction, may impose conditions on a supervisee it believes reasonably necessary to ensure that the supervisee will lead a law-abiding life or to assist the supervisee to do so. The Commission may also impose a condition of community service on a supervisee who was a Class F through I felon and who has failed to fully satisfy any order for restitution, reparation, or costs imposed against the supervisee as part of the supervisee's sentence; however, the Commission shall not impose such a condition of community service if the Commission determines, upon inquiry, that the supervisee has the financial resources to satisfy the order.

(c1) Repealed by Session Laws 2013-196, s. 2, effective June 26, 2013.

(d) Reintegrative Conditions. - Appropriate reintegrative conditions, for which a supervisee may receive earned time credits against the length of the supervision period, and repeated violation that may result in revocation of post-release supervision, are:

(1) Work faithfully at suitable employment or faithfully pursue a course of study or vocational training that will equip the supervisee for suitable employment.

(2) Undergo available medical or psychiatric treatment and remain in a specified institution if required for that purpose.

(3) Attend or reside in a facility providing rehabilitation, instruction, recreation, or residence for persons on post-release supervision.

(4) Support the supervisee's dependents and meet other family responsibilities.

(5) In the case of a supervisee who attended a basic skills program during incarceration, continue attending a basic skills program in pursuit of a General Education Development Degree or adult high school diploma.

(6) Satisfy other conditions reasonably related to reintegration into society.

(e) Controlling Conditions. - Appropriate controlling conditions, violation of which may result in revocation of post-release supervision, are:

(1) Not use, possess, or control any illegal drug or controlled substance unless it has been prescribed for the supervisee by a licensed physician and is in the original container with the prescription number affixed on it; not knowingly associate with any known or previously convicted users, possessors, or sellers of any such illegal drugs or controlled substances; and not knowingly be present at or frequent any place where such illegal drugs or controlled substances are sold, kept, or used.

(2) Comply with a court order to pay the costs of reintegrative treatment for a minor and a minor's parents or custodians where the offense involved evidence of physical, mental, or sexual abuse of a minor.

(3) Comply with a court order to pay court costs and costs for appointed counsel or public defender in the case for which the supervisee was convicted.

(4) Not possess a firearm, destructive device, or other dangerous weapon unless granted written permission by the Commission or a post-release supervision officer.

(5) Report to a post-release supervision officer at reasonable times and in a reasonable manner, as directed by the Commission or a post-release supervision officer.

(6)   Permit a post-release supervision officer to visit at reasonable times at the supervisee's home or elsewhere.

(7)   Remain within the geographic limits fixed by the Commission unless granted written permission to leave by the Commission or the post-release supervision officer.

(7a)   Not to abscond, by willfully avoiding supervision or by willfully making the supervisee's whereabouts unknown to the supervising probation officer.

(8)   Answer all reasonable inquiries by the post-release supervision officer and obtain prior approval from the post-release supervision officer for any change in address or employment.

(9)   Promptly notify the post-release supervision officer of any change in address or employment.

(10)   Submit at reasonable times to searches of the supervisee's person by a post-release supervision officer for purposes reasonably related to the post-release supervision. The Commission shall not require as a condition of post-release supervision that the supervisee submit to any other searches that would otherwise be unlawful. Whenever the search consists of testing for the presence of illegal drugs, the supervisee may also be required to reimburse the Division of Adult Correction of the Department of Public Safety for the actual cost of drug testing and drug screening, if the results are positive.

(11)   Make restitution or reparation to an aggrieved party as provided in G.S. 148-57.1.

(12)   Comply with an order from a court of competent jurisdiction regarding the payment of an obligation of the supervisee in connection with any judgment rendered by the court.

(13)   Remain in one or more specified places for a specified period or periods each day, and wear a device that permits the defendant's compliance with the condition to be monitored electronically and pay a fee of ninety dollars ($90.00) for the electronic monitoring device and a daily fee in an amount that reflects the actual cost of providing the electronic monitoring. The Commission may exempt a person from paying the fees only for a good cause. Fees collected under this subsection for the electronic monitoring device shall be transmitted to the State for deposit in the State's General Fund. The daily fees collected under this

subsection shall be remitted to the Department of Public Safety to cover the costs of providing the electronic monitoring.

(14) Repealed by Session Laws 2013-101, s. 1, effective June 12, 2013.

(e1) Prohibited Conditions. - The Commission shall not impose community service as a condition of post-release supervision.

(f) Required Supervision Fee. - The Commission shall require as a condition of post-release supervision that the supervisee pay a supervision fee of forty dollars ($40.00) per month. The Commission may exempt a supervisee from this condition only if it finds that requiring payment of the fee is an undue economic burden. The fee shall be paid to the clerk of superior court of the county in which the supervisee was convicted. The clerk shall transmit any money collected pursuant to this subsection to the State to be deposited in the State's General Fund. In no event shall a supervisee be required to pay more than one supervision fee per month. (1993, c. 538, s. 20.1; 1994, Ex. Sess., c. 24, s. 14(b); 1996, 2nd Ex. Sess., c. 18, s. 20.14(b); 1997-57, s. 6; 1997-237, s. 6; 2001-487, s. 47(c); 2002-126, s. 29A.2(b); 2006-247, s. 15(g); 2007-213, s. 9; 2010-31, s. 19.3(b); 2011-145, s. 19.1(h), (k); 2011-192, s. 2(c); 2013-101, s. 2; 2013-196, s. 1; 2013-363, s. 6.7(b).)

Vision Books Order Form

Fax Orders:	1-980-299-5965
Phone Orders:	1-704-898-0770
E-mail Orders:	www.visionbooks.org
Mail Orders:	Vision Books, LLC P.O. Box 42406 Charlotte, NC 28215

Shipp To:
Name_____
Address_____
City_____State_____Zip_____
Phone_____Fax_____
Email_____@_____

Bill To: We can bill a third party on your behalf.
Name_____
Address_____
City_____State_____Zip_____
Phone____(_____)_____Fax_____
Email_____@_____

Pamphlet Number ($15.00 Each)	Qty	Total Cost
_____	_____	_____
_____	_____	_____
_____	_____	_____
_____	_____	_____
_____	_____	_____
_____	_____	_____
_____	_____	_____
_____	_____	_____
<u>Full Volume Set 1-92</u>	<u>92 Pamphlets</u>	<u>1,380.00</u>

Free Shipping Shipping & Handling on Full Volume Orders
Add $1.00 Shipping & Handling per pamphlet $_____

Total Cost $_____

Thank You for Your Support. Management!

DID YOU ENJOY THIS BOOK?

Vision Books, LLC would like to hear from you! If you or someone you know has been falsely imprisoned, we would like to hear your story. If the 'North Carolina Criminal Law and Procedure' has had an effect in your life or if you have suggestions, we would like to hear from you. Send your letters to:

Vision Books, LLC
Attn: Staff Writers
P.O. Box 42406
Charlotte, NC 28215
Email: staff@visionbooks.org

Order Additional Copies:

Fax Orders:	1-980-299-5965
Phone Orders:	1-704-898-0770
E-mail Orders:	www.visionbooks.org
Mail Orders:	Vision Books, LLC P.O. Box 42406 Charlotte, NC 28215

www.ingramcontent.com/pod-product-compliance
Lightning Source LLC
Chambersburg PA
CBHW071406170526
45165CB00001B/191